SENSE WITH DOLLARS

CHARLES NEAL

DOUBLEDAY & COMPANY, INC.

GARDEN CITY, NEW YORK

1967

This is a revised and enlarged edition of SENSE WITH DOLLARS, originally published by Doubleday & Company, Inc. in 1965 as a Dolphin Handbook Original.

SENSE WITH
DOLLARS

THE DEDICATION

Millions of new consumers are pouring out of our schools and colleges. It is to these youngsters, including my own daughter, Linda, that I dedicate this book. May some of them profit from it.

THE ACKNOWLEDGMENTS

A great amount of the content of this book comes from what I have gleaned from other writers in the general realm of economics. I am most grateful. But I am particularly indebted to the Council on Consumer Information, a small but dedicated group devoting their time and energy toward consumer enlightenment. I have worked with the CCI for several years and have learned much.

I must also acknowledge the help received from the American Association of Credit Counselors, a group which has been working at the grass-roots level of family financial problems. The work of the AACC has been mostly unsung and often criticized. But now that work is being given full recognition by being imitated by its critics. Helping families get out of debt is as worthy a career as one can dream up in this complex, detached civilization.

And finally, I must thank my wife, Barbara, whose artistic leanings more or less crowded out a technical approach to money. She has been a source of inspiration and frequent rewriting.

THE APOLOGIES

This book is by no means complete. But who could write a complete book on family money? Then, too, by not sounding like a public relations man, I may have offended certain vested interests. I tried to be fair; and after all, each industry has its own "image" department anyway.

My real shame is that I am not a rich man. My problem is

that I don't really love money or wealth. If anything, I'm a bit of an iconoclast about them. But it takes money to survive, especially in a society with such a "financial character." Money is an essential, and one should always take more than a passing interest in the essentials.

You see, the days have passed when a girl could qualify as a good wife by canning fruits and keeping a neat broom closet. And gone are the days when a young husband could fulfill his responsibilities by handing his pay check to his wife. The wife of today must be a shrewd buyer and manager, because the home economics of today relate to money, not to making things in the home. And a wife needs a great deal of help from her husband.

So while in a sense I am writing about the domestic arts, I won't apologize for that. No man needs to be embarrassed when dealing with money and finances. And frankly, I am hoping for many male readers.

In gathering material for the section on investments, I made liberal use of friends skilled in real estate, insurance, stocks and bonds. Arthur Newfield, a vice president of Walston & Company, was particularly helpful on bonds. This is not meant to imply that any of my friends necessarily agree with my treatment of their specialties in this book.

CONTENTS

PART I

MANAGING YOUR INCOME,
or The Ins and Outs of Money

HIGHLIGHTING THE PROBLEM

The odds against you

The world is full of persons who look back and say, "If I'd only done this or that, I'd be in good shape today." But the point is, they didn't do whatever they now regret not having done. In some cases it was because they didn't know enough, in other cases, it was because they weren't willing to make sacrifices, take chances, or be different.

Yet an important reason why many people didn't go into business for themselves, buy that piece of land, or buy IBM stock when it was selling at bargain rates, was lack of ready money.

Look at it this way. Even the barely skilled worker approaching age sixty has probably handled over $150,000. To pretend he couldn't have saved some of that money over his working years is being unrealistic. Had he wanted to, really wanted to, he could have pulled rein on some of his spending habits enough to save a few dollars each week.

During fiscal 1965 almost 166,000 families filed bankruptcy proceedings. The cause in almost every case was overuse of credit; in other words, impatience to have all the goodies of life. In order to get credit, a family must have an income. Bankruptcies in these times usually can be blamed on poor management, not on lack of income.

A young person with a decent education and a vocational skill should be able to count on earning $250,000 over his working years, and many will earn double that amount. Sad to say, however, between now and the year 2000, some four million youngsters just starting out in business careers today will file personal bankruptcy proceedings—assuming that the present rate of financial failures remains as it is. Millions of other youngsters will stay ahead of the hounds, but just barely. They will lead unimaginative lives dodging bill collectors, constantly flirting with outright insolvency.

Once in this kind of a rut, it is very hard to get out. Habits are formed early and so are attitudes.

Having counseled thousands of persons face to face, I know how easy it is to get trapped on a financial treadmill. Every day we are urged to live better, higher on the hog—and immediately, not later. Keeping up with the Joneses is no joke; it is the very essence of modern-day American living. Even the most solemn and thrifty economists plead with us to part with our cash and use our credit liberally. After all, they say, if we don't spend freely, the economy may suffer, and who knows, we might all be out of jobs.

If you fall for this hogwash and get yourself into financial trouble, the same economists will chide you for being "economically illiterate" and hint that you are a threat to the free enterprise system. And the truth is, you would be. No society can survive when each year a higher percentage of its citizens goes under financially.

In fact, that's what all the shouting is about these days. As more and more Americans live in the shadow of debt and chronic insolvency, the battle between the extreme conservatives and the extreme liberals becomes more intense. Fewer families are able to carry their shares of the tax burdens, while the demands upon charity and government become ever increasing as millions of families fall into the dull despondency that results from "never getting ahead."

Why is it that a family from a poor section of Europe can arrive in this country penniless, and within a generation or so have a reasonable amount of wealth and a high degree of security? It happens over and over again, even in these times. And it happens simultaneously with the bankruptcies of hundreds of thousands of fourth- and fifth-generation Americans.

The answer is not necessarily better education. The answer, more likely, is that strangers to our culture have less trouble avoiding its booby traps. While they naturally want to impress us, they don't associate success with the consuming of fancy, short-lived status symbols. It seems to me that a healthy, well-educated foreigner has a better chance of success in America today, provided he is proud and determined, than does a native-born American.

The advertising industry, for all the good it has done to this country, can take much of the credit for our undoing. Our appetites are so whetted for the "good things" of life that patience has gone. To wait for a month or so, in order to have something, is unheard of. And to suggest waiting years is virtually subversive.

Compare, for instance, that attitude to the viewpoint of some of our early settlers. They were willing to wait, not just for years, but for generations. They were willing to build, not just for themselves, but for their children. And in the meantime, they themselves would simply do without.

Obviously this attitude did not destroy the nation. It gave it a depth and continuity. And above all, it gave it a clear purpose. The prevailing view today is that if a child or parent stands in the way of personal satisfaction, measured by unrestrained consuming, the human obstacle has to give way.

We like to pretend that times have changed, that the prosperity of our country depends upon all of us spending as fast as the money comes in, even faster. That pretense shows up in advertising, textbooks, government pronouncements, and editorials. And all too often, the pretense isn't that at all; the opinion is sincerely held.

To some of us it is laughable. As the nightclub comedienne said, "I can't stand my neighbor. He spent the money he could have used fixing up his backyard sending his kid to music school."

The situation has become so bad that the citizen barely exists as an entity. The citizen is called a "consumer," which implies that consuming is more important than exercising the rights of citizenship.

We worry a great deal about the national debt, which has increased very little since World War II. But we hear only praise when American families upped their short-term debts from $8 billion in 1945 to almost $90 billion by 1966.

The point is, from the standpoint of far too many influential persons, as long as you buy as many products as you can, it really doesn't matter how you do it. Just as long as you eventually pay for them, stay comfortably in debt, and don't ask any favors from society.

If that is enough for you, there's really no point in reading on. But if you are reasonably proud, ambitious, and sensible, I hope I can give you some thoughts on avoiding the nonsensical life patterns that too many Americans take for granted. I like to think you will be too proud to ever have to plead for cash, too proud to tolerate a bill collector at your door, and too proud to admit you have squandered all you have earned in any one year.

I also like to think you are too wise to try to impress other people with the obvious status symbols, the flashy auto, wall-to-wall carpeting, and the thirty-six button electric range. To impress sensible persons with these things is almost impossible anyway; in a mass production economy it is difficult to achieve distinction through purchasing commonplace goods. Trying to do so is admitting a serious lack of worth in your own character and personality.

How to plan the attack

The first step in money management is wanting to do a good job. The second is realizing how complex money management has become. After that, it is mainly a matter of learning how to deal with its complexities—and doing so.

Since life would hardly be worth living if every moment had to be devoted to some phase of financial management, the whole point of learning to do this correctly is to free yourself from time-consuming, irrelevant details, most of which arise from well-intended but misguided diligence or just plain mistakes.

There are hundreds of thousands of money managers in the country today offering to help other persons for a fee. This is not counting all the tax consultants and all the persons working for the government. These professionals specialize in particular aspects of finance, and their fields of concentration signal the basic outlines of money management.

There are experts who will help manage your income, although these specialists concentrate on high-income families. Some of these experts are called business managers. Others act as financial secretaries. The first section of this book deals with pure income management, the receiving and spending of income.

There are also a number of spending assistants, sometimes called professional shoppers. And in addition, there are numerous publications devoted to helping you get the most for your money. That is the subject matter contained in the second section of the book—not too technical, just common-sense guides.

With credit so widely used today, debt management is becoming an important specialty in our society. People use credit for everything from homes to paper napkins. And many people get in trouble with credit. So now we have debt counselors, credit counselors, court trustees, and social agencies offering to help families manage their debts. Debt management is the third area discussed here.

Finally, for those who manage to save money and accumulate net worth, we have the savings and investment counselors. This is the most complex field of all, with many types of savings plans and investment programs on the market. The final section of the book is called Managing Your Assets.

So there you have the big four in money management: IN-COME, SPENDING, DEBTS, and ASSETS. It may seem amusing that so many specialists have appeared to help with each of the four divisions of money today, but that's how complicated things are.

You should plan right now to learn as much as you can about money and its various relationships. As soon as you begin your adult life, you automatically need a basic knowledge of almost everything dealt with here. You will have income, you will spend money, you will acquire debts, and you will have assets to manage and invest.

To some readers, this book may seem too elementary. To some readers it will seem too complicated and technical. The author tried to hit a happy medium.

During your working career, you will have a river of money flowing into your hands and into your bank account. It can flow out as fast as it flows in, but you would be foolish to let that happen. Channel some of it off in the direction of your future and your security. You should divert some of your earnings toward fun and happiness without a guilty conscience. You will have earned the right to do that, and you can do it without being a miser or a skinflint.

THE BUDGET APPROACH

Explanation of important words and terms

Many words sound formidable until you understand their meanings. Take the word "budget" for instance. It conjures up all sorts of visions—green eyeshades, desks, books, red and black ink. Yet the word "budget" comes from the French word *bougette* or "little bag." In the old days a French merchant kept his cash in his *bougette*, and from that simple bookkeeping system came the present-day meaning of the personal, family budget.

How simple, or how complex, you decide to make your system is up to you. But I feel very strongly about this—simplicity in any money system mostly depends upon a reasonably complete knowledge of the principles of budgeting. You needn't be an accountant or a skilled bookkeeper to stay ahead of the battle, but you should understand the theories involved in balancing your books.

You will have made a good start by learning, and remembering, the general meaning of four words: ASSET, LIABILITY, INCOME, and EXPENSE. Sometimes these words are loosely used, but if you understand their precise meanings you will not only be well on the road toward better managing your own money, but you will have a finer understanding of modern business practices. And after all, a family unit is a small business.

An ASSET is anything having value. From a practical standpoint, an asset should have market value, in other words, be worth money. Naturally you will want to accumulate some assets if you are trying to get ahead. Here are some typical physical assets owned by the average family: home, automobile, furniture, cash, jewelry, and stocks or bonds. (Actually, a share of stock or a bond is not a tangible, physical asset, except for the paper it's printed on. But both stocks and bonds are backed by some sort of physical asset.)

A LIABILITY, the opposite of an ASSET, is about the same as a DEBT, an unpaid obligation. For instance, you may own an ASSET such as an automobile, but it may have a mortgage against it, which represents a DEBT or LIABILITY.

If the mortgage (LIABILITY) is greater than the market value of the car, from that standpoint alone, you are insolvent, or "in the red." The idea is to keep the total value of all your assets greater than the total of all your debts. That gives you a "net worth" or "solvent condition." I will explain net worth in greater detail later.

One way to do that is to control your expenses. An EXPENSE is something that "costs" you. Now, the word "cost" has a rather tricky meaning in its precise sense. For instance, the price of an ounce of gold is $35. So, loosely speaking, you might say that an ounce of gold "costs" $35. But if you were to buy an ounce of gold, there would be no EXPENSE whatsoever, since you would be trading one valuable ASSET for another—money for metal. In fact, an ounce of gold might hold its value forever, and in time might be worth even more than the $35 of currency.

Price is one thing; cost is another, when the word is loosely used; but cost, *as an expense,* is still another. Think of EXPENSE as a drain on your resources, as an act of spending your assets to your financial disadvantage. An EXPENSE is something that reduces your net worth, or the sum of money you could get by liquidating all your assets and paying all your debts. A vacation and a new refrigerator may both cost $300. In other words, the prices are identical. But a vacation would be a pure expense, even though a worthwhile one. The refrigerator, however, would be an asset, and would continue to serve you for years. You could even sell it immediately and get most of your money back. So a vacation represents a true expense, whereas the purchase of a refrigerator is merely trading one asset (cash) for another type of asset.

INCOME is more than just salary or wages. It can be from extra benefits such as free rent, food from a garden, and gifts of various kinds. When determining your "real" income, take into consideration the money value of benefits received from your employer, the cash savings you realize from not having to buy certain things you are realizing from your own efforts, and gifts. As long as your real income is greater than your real expense, you are getting ahead.

But there are two very important elements to this matter of keeping your income and expenses in balance. Failure to understand these two points can ruin you financially.

One is the matter of *depreciation,* the act or condition of losing value. Some things hold value very well over the years, and even become worth more with age. But other things lose value fast, and one of those things is an automobile.

The act of losing value is an expense, just as surely as the act of buying an ice cream cone is an expense. So no matter what your assets—your things of value—are worth at this moment, they must be revalued every now and then. You may be going in the hole without realizing it, simply because you aren't keeping track of depreciation—*value loss*—caused by age, use, fashion trends, or changing market conditions.

In fact, whenever you plan to acquire an asset, you should consider how well the asset will hold its value over the years. That is an essential to remember.

The second important element to consider in your income-expense ratio is that of psychological satisfaction. One should never be ruled entirely by money considerations. If certain spending habits give you a great feeling of satisfaction, you should weigh that in your decisions. But remember this: there must be a limit to that sort of spending and that sort of rationalizing. There is no place in a financial statement for "psychological satisfaction." A banker would look at you in amazement if you listed such in your assets.

So no matter how much satisfaction you get from certain expenses, limit them to your means, and to what you hope to achieve from your overall spending and savings plan.

The truth is, the terms "psychological satisfaction" and "psychological income" are often used by some businesses to justify the products and services they offer the American public.

To sum up: you measure expenses against income and you measure assets against liabilities. You *cannot* measure either expense or income against either assets or liabilities.

A business firm keeps two types of records in its bookkeeping system—the expense versus income record, and the asset versus liability record.

Overspending soon shows up as a minus in your value, your net worth. And the act of saving—spending less than you earn—soon shows up as a gain in your assets or a decrease in your debts, which means your worth is increasing.

If this sounds too much like a course in bookkeeping, bear in mind how often you use the words EXPENSE, ASSET, INCOME, and LIABILITY in your everyday speech. In speaking of a man's wife, it is often said she is an "asset" to him, meaning she increases his worth. Or conversely, a wife may be said to be a liability to her husband, and the meaning is clear there.

The truth is, no one can get ahead in the world, unless he has a lot of luck or windfalls, without a fairly good idea of the meaning of bookkeeping terms and their application to his everyday spending and saving.

The techniques of budgeting

Back in the "good old days" (?) about a hundred years ago, budgeting was fairly simple. Almost everything was on a cash basis for consumers, and life consisted mostly of pure survival. No cash, no groceries.

In fact, shelter, food, and clothing were about all a family of average means concerned itself with, plus perhaps giving to the church and saving a few dollars. Shelter, to most persons, meant rent, since few families owned their own homes.

Food was prepared in the home; only the raw ingredients were bought at the store. And clothing was simple, durable, and often home-sewn.

To be sure, there were medical bills, but doctors rarely got paid promptly, so budgeting for illness was virtually unheard of. As to transportation, it was horse or foot. In short, budgeting meant not spending more than you had on hand.

Now even a fairly simple family budget looks something like this:

SHELTER
FOOD
DRESS
TRANSPORTATION
MEDICAL
LIFE INSURANCE
SAVINGS
BETTERMENT

1

Many a modern budgeteer struggles along with even more elaborate divisions of spending, including such as these:

HOME UPKEEP

PERSONAL CARE

INSTALLMENT PAYMENTS

VACATIONS

CHURCH AND CHARITY

PERSONAL ALLOWANCES

ENTERTAINMENT

FURNITURE AND FURNISHINGS

My advice is to use the first list of the eight major categories. Under each of the major ones, you can list subdivisions from the second list.

For instance, home upkeep is really a part of shelter. As to installment payments, there really is no such category in a true bookkeeping sense. *Money paid on a debt is a form of saving,* once the debt is incurred. When you pay off a debt, you reduce your liabilities. And that has as good an effect on your net worth as adding more assets. Net worth, as I mentioned before, means the difference between what you "own" and what you "owe."

In the second list shown, all but home upkeep (shelter) can go under BETTERMENT, sometimes called IMPROVEMENT. Betterment is the section of the budget requiring the most decisions, wherein *you* must decide which things are more important than others. With some expenses, such as utility costs, you have little choice. But under BETTERMENT, you may have to decide between church contributions and personal allowances, between vacations and entertaining, or between better furnishings and less costly personal care.

Many budget guides are set up in a simple but often misleading manner, for many teachers are apparently afraid that genuine family bookkeeping is beyond the understanding of most of us. In this way budget instructors help to compound our errors and help to perpetuate the confusion.

What is being taught today, under the name of budgeting, is mostly a "cash-in, cash-out" system. Under the *outgo,* or breakdown of spending, column may be lumped such things as debt payment and vacations. Paying on a debt (except for the interest cost) is actually a *savings,* whereas vacations are an *expense,* even though necessary. It is totally unrealistic to lump savings with expenses, unless we carry the whole analysis one step further. And that step is to separate the true expenses from all other forms of parting with cash. To know whether you are on sound financial ground in the way you spend money, you must compare your expenses—your *true expenses*—with your *real income.*

And that is why, at the back of this book, I have prepared some forms, to be used monthly or once a year. These forms show what is an expense and what isn't.

Whenever you part with money, cash or check, you need to ask yourself: Am I parting with my money as an expense? Am I paying off a debt, thereby increasing my net worth or liquidation value? Or am I simply trading one of my assets, cash, for another asset, something which I could sell and get my money back?

You will discover that every time you part with cash or write a check on your bank account, your action fits one of the three descriptions. It is either an *expense* act, such as buying food; an act of *saving,* placing money in a bank or paying your debts; or an act of *trading assets,* in which case, for a while at least, no cost or expense is involved.

Sometimes the definitions of spending are not clear-cut. Even highly paid accountants have trouble with the definitions sometimes. Take, as an example, the act of paying cash for a secondhand vacuum cleaner. At the moment of purchase, there really isn't any expense involved. You could sell the cleaner to someone if you tried and get your money back. On the other hand, the cleaner may not last very long and there isn't much money involved. Most persons would decide to show the transaction as an expense and forget about it.

But on the other hand, suppose you paid cash for a $3000 automobile. There certainly wasn't $3000 in expenses involved. You still have the car and you certainly could sell it for almost as much as you paid. So obviously you are simply trading assets for the time being; no expense, no savings—just a different asset from the money you had in the bank.

Some of this may sound like splitting hairs, especially if you are used to spending your money fast and ignoring the consequences. But the point I am making is this: If you can't identify the types of your spending, and see the effect expenditures have on your financial picture, you will become a victim of every skin game imaginable. Identification is important.

The average person thinks he is saving money when he buys all sorts of consumer goods. And it is true, as I pointed out, that buying things of value that last for a while, is simply a matter of trading assets. But most products today have built-in obsolescence. If they don't actually wear out fast, the manufacturer remedies that by making his new product fancier and prettier than his older ones, thereby creating a "psychological" obsolescence. You fall out of love with what you already have.

One way to whip the system is to budget for the fast replacement trends of today by keeping track of the amount of depreciation. Whereas years ago, persons accepted the fact that most of their wages were used up in day-to-day living, we tend to kid ourselves. Surrounded by all the goodies of modern living, we ignore our debts, and we overrate the value of our assets. Budgeting today is mostly *keeping track of how fast our possessions lose value,* and then setting aside money to replace them.

This does involve skill, time, and understanding. So is it any wonder a higher percentage of wage earners get in financial trouble each year? If you are a young person, you have a great opportunity to get started properly. If you understand what things cost, through proper record-keeping, you will eventually learn to offset the costs through better buying, better care of products, and avoiding items which cost a great deal in maintenance and insurance expense. Otherwise you will be in the same fix as most adults, always complaining about the high cost of living, relying on pay raises to cure their problems, and, in general, forever wondering what hit them.

As to how much to spend for this or that—the various categories in your budget list—just remember one thing. You have only so much income, which represents 100 per cent. You can't spend more than that without going in the hole.

Break down your projected spending by trial and error. Start by keeping shelter and food combined within 50 per cent of your monthly take-home pay. The rest will fall into line by adjusting percentages.

But I can assure you of this: Unless you start out with a fantastically high income, you are going to meet with some disappointments in adjusting your spending. Despite all the propaganda, few American families earn enough to buy the best housing, the best transportation, the finest clothing, etc., and still entertain a great deal between vacations.

To put it more bluntly, you are going to have to make some sacrifices. You may have to keep a car longer than you originally hoped. You may need to postpone vacations for several years. And so on. I don't know why some young people get married and expect to begin life with everything, but many young persons expect exactly that.

Who should keep the records—husband or wife?

There is a certain amount of dirty work involved in being the family bookkeeper. It also takes time and skill. So we come to the question of who should assume the work and responsibility today—the husband or the wife.

In general, and I say this with the kindest of intentions, women like to shop more than men do. And women, therefore, do most of the spending in this country—80 per cent of it according to one estimate. So if you were the public relations man for a large consumer industry, wouldn't you take advantage of this fact?

You might decide to work even harder to keep the family purse strings in the hands of women, and what better way to do that than to flatter women about their money-management abilities? Even security-conscious husbands might be led into letting their wives handle all the money and keep the books. And this is just what has happened in a high percentage of American families.

Not that wives want to bankrupt their husbands—far from it. But most young wives come from families where Daddy has always somehow managed to provide the necessities, so why can't young hubby do the same? And, after all, Mamma always did the shopping.

To many young girls, saving money means getting a better bargain than usual at some store, which is great; but somehow that kind of "savings" doesn't show up in the bank. It more likely shows up in a balance owed on a credit account. Men, unimaginative creatures that they are, think of savings as piling up in a bank —not spending, in other words.

The moral is, unless the wife in your house is more practical about money than most young women, let the husband have a firm say about how money is spent, bargain sale or no bargain sale. It makes for better balance that way.

That does not mean, however, that wives shouldn't keep the records and pay the bills; whether the husband or the wife handles the details of family money management should depend on which has the greater aptitude and willingness. In many cases that problem resolves itself into which member of the team has the best education and knack with figures. We are, of course, talking about the bookkeeping, not the decision-making. A bookkeeper in a large firm pays the bills, does the filing, and keeps the records, but he is not necessarily the purchasing agent or the comptroller.

So, decide who will handle the details first. Then agree early in the game to talk things over with each other on major purchases. And by a major purchase, I mean any item which could make a dent in the budget or the savings plan. Even a $25 item could disrupt a $500-a-month budget, since it is 5 per cent of monthly income.

In my opinion, neither husband nor wife should buy a new outfit, a piece of furniture, an appliance, an expensive gift, and certainly not an automobile, new or used, without a family discussion.

One major obstacle to complete frankness about money is the feeling on the part of many husbands that if a wife knows there is money in the bank she will want to spend it. That subject should be talked about before the savings build up.

And too many wives want to build a private nest egg for little personal whims of spending. This is fine in theory, and gives an individuality to marriage. However, if personal whims give way to a desire for complete independence, trouble soon follows. If a marriage is to work, the fewer secrets the better. Of course, the finest, most logical, money agreement in the world won't hold two incompatible persons together. This you should accept in the very beginning. But why complicate a marriage with friction over money in times when marriage as an institution is fighting for survival?

The best-adjusted young sophisticates of today realize that money is no guarantee to a happy marriage, and that money should best be treated as a necessary evil. Earn it, plan to handle it, save some of it, put it to work as soon as possible, and then get on to the more important phases of living.

If this sounds a little anti-Horatio Alger, let me be the first to admit it. Alger never seemed to portray the wives of his money-hungry heroes. They must have been busy clipping coupons off 6 per cent bonds. There's a heap more to living in twentieth-century America than "luck, pluck and a buck."

Shortcuts for lazy people

It is precisely because many young Americans want more out of life than being dominated by money, that I offer a few ideas on how to simplify budgeting.

First you think in terms of your annual income. Then, for one time only, you divide that income into the various spending and savings areas I set forth earlier. If you decide you can afford so much in rent, you spend that much and no more; at least, not until you get a raise.

Then figure what you can afford for pure eating, first on an annual basis and then dividing the sum into weekly and monthly spending allowances. Spend that much and no more. The same treatment should be given to clothing, life insurance, etc.

If you hold your spending to these figures, stay out of debt, and save regularly as part of your overall plan, you really needn't keep many records. All you need do, once a year, is add up your assets at their current value to see if you are gaining or losing.

That's really all there is to staying ahead of the game. But the day you become impatient and begin using installment credit, you had best start using a more detailed—and more time-consuming—system. Since most persons use credit these days, we assume you will, too, so the rest of the book is devoted to helping you cope with that and other problems of money management.

But first, while we're still on the general "ins and outs" of money, and the subject of budgeting, let me remind you of one thing. The installment credit system, as we know it today, came into being because most Americans either can't or won't budget.

It takes some sort of budgeting to save money in order to pay cash for things later. So the credit men offer to do the budgeting for you. They say in effect, "O.K., so you won't budget. Then buy whatever you want now, on credit, and then pay back later."

But the amusing aspect of all this, or maybe it isn't so amusing, is that the credit buyer, or borrower, then has to budget in order to save enough from his income to repay his debts. Actually he hasn't gained a thing, except that he is able to fulfill his wants a little sooner by using credit than if he waited to save in order to pay cash later. And under the credit system, he *pays* interest rather than *receives* it as a reward for saving.

So, one way to budget is to let credit firms do some of the work for you—at a price, of course. But we'll get into the details of that later in this book.

HELPFUL IDEAS ON PAYING BILLS

Don't make a career out of keeping creditors happy

A few hundred years ago, English gentlemen settled their accounts (bills) once a year. It was considered poor taste for a creditor to press for payment until shortly after the first of the coming year. But back in those days, tradesmen and merchants were several notches down the social scale from their positions today, and wouldn't have dared offend the big spenders of that era.

Now this situation is reversed. Businessmen, especially financial ones, are in the saddle and have altered the economic scheme of things to fit their accounting machines. The big spenders of our day, the credit-card-carrying consumers, are expected to pay up at least once a month. Not only that, but if your name begins with an A, you may be asked to settle your account at a department store by the twenty-fifth of each month. If your name begins with a G, your monthly due date may be the seventh. It all depends on how each creditor gears his billing cycle.

Since few credit firms have exactly the same systems, if you use credit liberally, you may find yourself slaving over a hot checkbook twenty or thirty days out of each month. My research shows that few family bookkeepers find this very stimulating. For one thing, that phase of money management is further complicated by the credit system itself. Each year a greater number of families live from payday to payday because they use credit right up to the hilt and beyond.

The fellow whose name begins with G rarely can pay his department store promptly on the seventh because Friday, his payday, falls on the fifth one month and on the tenth another. So most of the time Mr. G is a little slow in paying, a little worried about his credit rating or kiting checks.

There are ways to whip this system. I wouldn't dream of going back to the old "once a year" bill-paying approach, even for gentlemen, although it might make a fine platform for some opportunistic politician. But isn't once a month reasonable? By that I mean setting aside one day out of each month to pay ALL creditors. On that one day, you could sit down with all your unpaid obligations and pay the most important first, the second most important next, and so on. It might take two hours at the outside. Then, if you need to wait for another payday to make the rest of your creditors happy and solvent, fine. Pay them the following week.

During the remainder of the day, and the rest of the month, you take on other and more enjoyable business, like just living.

How does one go about getting control of a bill-paying mess? First let me show you how to avoid getting into such a trap in the first place. Then I'll show how to rearrange an already bad situation.

We'll start by giving a nod to those business establishments which still cling to businesslike practices, even when dealing with consumers. By that I mean those firms which accept the tenth of the month as a decent time to settle up. The tenth has been used for years as a due date; some businesses continue to give discounts to customers who pay up in full on that date. We, of course, aren't asking for discounts, just freedom. But let's gear this entire philosophy around the tenth as a good date for draining our bank account.

Next, we'll analyze those bills we consistently pay every month. Generally they fall into three classes: (1) current living expenses, including rent or house payments, utilities and phone, and gasoline and food; (2) contracted loan and installment credit payments, with a fixed sum due each month; (3) charge accounts, including those so-called revolving accounts which fluctuate a bit in monthly payments.

Now that the bills are categorized, we can tackle each group with the idea of harmonizing the due dates so that we can pay them all at the same time of the month.

On current expenses, you can simply pick your own due date to begin with. If you rent a house or apartment, tell the landlord you desire to pay him on the tenth. If you move in on the twentieth, pay him the remainer of the first month's rent, plus the full next month's rent, up to the tenth if necessary. Most landlords won't object to that system.

Or if you're buying a house, tell the mortgage company when you want to pay the house payment. It's about that simple.

As to utilities and phone, it may just be that after your deposit, the regular billing date will come close to your goal, within a few days before or after. If so, no problem. If it comes, for instance, on the twentieth or twenty-fifth, pay a little in advance. Then whenever you receive your first billing, pay it on the first tenth of the month that comes around.

As to loan and contract payments, when starting off you always have the right to pick your due dates. A good credit manager always asks for your preference, if for no other reason than to avoid the expense of chronically chasing you with notices and collectors.

If you already have your payment dates thoroughly scattered over the month, start renegotiating with each credit firm. Take another look at your due dates on each bill. Those due from the fifth to the fifteenth will fit into your system of the tenth without a phone call. Some you will be paying a few days late, some a few days early. Only those billing dates falling between the sixteenth and the following fourth will need to be revised.

Some mortgage and loan companies will agree to a due-date change willingly, especially if they've been sending you expensive follow-up notices. And a few credit houses may charge a *one-time-only* (make sure it's that) late fee, to change your payment date. My point is: All due dates can be changed with a little effort. Even if a few creditors won't cooperate, the worst that can happen is that you'll write checks twice a month.

Regular charge accounts present the toughest problem. Stores just love "cycle billing." It makes it easier to spread the work load of billing, as well as the work load of collecting. But remember, this book was written for you, not retailers. Billing clerks are paid to work five days out of every week, but nobody is paying you to fiddle with your checkbook when you ought to be out making a living or having fun.

You may have to argue with your charge creditors to make them see the light, even to the point of picking stores which consider individual customers more important than IBM machines. But I can assure you it is possible to arrange all your due dates to fit your system with a little effort and persuasion.

Now that you have tamed all your creditors into gearing their systems to yours, what next? Mainly, it's a matter of keeping enough money in your checking account to handle all those bills when your due date hits. To be specific, if your monthly outgo amounts to $700 regularly over the year, you must have at least $700 in your account by the tenth of each month.

So sit down with an adding machine, if you can find one, or with a sharp pencil if you can't, and add up all those regular monthly contributions you make to landlords, loan companies, utility companies, and charge account creditors. Go back over your checkbook to estimate amounts if necessary. Then *start out with that amount*—and this is the key—EVEN IF YOU HAVE TO

BORROW THE MONEY AND INCLUDE THE REPAYMENT IN YOUR TENTH-
OF-THE-MONTH SETTLEMENTS.

Then, until you get into the swing of this system and find
you have it mastered, with money enough to keep your creditors
content, don't take on even one more obligation—not one.

In case you feel all this is too much trouble—this business
of paying all bills once a month, with a reasonable leeway—
let me recapitulate and emphasize the advantages it holds for
you over the old catch-me-when-you-can system.

1. It frees you of constantly and chronically fighting with
your checking account. No person should have to spend more
than a few hours once a month, during the same day, settling his
accounts. Anything more is checkbook slavery.

2. By having all your bills in front of you at the same time,
you can give preference to the most important ones in a crisis.
And while all creditors have an equal "moral" claim against
your pay check, let's be realistic. If you don't pay the rent, out
you go. If you miss the car payment, you're likely to be afoot.
On the other hand, shorting a doctor or dentist for a few weeks
won't bring your house down, especially if your short payment
is accompanied with a nice word of explanation and a promise.
Perhaps the most valuable part of my system is selectivity, paying
first bills first.

3. The once-a-month system is a great discipline. If you find
yourself continually short by the tenth, it's obviously time to
pull rein on spending and charging. On the other hand, simply
paying the bills when they arrive tends to confuse people. They
think everything will be straightened out by next payday, which
won't happen, of course.

4. Another advantage is this: When you pay the bills, you
can also do some filing for tax purposes, record-keeping for
budget purposes, and thinking for your future purposes. Having
all your past and current spending before you at the same time
gives the whole picture, something you must have to improve
your financial position.

So much for the merits of my suggestions. You could sum them up by saying it is just more businesslike to tackle bills systematically than it is to jump erratically to your checkbook and pen every time the postman rings. And contrary to that old saying, the postman rings quite often these days, financially speaking.

As to the mechanics of the system, buy a sharp spindle and stick the bills on the spindle until bill-paying time. You don't even need to open the envelopes until the tenth. And remember, the tenth is only an approximate date to use. The eighth or ninth are fine times too.

To those who decide to give this a try and who succeed, I can state one thing with certainty—they'll wonder how in the world they ever muddled through before. And they'll also be ashamed they let *other* people's systems dominate so much of their lives before.

A *checking account is a must*

I can't for the life of me see how any modern-day credit-consumer can manage without a checking account. To be sure, checks cost money, but not nearly as much money as driving around town leaving bits of cash here and there; and not a fraction of the cost of buying money orders at from twenty to thirty-five cents each.

So decide right now to use a checking account. And that, of course, means learning something about the various kinds of checks and accounts.

A few banks, mostly new ones, offer free checking accounts for new depositors. But that promotional scheme isn't likely to take hold on any large scale, so we'll ignore it. If you happen to have a free account, fine, but ordinarily we must expect to pay something to maintain a checking account.

There are two basic types of checking accounts. One is the

type where you pay for the checks in advance, at so much a check. Or you may be billed for such special checks later. The other is the kind in which you are charged according to the activity in your account—the number of checks you write—and the size of your average balance. Personally, I prefer the latter kind, for two reasons, even though the special account checks may be slightly less expensive for those persons using only a few checks each month. One, the buy-your-checks-in-advance account is for more or less unsophisticated persons, and I'm trying to write a book for those who want to be somewhat more sophisticated about money in general. And two, the type of account in which the cost depends on how you handle it affords greater opportunity for savings and efficiency.

The latter and more sophisticated checking account may have a number of variations. You can obtain the large three-on-a-page book, or you can get the single-check-per-page, pocket-size type. Either one will do, although I favor the larger book. Since you can't carry it around with you, you can't be writing checks all the time, a money-saving feature. Of course, you can always get counter checks, the ones on which you have to write in the name of the bank and so on, but this can be deadly. It's too easy to forget to subtract counter checks from your records.

But whichever type of check or checkbook you use, all checks have this in common—they either have stubs, or come with booklets in which to record the details of each transaction. As you write a check, always record on the stub or record book the *date*, the *amount*, to *whom*, for *what*, and in some cases, *why*. Even the best memories may fail. Put it down in writing.

Better yet, fill in the stub or record book *before* you write the check. And after you write the check, subtract that amount from your balance immediately. If you ruin a check, or void it, show on your stub records that the particular check was destroyed.

Of course, if you follow the once-a-month method of paying bills, most of your check-writing will be done at home. You can do your stub records leisurely and carefully. And you can bring your balance up to date without so many chances of error.

An important point in keeping accurate and fairly detailed records on your stubs is this: Once a month or once a year, you can also bring your budget up-to-date—control your spending, in other words. As an example, as you write your checks, you may come to the account at the Big Store, where you owe $65.36. A quick glance at the invoices or sales slips accompanying the billing shows that $33 went for clothing, $15 for toiletries and personal care, and the rest for household expenses. Why not put those notations, the spending breakdown, right on the stubs too? It will really help your budgeting when you decide to bring your budget book up-to-date and record your spending.

Also, when you pay an account with some interest included in the bill, make a notation of how much interest you pay. This not only helps in your personal bookkeeping and in tax records, but it helps to spur you into paying off the more expensive interest-carrying bills as fast as possible.

At this point we come to a controversy. Many banks urge you and your wife to use the same checking account—it is called a "joint account." It may be a little cheaper to combine a wife's bank account with that of her husband, but the possibilities for trouble are unlimited. Many a divorce has been sealed by a husband's or wife's failing to remember a stub for that counter check.

Two check-writers on the same account spell trouble to me, no matter what other virtues the system may hold. I say use separate accounts for man and wife, if two accounts really are needed. But it seems to me that one account would suffice for a family, unless both husband and wife are working and wish some small degree of financial independence.

As I said earlier, one member of the family, the most competent, should act as family bookkeeper, and that person should be in overall charge of the checkbook.

One great advantage of the check-writing method of paying bills over all other systems, is that it rules out the need for keeping most sales slips, receipts, and billings. The check is the record, once it is canceled, endorsed, and in your possession. And checks, being small, are easy to file and store.

Once the canceled checks are returned to you, they should be immediately reconciled. By that I mean you should attempt to prove that the balance shown in your account by the bank is the same you show on your stubs. This seems to frighten some persons, especially those who claim to have no aptitude for figures.

As you may already know, once a month the bank sends you your past month's checks, around which is an accounting statement. The checks are usually not in numerical order, but the checks are in the same order as they are listed on the bank's accounting sheet, the sequence in which the bank honored the checks. To reconcile your bank account, take the following steps, in order:

1. Match the amount of each check, as it comes up in the stack, against the bank's listing (from the top of the sheet down, usually). As you turn over each check, make a pencil or pen mark against the bank's list. Make sure the bank hasn't charged you with other persons' checks.

Then see if the bank correctly credited you with each deposit you made. These, too, will be in chronological order. See that the amounts match exactly with each of the sums you deposited.

2. If your pile of checks and your deposits match those on the bank's records, then sort the checks by check number. These should be chronological, too, in the order you wrote them, not as the bank received them.

3. Then go back to last month's reconciliation to see what checks were outstanding from the previous month's accounting. Usually they will be in by this time. If some are still outstanding, list them on this month's reconciliation column as still out. Now you are ready to see how many of your most recent month's checks are still uncashed.

4. Since now both your stubs and the checks themselves are in

numerical and chronological order, it is a simple matter to see which are still out. List those that are missing, in the space provided by the bank form. If you've made notations on voided checks you'll be spared trouble over that confusing aspect.

5. Once all outstanding checks are listed and then totaled, you follow the instructions shown on the bank reconciliation form. Subtract the outstanding checks from the balance shown on the bottom of the bank form (your balance); it should agree with the balance shown on your own check stubs. You can either reconcile up to the final check the bank cleared and returned to you, or you can carry it up to the end of the month and list all checks written up to that period in your outstanding column.

But in many cases you'll still show a slightly higher balance than the bank, even if your arithmetic and accounting are perfect. That's because of the bank service charge (analysis charge). Deduct that from your check stub account, by actually entering it as a check written, and you should be in balance with the bank.

Do this every month, without fail. If you can't do it immediately upon receiving the statement, do it just before that big bill-paying session once a month. But do it before you write more checks, for obvious reasons.

A checking account does cost money. Just $2 a month means $24 a year, the price of a new dress or a pair of shoes. Consequently, you should try to keep your bank service charge (analysis charge) as low as possible.

As I said before, two factors determine the cost of the regular checking account: *activity*, and the *size* of your average monthly balance.

To control the activity, make as few deposits as possible and write as few checks as possible. That could mean writing your spending allowance checks only once a month, for instance. And instead of writing checks every time you go to the store for groceries, you could write one check each month large enough for the month's groceries, and pay cash at the store each time. That would mean keeping cash around the house in a safe place.

As to keeping your balance high enough to offset the monthly service charges, that is almost impossible, and in many cases downright uneconomical. Many banks require as much as $500 to be in an account at all times, and if the balance slips below this point, even for a day or two, they use the *low* figure as your average, or minimum balance.

And it is usually penny-foolish to transfer money from a savings account to a checking account. Savings accounts pay from 3 to 4 per cent per annum, while a bank paying 3 per cent on savings may allow you only 2 per cent, or even less, as a credit for the balance in your checking account, as an offset against service charges.

Keeping the activity in your checking account down—the number of bookkeeping transactions the bank must make—is the key to a low service charge, not keeping a high balance in your account.

One checking account will do for most families, but I mean just one for regular monthly use. There is a kind of supplemental checking account that I have recommended for many families, one to use for those irregular bills that come due once or twice a year. I mean bills such as life insurance premiums, property taxes, vacation expenses, and others which aren't smoothly amortized (spread evenly) over each month. (Incidentally, *amortize* comes from the Latin words meaning "to kill." When you amortize a debt, you arrange for its burial.) For unamortized bills I suggest a second checking account, perhaps in a different bank. I'll cover that in detail next.

How to smooth over the rough spots

Many times during your life you'll have some tough sledding, financially speaking. But many a so-called emergency is nothing but the result of poor planning—failure to prepare for the inevitable.

"It seems like something throws our budget out of whack every month," complained one of my clients. But when I asked her to give me some examples, she listed such things as car repair, life insurance premiums, property taxes, an unexpected and unusually large dental bill, a vacation, a new refrigerator, and state income taxes.

Then I asked her to go back and add up the cost of all those things she mentioned as budget-breakers. It came to almost $1800. Next I asked her which of the expenses in the list could have been avoided. "None," she replied, "although I suppose we could have skipped a vacation."

Then I asked her which of the items really surprised her, which of them she could honestly say were unusual emergencies. Her answer came back, "Well, none of them, I guess, except for the refrigerator giving out, although we knew it would happen sooner or later—the thing was fifteen years old."

She admitted her husband's teeth had needed work for two years, and that they had been nursing the family car along for some time, hoping to stall off a repair bill.

It was just a matter of trying to ward off the inevitable, hoping against hope that a certain number of predictable, yearly expenses would not materialize. I finally convinced the lady and her husband they should set up a separate checking account, in a separate bank, and deposit $150 a month into the account.

And they did just that, not without encountering a few problems, however. What they learned was this: They had been spending on high living the money they should have been saving for the so-called emergencies. They'd been eating out a little too much, seeing too many shows and plays, spending carelessly for a number of things, and in general parting with some of their money quite frivolously.

But in a few months they felt compensated for their efforts and their discipline. There was money in the bank to meet various expenses as they arose, and they didn't have to rush down to the friendly finance company to rejuggle their budget just to meet the expenses they should have been providing for.

The point is, almost all financial "emergencies" can be predicted in advance. All a family needs to do is go back over the previous year's spending to identify the trouble areas. The next step is to add up the annual expenses not due in even monthly payments, and set aside that much money to meet the expenses as they come around.

I did not suggest the emergency money be placed in a savings account for a good reason. Almost every month a withdrawal is required. And setting aside money in advance, for spending that is soon to occur, isn't really "saving." At best it is short-term saving, and bankers understandably dislike cash going in and out of a savings account with great frequency.

A separate checking account would cost very little for most families using the system suggested above. The balance would stay reasonably high for one thing, offsetting a service charge, and in most cases there would be very little checking activity—one or two checks a month.

Why not leave enough cash in a regular checking account to meet those big unamortized bills? Human nature being what it is, the temptation would be too great to spend the money. Not only that, it would require a tricky set of personal books to know if there was enough money at all times in the general "pot."

Business firms have set up other and more simple ways for families to smooth out the rough spots in their budgets. As an example, you can have the annual property taxes on your home included in the monthly mortgage payment. But that can mean slow reduction of your mortgage and added interest expense. You can pay your life insurance premiums monthly, or even weekly, but at a stiff cost to you. You can even "prepay" your medical and dental bills under some form of prepayment insurance, but remember this: The insurance firm or association will add at least 10 per cent to your regular cost, just to handle your bookkeeping for you.

And, of course, there are all kinds of lending institutions ready to loan you money every time you become endangered by your own lack of planning. Such loans usually cost from 12 to 36 per cent interest, far more than the cost of an extra checking account and a little planning on your own.

If you try setting money aside in advance, your first reaction will be: "I just don't earn enough money to do that and live decently." What you really mean is: "I guess I've been living beyond my income and didn't realize it."

Either way, the solution has two aspects: either earn more money, or cut down on your spending. That is why almost two out of three young wives are working outside the home, and why millions of American men take on extra jobs.

The truth is, the American standard of living, as depicted in the ads, is beyond the reach of most one-income families today— a fact that shows up in the billions of dollars we owe to credit houses and lending institutions.

You can meet the problem head-on by providing in advance for the big expenses, and perhaps by cutting your living costs, or increasing your income, or both. Or you can just slide along and end up heavily in debt. It's up to you.

I can say this with certainty. If most businesses operated in the manner most families operate—not accruing money for predicted expenses—few of us would have jobs. There would be very few businesses operating.

HOW TO STOCK A "HOME OFFICE"

Items to keep on hand

Today a home is a small business. And to stay in business, the family money manager, or bookkeeper, needs to have a plentiful inventory of supplies. Coming under that heading would be pencils, pens, envelopes, stationery, stamps, erasers, a dictionary, and of course, little things like the spindle I suggested for holding unpaid bills.

Each time the family shopper goes for groceries, she should take inventory of what is short in the financial department. Since a copy of every business letter should always be retained, carbon paper is a necessity these days too, even for handwriting.

There should be some sort of a filing cabinet to hold records; secondhand filing cabinets can be bought inexpensively. One drawer in the cabinet should be for folders to keep carbons of letters, important receipts for tax records, and general correspondence, business and personal. And the folders should be clearly labeled, easy to read.

Take a look at the desk of any efficient bookkeeper or secretary and you will find an orderly arrangement. No one can work in confusion. A box is needed for stamps, a tray for paper clips and erasers, a desk calendar for important reminders, and a large wastebasket for toss-outs.

Two other little items help to round out a good family business center—a stapler and a sticky-tape holder. You'd be surprised how often you want to staple or stick things together.

These are the basics, the things you really need to tackle the bills and the family books, not to mention the annual chore of assembling and preparing your tax information and returns.

However, a good portable typewriter is almost a "must" these days too, even for persons who have to "hunt and peck." Typewritten letters and memos carry more weight and get better responses than handwritten ones. Not only that, but the person or firm getting the correspondence has a better chance of deciphering the message. And a small adding machine, if you can afford one, will really help.

Young persons may feel that all this preparing should come later, when family life gets more complicated and organized. But today married life becomes complex right from the start. The bills start rolling in, taxes come due, a young mother is flooded with all sorts of instruction sheets and pamphlets, and the husband finds himself looking for places to file things. So, get organized right away, not later.

Picking the right spot

No matter how well-prepared you are for work, it takes the proper surroundings to get a job accomplished. This means that great thought should be given to setting aside some part of the home for the family business section. No husband or wife can attend to detailed writing and arithmetic with children under foot. If space is a real problem, it's better to use a part of the parents' bedroom, assuming the door can be closed, than to put the desk and equipment in the so-called family room. Togetherness and budget-figuring are not very compatible.

An ideal arrangement, of course, is a separate room for bill-paying and record-keeping. This same room can hold books and various other things used for study. But such a luxury is not often possible for families just starting out, so the main thing to arrange is privacy and quiet.

There should be a desk, even if it is no more than a flat wooden door stretched across two boxes or filing cabinets. And if you have a typewriter, be sure it is on a stand or typing-level desk. The next most important item is a good desk lamp, one which doesn't glare into the eyes. If this is not possible, check the regular room lighting to see that there will be no eyestrain or blinding.

It is my opinion, based on experience, that a family business center should be that and that alone. Once it is used for another purpose, it loses its main value, that of being an inviting, convenient place in which to transact the family business.

Up to now we have more or less set the stage for other important aspects of money management. So far, we have dealt with the "ins and outs" of money, the actual handling of it. Now we'll get to another important phase, the spending of it.

SPECIAL SITUATION:
INCREASING YOUR INCOME

Does it pay a wife to work?

When a young husband and wife finally decide the family income just isn't grand enough to provide the standard of living they desire, the wife usually says, "Well, I can always go back to work." Most husbands at this point develop a sinking feeling in their stomachs, partly from embarrassment at not being good enough providers, and partly from reluctance to expose their wives to the temptations of the world. On the other hand, they reason, an extra $350 or so a month would go a long way toward clearing up some bills and raising the family standard of living. So back to the secretarial pool goes Elsie, a bit defensive, but somewhat thrilled to renew old acquaintances and get back in the swim.

If there are no children to care for, Elsie can indeed elevate her standard of consuming. Not as much as she thinks, of course, but considerably. Nevertheless, she ought to get out her pencil and do some figuring. Here is an actual example which came to my attention in the summer of 1966. The young wife was paid $350 (gross) per month for her work at a bank. First, let's take a look at her net paycheck.

Gross Wages:	$350.00
Social Security (4.2%):	14.70
Disability Insurance (2%):	7.00
Withholding-income tax:	48.90
Misc. Company Deductions:	12.40
	83.00
Net monthly pay:	$267.00

Thus, $83 disappeared right off the bat. Her income taxes were higher than when she was single because her husband was already claiming her as an exemption, and she couldn't claim herself. Even the company deductions were mostly extra expense, duplicating certain insurance protections her $10,000 per year husband was already providing.

Now let's see what happened to the remaining $267.

Elsie's net monthly pay:	$267.00
Lunches ($1 per working day average)	22.00
Extra gasoline for second car	10.00
Clothing, nylons, cleaning	30.00
Contributions and pools:	5.00
State Income Tax (not deducted)	8.00
Cleaning lady (once a week)	44.00
Extra meals out (from fatigue)	40.00
Net income after obvious costs:	$108.00

My, how $350 disintegrates when you finally count what's left. To be sure, this Elsie was building up her own social security credits, which is to be considered. She was dining out more frequently, although she sometimes was too weary to enjoy it. And, she did escape some of the drudgery of housecleaning. But to put in 37½ hours of work each week for only $25 left her somewhat disturbed. She decided to quit work after six months, much to the chagrin of her husband. Having become used to his wife fraternizing with office workers of both sexes, he no longer worried about that, while that hard-earned $108 a month did make the car payment. Anyway, back to the badly-bent budget.

Now, let's assume that Elsie was also a mother—of a child under five years of age. Chances are it would have cost her at least $70 per month for a full-time baby-sitter and/or for day school. Thus her net would be less than $40 per month. She would have been working for less than 25 cents an hour after taxes and expenses.

Forget it, you say? Not necessarily, as I'll show you. There's no way to whip the taxes and mandatory deductions, so let's work with the $267 and assume there will be no small child involved. Elsie could pack her own lunches and save at least $11 a month. There is no law saying she has to have a cleaning woman, at least not that frequently. Being too tired to cook dinners is sometimes an excuse to spend money. That expense could be reduced considerably. As to the $30 a month for clothing and cleaning, a little more homework could knock that in half. All in all, a wife who genuinely wants to help with the family finances could easily take home one-half or more of her gross paycheck—$175 a month in the example given. Even if she had small children she could net at least $100 per month from a $350 salary. The U. S. Department of Agriculture made a survey in 1966 to learn how much working mothers netted after taxes and job-related expenses. It turned out that 40 to 50 per cent of each gross check went for such expenses. The conclusion was that the working wife with children doesn't have a big profit to show for her efforts. But she still nets "something."

Whether that would make working worthwhile depends a great deal on what a wife is capable of earning. If she has no valuable job talents, she's merely trading her own unskilled labor for the unskilled labor of baby-sitters and cleaning ladies. If she is a highly paid secretary or an executive type, that's a different matter. And there are several ways of looking at this too. Netting only one-half of a paycheck sounds rather pathetic until you look at it from a business point of view.

Most any business would be happy to net 50 per cent on sales. So would many professional persons. Therefore, the mother who is able to trade her specialized services for those of other specialists, and come out 50 per cent ahead, is operating in the finest tradition of our society. That's assuming she enjoys her work to a reasonable extent and isn't depriving her children of a proper upbringing. (The widowed or divorced mother presents a different problem, and that will be discussed in a later chapter.)

There are several other aspects of the working wife situation worthy of mention. One has to do with the ability of a one-paycheck family trying to keep up with a two-paycheck society. More wives than ever are back in the commercial arena trying to supplement the family income, prodded on by other working wives who pay for otherwise impossible-to-obtain luxuries and conveniences. Entire industries are now based on the two-paycheck system, and among them are convenience foods, automatic dishwashers, and "instant" everythings. The husband who puts his foot down and says "I'm simply not going to allow my wife to leave home to work; she should be minding the house and children as woman always have done" needs to be a darned good provider and manager. Otherwise his standard of living will suffer noticeably from those of his friends and business associates. He will, in fact, often be embarrassed by his need to be frugal.

What's more, he best be married to an understanding, motherly, home-oriented type—preferably to a female philosopher who is beyond the material temptations enticingly displayed by television, newspapers, magazines, and neighbor ladies. There is always the possibility that away-from-home mothers present a sociological danger to our society—that their children will develop into neglected, urban monsters. Sociologists and welfare workers beat this drum rather regularly for many years. But looking at it logically, away-from-home daddies present a sociological danger, and I know of no way to cure that.

And here's another reality we must face. Most young wives are better educated than their mothers and grandmothers. Today's rather typical young wife is rarely content to stay home and play the role of a domestic. She demands greater challenges and greater rewards. Mother or not, she's eventually going to spend a great deal of time away from home, and she might as well spend it earning as yearning—or merely spending. What's more, the genuinely "educated" woman recognizes the implications of being away from her children most of the day. During the time she is with them she tries to make up for when she's away. A part-time, but devoted mother is far better than a full-time, but always complaining drudge.

If I seem to be making too strong a case for the two-paycheck family, it isn't that I welcome the trend without question or strong reservations. It's mainly that the clock can't be turned back. Except in rare cases, it takes two regular incomes to reach the so-called American Standard of Living. We can't educate young women to achievement and then turn them loose with vacuum cleaners and wet diapers. Perhaps even more importantly, we ought to stop making nervous wrecks out of young men by pretending it is within their abilities to live in the grand style on limited incomes, while remaining married to well-educated motherly domestics.

There also is this important point to bear in mind: considering all the automation and technological change, no man's job is really secure. Even a mature man has to face up to having to change not only his job, but his actual line of work, several times before he retires. A young man just emerging from college may have to change occupations five or six times before receiving his social security checks. And during that span of time, the odds are heavy that he'll be completely without income more than once. Isn't it wise to have another source of income, just in case? Knowing there'll always be *some* income to pay the bills and buy the food takes much of the frustration and fear out of the modern existence.

This relates to the matter of life insurance protection. The husband who loves his old-fashioned domestic life, to the point of insisting his wife remain at home, assumes an enormous security burden. What if something happens to him? Just thinking about that possibility often leads him to buy more insurance than he can comfortably afford. He may subscribe to the full (and expensive) treatment—guaranteed monthly income, disability insurance, double indemnity, options to buy additional protection without a medical examination, and huge face-value coverage. All of which are great if you can afford them. With the family's future so totally dependent on his earning power, the husband feels he dare not gamble. So he channels a great deal of his salary into the "expense" of hazard insurance, rather than into estate-building or better living. He does this even though his now completely domesticated wife once worked and had a job skill, because he knows that old job skills become obsolete rather quickly these days.

But the husband with a wife already working doesn't panic so easily. He knows his wife definitely has some earning power, that's it's already established and adjusted to. If something happens to him, there will be shock and emotional upheaval, but you can't insure against those. The economic disruption will be manageable, however, and that's important. Instead of having to spend so much guarding against the unthinkable, a husband with a wage-earning wife can begin to build a security estate almost immediately.

A near perfect situation could arise from a wife's being able to earn extra money without leaving home. But such work is hard to find, and unstable at best. A woman could search for months without finding profitable home-typing or sewing. Now and then such opportunities present themselves to properly qualified women, but in my experience they are rare indeed. Enjoy the best of both worlds if you can, but you may not have a chance.

What about the marriage itself? Will it suffer because of the pressures of two jobs? Will the two wage earners bore each other with personal job problems? Will they become estranged or hostile? Will sexual temptations split their happy, solvent marriage? The answer is, of course, "quite possibly." That is the kind of world we live in. It takes determination, understanding, and sophistication to stay married under the most ideal of conditions. The husband will have to acknowledge that he's only one part of a domestic-commercial partnership, and the wife will have to recognize that her husband is bound to suffer some misgivings about it all. But if it's necessary to quarantine a woman in order to keep a sparkle in her eye, there really isn't much to the marriage anyway.

Not too amazingly, most of our recent college graduates have thought out many of these things. They know the old rules of the game are dead, that neither "Father Knows Best" nor "Mother's Always Right" has much pertinence today. You make up the rules as you go along, kicking aside sacred cows as fast as they get in the way. Just because a man's mother worked exclusively in the home is no reason his wife should. And simply because a girl's father managed dandily on his job at the store is no guarantee her husband can or should.

There are plenty of other dangers associated with the working wife question. Should her income suddenly cease, spending habits might have to be drastically adjusted. This is particularly true if the husband has little chance of substantially increasing his own income. Budgets should be prepared with this in mind. To incur debts based almost entirely on the second income is living dangerously.

It used to be that a working wife secretly felt the need of a psychologist. Was she working primarily to escape her home life? Was she working mainly to afford luxuries not obtainable on her husband's limited salary? Well, she can go to a head-shrinker if she chooses. But in my opinion, "economic need" is not the only acceptable excuse for choosing a typewriter over a mangle. A woman *can* be a good wife and mother even as she aspires to the finer, material things in life. Provided, of course, she recognizes her primary responsibilities. And no, she's not stealing another person's job by working when she really doesn't have to. Everyone who works and creates makes a job for someone else, because of the wealth and purchasing power added to the economic mix.

It has already been established through research that about two-thirds of the married women without children are currently working outside the home. When and if children arrive, many of these women will choose to leave their employment to become full-time mothers, at least temporarily. A great many will go back to work when the children are old enough to enter nursery school, which comes at age two to three. Others will remain at home until the children have graduated from high school or college. The second career of women is a phenomenon of our age, but it is easy to understand. The home conveniences and gadgets which make it *possible* for a young wife and mother to work make it almost *mandatory* for an older woman. There's simply nothing to do when the children leave home. Unless the mother of a matured family has the money and inclination to pursue hobbies, work for charity, or become a clubwoman, time hangs heavy on her hands. She usually chooses to go back to work in order to help build the family security, not because she has to but because she wants to.

Such women, as most employers will surely agree, usually make fine employees. Not so, the younger woman who is forced back to her job because of pressing financial problems. She may be resentful and hostile. She may be counting the days until she can stop working again and stay home. It is one of life's little ironies that when a wife's earnings are needed the most, during those expensive younger years, circumstances make it hard to accomplish.

In the final analysis, and no matter how you measure it, a working wife usually is a better answer to supplementing the family income than is the practice of "moonlighting," where the husband attempts to work two jobs. While it is true that a working wife is holding down two jobs when laboring outside the home, the moonlighting husband has to work at three. Being a husband and father ranks almost equally with being a wife and mother. There is little left of a man who tries to hold down two paying positions, not enough to play head of the household when he arrives home to rest for a while. As a rule he is also deceiving one or both of his employers and this weighs on his conscience. Up to a point, of course, a man can supplement his regular income with occasional outside work, without sapping his energy or his emotions. But as a regular practice, it puts an enormous strain on his ability to measure up as a human being.

We are by nature a dynamic, restless breed. Contentment is not part of our heritage. It hasn't been since this vast continent opened up to our ancestors. There's a little of the Horatio Alger in most of us, stimulated by the incessant naggings of the commercial advertisers to upgrade our standards. Whereas in the older cultures a man would adjust his spending to his income, we aren't patient enough for that. We have to do better immediately, even if it means going into debt, working at two jobs, or encouraging our wives to work. No matter how much we earn, it's never quite enough. If we begin to suspect we've reached an earning plateau, we switch jobs or slip into a blue funk. There's a lot to be said for this sort of dissatisfaction, and a lot to be said against it. It depends on your personal view of life. But when personal ambition is carried to the extremes of gambling, stealing, and embezzling—which it often is—there's nothing to be said for it. Far better to break with the old patterns of living and start all over again if necessary. Men often do just that—win or lose.

On being your own boss

Wanting more money, through eliminating an employer's "profit," is only one reason why a man would struggle to become his own boss. It is *one* reason, however. Another and perhaps more important reason is the unwillingness to accept the discipline imposed by the corporate structure. A third reason is the abhorrence of corporate infighting, back-biting, and hand-kissing. As I labor with this chapter I am also reminded that one-half the people in America are under twenty-five years of age and that the majority of the better-educated youth of this country already have gone on record as being thoroughly disenchanted with the commercialism and the business way of life.

To write this chapter in the inspirational manner of Horatio Alger would be old-hat and downright dishonest. I would prefer to state the facts as I honestly see them and then to offer some personal observations. Having spent much of my life in the world of commerce, I certainly am not "anti-business."

Business has always been dog-eat-dog to a great extent. We shouldn't pretend otherwise. Nevertheless, an entire generation of Americans was weaned on the glamour, courage, and integrity of the business way of life. "My boy's going into business" was a prideful thing to say. Our children appear to be a bit more cynical. One recent poll showed that only a small minority of college students wanted any part of commerce, feeling that it was either too dirty or too lacking in inspiration. When the business "fraternal organizations" try to lure young men into their rituals they often come up with the misfits and lemons.

I could pussy-foot around for several chapters trying to dodge the real issues, but why bother? American business is a bit tarnished. It does lack inspiration in many instances, and it does leave much to be desired even when it comes to security. Many large corporations respect only one guideline, the P & L statement. The small entrepreneur faces a dismal future, unless he gets in and gets out fast. If he has a hot idea, it will soon be copied by giant firms with decided competitive advantages. Even the big corporations have to run pretty fast to keep from being gobbled up. Business mergers were taking place at the rate of nine a day during June of 1966 (over 2000 per year), with only occasional challenge from the anti-trust boys. Business cannibalism is rarely criticized; it is more often defended as a boon to the consumer and the economy in general. Efficiency is the password, no matter what it does to the human beings involved. One cannot help but admire the drive and ambition of these corporate executives, for those are the qualities you will need too.

At the opposite extreme, assuming you care to buck the odds and plunge into profit-making, is the "world owes me a living" crowd—those who think they were born with a proprietary interest in any job they select. These are the people you will have to hire if you get big enough. Many of them are poorly educated youngsters who never had to fight for a nickel or go without a lunch. They are the real victims of our society. They seemingly were born to consume and pay taxes, the perfect "epsilons" of Aldous Huxley's *Brave New World.*

As a fledgling businessman, you may develop a split personality, hating the established giants who are crowding you to the wall but also despising most of your employees because they evince no sympathy over your problems, and because they insist on being paid more than you feel they are worth. You'll often wish you had stuck to your job and your punch card or gone into the Peace Corps.

These are just some of the things every teacher of business or economics should say to his students, in my opinion, because anything less is shoving them into battle without weapons or armor. Then, if he is any kind of a philosopher, he might add something like this:

"Commerce is neither good nor bad in an abstract sense. It depends upon the product, the service, and the results. Profit-making is not to be condemned either, because it is only the means to better ends. Humans demand rewards for both effort and excellence, and rightly so. Who can say that wanting an extra million dollars is any more selfish than wanting a doctorate in philosophy?

"There will always be commerce of some sort, and to abandon it to the rascals is a short-sighted cowardly view. Even if you sneer at commerce and try to avoid it, you will have to live off it, which could make you somewhat of a parasite. I can't force you to like the world of business, but don't avoid it simply because it has attracted a certain number of bums."

To which I might add the following thought. Many an executive has blamed his unethical dealings on unswerving loyalty to his corporation. A corporation is by law an "artificial person," created by consent of live human beings. If each corporation were required to include in its articles of incorporation a pledge to respect and uphold the dignity, legal rights, and entitlement to fair play of every employee and customer, humanity might be better served. At least an executive would be hard put to blame his alligator tactics on the cruel corporation. Perhaps this is dreaming, but it's no more far-fetched than the loyalty oaths now required of many dedicated public servants.

I am filled with hope when a giant corporation such as Xerox will sponsor a controversial but informative television program, over threats of order cancellations. This is American business at its best in my view. Size need not be a danger, but eternal vigilance on our part is the best insurance against abuse. Whether you think of business as an interesting challenge and wish to become a part of it, or view it as a disgusting spectacle of unrestrained greed, there is absolutely no way to escape its impact on your life.

You may prefer to confine your activities in the P & L arena to those of carrying the swords or keeping score. And even if you choose not to become a gladiator, you'll sooner or later have to lay some bets on your favorites. That is precisely what we do when we invest or speculate in the stock market. I refuse to make a case for bad business tactics, and there are plenty of them at every level. But I can't help but remind you that our economy is the envy of the world, that it has helped create the leisure, education, and wealth which make it possible to indulge in self-analysis. We've done so well that most all other nations are trying to copy us, even the socialistic ones which are gingerly experimenting with the material reward "incentive system." No, business isn't necessarily bad, it has simply attracted a disproportionate number of one-dimensional men. You can't escape the business ethic by fleeing from the "corporation." It is here to stay, if for no other reason than because it is the most efficient form of doing business yet devised.

Furthermore, the odds are rather heavy that you'll make more money by adjusting to a giant organization than by striking out on your own. If you are nursing a personality problem, having trouble finding yourself in the extroverted organizational setup, that very problem will hamstring any effort to be your own boss. No matter what you do, you'll have to deal with people—good ones, bad ones and so-so ones. If it's just more money and recognition you are after, you can go after these before you even get involved with big business or while you're still an office boy, even after you become company president.

Here again, I wish I could come up with some exciting odds in your favor, but I can't. But it at least helps to know what you are up against, even if you do think "positively." The pragmatics of becoming a success are elusive at best. It helps to be handsome, personable, and well known. It also helps to be determined. But even these attributes are often not quite enough. Success quite often depends on luck, timing, and a boost from the right people. A new freeway can ruin one business and enrich another. A politician can put you out of business almost overnight, by pushing through a piece of "special interest" legislation. An electronic genius can make your own invention obsolete before you get it on the market. There are several cases of this happening. Even in the field of personal services, new inventions and big money cast their shadows. No matter what field of endeavor you pick— travel service, employment agency, bill collector, bookkeeping service, or whatnot—they are all being updated to include the latest equipment and techniques, which means a large capital investment and intense competition. What's more, most of the actual services performed by human beings will soon be handled by computers and automatic equipment.

It has been assumed until fairly recently that the "service industries" would be the last refuge of the small entrepreneur, but there are few things man can do that machines can't do better. Machines are "capital" rather than "labor," in the economic sense, which means, in essence, that we've finally accumulated enough wealth to replace ourselves. It may finally boil down to who owns the machines. You can still make money operating a service-type business, but not as much as you might think, or for as long as you may hope.

If selling your services or talents doesn't appeal to you, there always is the alternative of making something, going into the manufacturing business in other words. Or, you can go into construction work, publishing, or just about any field of business now operating. You can even make a "business" of starting businesses and then selling them.

So, what are your odds? The average new business venture survives about four years. According to the U. S. Department of Commerce, only half of all new business enterprises last for two years. One in three survives for four years, and only one in five lasts for five years. Those which do succeed help balance the averages by lasting for a good many years.

The predominant reasons for failure are lack of ability and lack of capital. According to Elmer L. Winter, in *Your Future in Your Own Business* (Rosen Press), of the 13,501 businesses that failed in 1964, 56 per cent had lived for less than five years. And in analyzing these defunct concerns, it became apparent that management inability was the primary cause of failure, followed closely by lack of capital. In many cases the management was capable in a general sort of way, but not competent in the particular field involved. And most men underestimated the amount of money required to swing a new business deal today.

Having been a trustee in bankruptcy for a number of insolvent small businesses, I can testify first-hand that lack of capital can ruin the most promising new endeavor. I've tried to salvage concerns that began life with barely enough cash to cover the second month's rent. There are other common characteristics of failure, such as refusing to keep a decent set of books, trying to skip the services of a good lawyer, and cutting prices merely to increase volume. Always try to learn what those in similar fields net. The U. S. Department of Commerce has a wealth of material on those statistics. Hire a lawyer who will help you set up the proper legal structure. If you need large amounts of capital, the corporate form of business is almost a must, even if you yourself are a fugitive from the corporate way of life. Contact an accountant and ask him to set up a set of books for you. Either learn to make the proper entries on a regular basis or hire someone to do it for you. The more frequently you obtain a detailed profit and loss statement, the less likely you'll be to sink too much money into a doomed business. And the more likely you'll be to correct mistakes before it's too late. Make certain you understand the fundamentals of the business you choose before you hang out your sign.

If, for instance, you decide to open an eating place, it would be wise to work as a waiter, man in charge, and purchasing agent—even as cook's helper—before you go it on your own.

Getting paid while you're an apprentice is an inexpensive way
to learn. But even then, be sure to read some good books on
how to succeed in that particular field. The most successful farmer
I know had never been on a farm until after going back to
college and getting a degree in agriculture at Iowa State College.
And even after that he worked on a farm before investing in his
own acreage.

In case you think you'd like to operate a small motel on your
own, the Bank of America recently stated that it's no longer a
"Mom and Pop" game. During 1966, the older and smaller
motels were being "phased out" at the rate of 2000 to 3000
per year. The big chains have taken over. The same is true of
the small neighborhood grocery store. A few such stores still
survive, concentrating on either luxury items or easy credit.

Maybe you'd like to be an inventor. I've had some experience
at that worth repeating. A friend of mine formed a small corporation to market a product for home use. The item was useful,
cleverly designed, and highly unique. First he tried to produce
and sell it to retailers, since that would net the most profit over
the long haul. Therefore, he contacted a plastics manufacturer
for an estimate. The men in charge of such things quickly informed my friend that an estimate would be impossible until he
had studied a set of precise engineering blueprints, which at the
lowest figure would cost about $4000. That seemed like quite a
financial gamble *just* to obtain a production cost estimate. What's
more, even with the proper blueprints, the molds for the item
would run into at least another $75,000.

It soon became obvious to my friend that he ought to do
some believable market research before raising that kind of
money for a new and untried product. But a research firm wanted
$5000 to do a professional survey. So that idea was abandoned
too. It eventually boiled down to one of two things: interesting
a going concern into making the product on a royalty basis, or
selling out to one of the giant retailers, who have their own
manufacturing connections. He hoped to get 5 per cent of the
production costs as a royalty. The manufacturers were almost

impossible to deal with. In each case they wanted to keep the item and study it for several weeks, and since the patents hadn't been officially approved, that would have been a rather naïve gesture.

Since most large manufacturing firms have their own research departments, the usual reaction was N.I.H., or "not invented here." In fact, in order to interest a manufacturer in a new product, you almost always have to go through its own research department. The response is what you might expect. As of this writing, this particular product is still in limbo, but I am certain the situation is far from unique. It takes really big money to get anything on the market today, far more "risk capital" than most inventors or small business firms can raise. In addition, there are the problems of packaging, inventorying, merchandising, and mass advertising. To go into the manufacturing of a new product often takes an initial investment of around $250,000, and that can disappear in a few months. Worth bearing in mind is the actual case of a hand lotion dispenser which met every market test and eventually appeared on the department store shelves—at a cost of close to $300,000. Every problem of production and merchandising had been whipped, except one—hardly anyone wanted it. The firm folded shortly after its first big bang. There are many cases similar to that one. There are plenty of success stories too, such as the hoola-hoop, which is simplicity itself. My point here is to show what you face when you try to get something new on the market.

Because of all the requirements needed to make a success of any new business, including money, knowhow, and experience, the franchising system would seem promising. A franchise is a contract to operate a business under prescribed methods established by a franchising company. Under this arrangement an investor can obtain advice, systems, and practical experience— for a price, of course. Some franchises have proved valuable beyond exaggeration. Others proved to be utterly worthless.

For about $2, you can obtain a book listing hundreds of franchises, with classifications by both "line of business" and the cost involved. The book is the Franchise Annual, published by the National Franchise Reports, 333 North Michigan Avenue, Chicago, Illinois. Usually one pays an original franchise fee to the parent company, plus a monthly fee based on the volume of business. Quite often you have to order all your supplies through the franchising firm. Aside from the honesty of the company, and its commercial knowhow and experience, you have to rely a great deal on its market research regarding location and profit potential.

And, unfortunately, the franchise field recently has been flooded with frauds and questionable operators. The Federal Trade Commission has been busy trying to weed out the bad actors. Vending machine concessions in particular have been oversold under franchising, and so have many automatic laundry operations. The factors most investors seem to ignore is the cost of replacing and servicing their machines. They also ignore the value of their own time and effort.

Some restaurant franchises have proved to be highly profitable. As just one example, the International House of Pancakes, which is actually owned by International Industries, Inc., had over 100 outlets franchised during 1966. Some Pancake House operators were netting more each year—after paying themselves a salary—than they originally paid for their franchises. Some Orange Julius franchises also have been very rewarding to investors. Any honest franchising firm should be as careful in selecting its business connections as investors would be in parting with money. You should be able to see figures to back up the claims made and to visit with other franchise owners.

There are a number of "franchise schools" operating throughout the country, some honest and some not. A few are merely "fronting" for questionable franchising outfits. During early 1966, forty-nine persons were under Federal indictment for selling, or attempting to sell, worthless franchises through the mails. One hundred ninety-one other persons or firms were being investigated by postal authorities. The franchise field has become so risky that only the most thorough investigation would warrant an investment.

Even if you don't care about going into business in a big way, choosing instead to run a one-man operation with perhaps one or two employees, things won't be easy. The world of business has become tremendously complex, and there are few men capable of acting simultaneously as sales manager, personnel manager, bookkeeper, and general flunky. Even were you that talented and diversified, there are limits to time and energy. You would be competing, sooner or later, with much larger enterprises better able to delegate duties and responsibilities.

You should also be aware of some of the newer pitfalls to being a modern-day success story. While most of our less populated states encourage the formation of new enterprises, some of our larger states seem to view it with alarm. New York and California both regulate almost into the ground. Forming a small corporation often costs $1000 or more including the attorney fee. Most large states will check their statutes carefully to see if you don't come under some licensing arrangement. If you handle public money or trust funds, you'll likely have to be bonded, both to the state and your clients. You may even be audited by the state every year. In California this costs $100 per day per auditor. The county assessor will want his cut, taxing the value of your office equipment. The city may require a "business license tax" based on gross volume, rather than on net profit.

A number of states screen applications to do business very carefully. An "Investment Counsel" certificate in California costs $50 per year, but that's the least of it. Such an applicant will be interrogated, fingerprinted, and checked back to the day he was born. Not all of this care and red tape come from wanting to protect the public. Some come from established bureaucracies trying to expand their powers and increase their revenues.

Some of the problems, too, arise from the influence of established industries within the various state agencies. All businesses are very alert to the dangers of potential competition, and they make it as hard on newcomers as possible. In time, most regulatory agencies come to serve the industries they are set up to regulate.

And finally, the so-called "consumer protection lobbyists" often defeat their own goals. In an effort to erase business abuses and to screen out bad actors, they make the rules of the game so complex and costly that only the big operators can survive. Thus, the consumer suffers from lack of competition and the small entrepreneur has to abandon the field. One of the worst requirements being imposed on certain service industries is the "minimum capital" rules. If a man has to put up $25,000 or more in order to hope to earn $10,000 per year, he's whipped before he starts, especially when you consider his chances of failure. This "minimum capital" requirement is probably unconstitutional if you want to carry it high enough, but in the meanwhile it is proving to be the best gimmick yet to restrict competition within any one field. It's almost as bad as the "convenience and necessity" laws under which state officials have the power to deny a new license simply because the public "appears" to be adequately served by the existing number of firms.

If, in spite of all the warnings and philosophical observations I have offered on business in general, you decide to have a try at it on your own, let me be the first to compliment you. Being willing to try is very nearly its own reward. Money will likely be your first hurdle. Don't make the mistake of being under-capitalized. It is always better to start with more than you think you'll need than not enough. You can always return some of the capital tax-free.

Keep in mind that banks rarely, if ever, make loans to start up a business. That is considered "risk capital" and you'll have to raise it elsewhere. Unless you have plenty of funds yourself, you may have to rely heavily on friends, relatives, and business associates. The Small Business Administration can be helpful, but unless you have a very good idea, a fine chance of success, and quite a bit of capital already, don't waste your time applying. The same goes for the Small Business Investment Companies, or SBICs, licensed by the SBA. In 1966, some 200 of the SBICs, out of 700 in total, were virtually insolvent or in a shaky condition. Many of the others weren't making loans except to affiliate concerns and "sure things." Some of the SBICs were quite obviously "holding companies" for miscellaneous enterprises of the chief stockholders. Just before getting into this book I phoned twenty different SBICs and not one was interested in making a loan to a stranger.

If it's capital that's holding you back, forget about the easy ways; get out and sell your idea to people with money who trust you. Make up a brochure outlining your requirements, experience, chances for success, and proposed method of operation. Document your reasons for thinking the venture will succeed. Draw up a month-by-month profit and loss projection covering at least six months, or until you hope to break into the black. This alone may convince a fence-sitting prospect.

And if you do raise the necessary money, go easy on your own draw or salary. Acting like a tycoon before you're out of the red ink is a legendary way to go broke. Wait awhile before buying a bigger home and moving up in the world. Cement your future with a good solid cash reserve. That's one sure way to expand, because bankers love to lend money to borrowers who don't seem to need it. If you've got a good thing going, don't be too conservative when it comes to borrowing money; using the capital of others is a time-tested method. Be hard-nosed about the terms and the interest rates, however, and keep the due dates on your calendar. Pay a loan in advance once in a while. Play one bank against another now and then.

Keep track of your profits-to-sales ratio, and make sure the capital you have is paying its own way. When it comes to business, there's no substitute for being businesslike. Generally speaking, money is where the people are, which is why I stressed the trends within our larger states. But when you consider the more laissez-faire attitude of the smaller states, without all the red tape and bureaucracy, you may do better in Middletown than in Megalopolis.

I suspect it takes a unique breed of man to succeed in business today. Just like a football player, he has to love rough body contact. If you're that kind of guy, nothing I've said should deter you. It should, in fact, stimulate you. All I'm trying to do is point up the newer rules of the game.

PART II

MANAGING YOUR SPENDING,
or Where the Money Goes

KEEPING A ROOF OVER YOUR HEAD

Renting versus buying

Shelter, or housing, is one of three big necessities of family spending. As such, you should approach the subject coolly and economically. Yet there is more fuzzy thinking on the subject of housing, particularly as to the merits of renting versus buying, than on any other aspect of family spending.

Young people particularly hate to rent, even for a short time. The reason for this fixation can be traced to a popular myth—the one about rent receipts being pure "waste." Rent money is no more wasted than the money spent for bread or for medical care. Yet despite that fact, too many persons think of house payments as almost pure "savings," and of rent money in terms of a leaky faucet. Some persons may be deliberately closing their minds to economic reality in order to "own their own homes."

The hard truth is that in normal times it is almost as inexpensive to rent a single-family unit as it is to buy such a place. In order to prove this, we'll examine the whole landlord-tenant relationship.

A landlord renting out a one-family dwelling would be lucky to earn a net of 6 per cent on his equity—the home value less the mortgage—and only then if he received his rent promptly and kept the place tenanted most of the time. And you notice I said on his "equity," not on the value of the home.

Thus, a landlord with a $5000 equity in a $25,000 home *might* hope to earn about 6 per cent on his $5000 each year, or a mere $300. Or to put it another way, if you had that much equity in your $25,000 home, you'd be saving that same $300, or $25 a month, by *not* renting the house from a landlord. And you might not save that much, because you can't claim as many tax deductions as a landlord.

You may be sophisticated enough to answer that at least you'd be able to deduct the interest and property taxes from your income tax return. Well, so can a landlord, and what's more, he can deduct the insurance, the upkeep, and the depreciation on the home, too, which you can't. Depreciation is the amount by which the home loses value. Yet he'd still be lucky to net 6 per cent on his equity, even after utilizing these tax advantages.

The only exceptions to this are the slum landlords, many of whom charge outrageous rents on run-down houses. Middle-income persons are more careful in what they rent and in the rents they pay.

Let's put it in another way. Every house has a potential "rental value," the sum of money that could be realized by renting it out to a tenant. As a rule, the rental value of a house is about 10 per cent per year of the market value. Thus, a $25,000 home has an approximate annual rental value of $2500—a little over $200 a month. If you continue to live in the $25,000 home you own (or are buying on mortgage), the real cost to you each year is about $2500.

Why? Because, quite logically, that is what you could earn each year by moving out and renting your place to a tenant. So, if you choose to live in your own place, thereby passing up or consuming the possible income from renting, your costs are easy to measure. They are the sums you lose by not renting out your place.

I know—you'd just have to find another place to live. But you COULD collect the $2500 from a tenant and then move into an economy rental unit yourself, saving perhaps as much as $1000 per year. I'm not suggesting anyone do that, of course; I'm simply trying to show what it really costs to live in your own house. You are, of course, your own landlord when you live in your own investment.

If the landlord in the make-believe case had his $25,000 place completely paid for, he would net a little more money. He would

net about $1500 per year. But remember this, he would be tying
up $25,000 to make that $1500 a year. He could do about that
well or better by selecting some good common stocks, and have
far fewer headaches. He could earn 4 per cent or more in an
insured savings and loan company.

Which brings me to another point. If you have a high mortgage on your place, you lose much of the advantages of home
ownership. The interest you pay the finance company comes out
of your potential profit or savings.

On the other hand, even if you own your place free and clear,
you are just sitting on top of a lot of equity which could be invested otherwise.

The truth is, a single-family dwelling isn't much of an investment, in the real sense of the word, either for landlords or for
homeowners. Homes these days are more hobbies than investments.

Then why do so many families buy their own homes? Partly
for the reason I just gave, because of misconceptions about economy. But there are other reasons, one of which has to do with
land inflation, especially in booming areas. If you live, or want to
live, in an area which is growing fast, you may be able to count
on your land increasing in value. But there is a limit to the rate
of increase in value of land.

You take your chances when you count on inflation to bail
you out of a costly real estate purchase. And while you're waiting for the land to inflate, taxes and interest can murder your
budget.

Another reason so many persons buy homes today is the tax
angle I mentioned. But only persons with substantial incomes
can save much on their income taxes by paying high interest
costs and high property taxes. The fellow making $10,000 a year
doesn't get much of a break from the extra deductions for this
reason. Even the top part of his income, after allowing for his
personal exemptions (the number in his family) and his regular
deductions, doesn't get into the really high tax brackets. Middle-
income persons sometimes save as much as 10 per cent of the net

cost of their interest and property taxes by deducting them from gross income.

But the Federal Government allows each family a 10 per cent flat deduction anyway, and unless a family has enough deductions to itemize, including mortgage interest and property taxes, these last two costs become pure expense.

The income tax break on home ownership usually goes to those families with quite high incomes, say $20,000 a year on up. Lower income persons may think they save on income taxes by owning their homes, and some do, but not as much as they believe. For one thing, many persons think of interest and property taxes as being deducted from the net income taxes themselves, sort of substituting for income taxes. This is not the case. These two big costs of owning a home are merely deducted from GROSS INCOME, thereby reducing the income taxes by only a fraction.

In addition to thinking they are saving most of the money they'd be spending on rent receipts, overestimating the amounts they save on income tax deductions, and hoping for land inflation, many persons have other and more valid reasons for buying homes. They feel a home is a better place to raise children than a rented apartment, and this is often true.

Some persons want status, and a fancy home is a sort of prestige symbol. It always has been and probably always will be.

Some persons plunge into home ownership simply because others are doing it, a kind of follow-the-leader thinking. And many persons buy homes because they have no choice; they have too many children to please any landlord, or live in cities where decent rental units are scarce.

There are a number of valid reasons for home ownership—mostly sociological reasons—but there are very few genuine economic reasons. If owning a home makes you a better and more responsible citizen and gives you more privacy, then buy a home. But if you get the urge to boast about all the money you are saving, don't tell your tale to an economist. Not at least until you've done a lot of figuring and comparing.

But if nothing else, the rather cold-blooded treatment I've

given home ownership so far should prove one thing to you: The size of the monthly payment has little to do with the real "cost" of owning a home. You should know enough now, for instance, to compare the cost of an apartment with the cost of a home you might buy.

And the way to do that, of course, is to compare the *annual rental* for an apartment, with 10 per cent of the *value* of the *home* you are considering. If you foolishly compare the monthly apartment rent with the monthly payment on a home, you are in effect comparing pounds to inches. There is no comparative relationship, none whatsoever. Mortgage payments have nothing to do with "cost" of home ownership. They are simply a measurement of debt reduction.

As any professional landlord knows, the real costs of owning a house are these:

> Upkeep and repair
> Fire and homeowner insurance
> Property taxes
> Depreciation (value loss)
> Equity investment

These expenses are just as real to a homeowner as to a landlord. The big difference is that a landlord recognizes them and includes them in the price he charges for use of his property, whereas too often the homeowner pretends the expenses don't exist.

The landlord knows he must get about 10 per cent per year in rent for his property to cover his expenses and net him a profit, even a small profit, just on his equity. Homeowners would be wise to think as landlords do.

And this presentation should do one more thing for you. If you are now living in an apartment, itching to buy your own home and save the rent money, take heart. The drain on your solvency isn't as bad as all that. You can afford to help the landlord pay his own bills for a while, without prejudicing your future.

If you have a reasonably good deal where you live, the most you are losing is perhaps 10 per cent of what you are paying in rent each month. Don't jump into a home mortgage until you are ready, financially and philosophically. At least by renting you'll be free to move in the event of a job transfer. You may want to remain mobile for a while.

As a final clincher, let me resolve one problem that is probably still worrying you. You may by now have conceded that home ownership isn't free, that it does cost money. But you still feel that at least by buying a home you'd eventually have something to show for it, whereas you'd have nothing but rent receipts otherwise.

But that needn't be. After all, I've been comparing the "cost" of renting with the "cost" of owning. You can save money and acquire net worth in other ways than by paying on a mortgage. You can simply open a savings account.

How much house can you afford?

Now that you know how to measure housing costs, the logical question is: How much can I afford? There is no magical rule as to the percentage of one's income which should be spent on rent or housing. But a number of consumer economists stick to the 25 per cent rule.

It is a fairly good rule, for this reason: While it is possible to spend 50 per cent or more of your income on home ownership or rent, you probably wouldn't carry it off very well. It would mean scrimping on most other areas of the budget, and actually doing without a number of essentials. Those who like to stretch their housing capacity to the limit usually like to gamble on other things too.

Most Americans want to live the well-balanced life today, which means, in essence, fine clothing, good food, the best medical care, decent transportation, and expensive vacations. So, it becomes a matter of giving a certain percentage of one's income to each aspect of the budget. Twenty-five per cent for housing is a time-tested and reasonable figure. After all, a roof is only one part of living.

Assuming you are willing to limit your spending on housing to 25 per cent, all you need do is arrive at one-fourth (25 per cent) of your gross annual income, and then multiply that figure by 10.

Let's assume you earn $8000 per year, for example. One-fourth of $8000 is $2000, which multiplied by 10 comes out to $20,000. That figure is about what you can afford to pay for a home and stay within the 25 per cent budget allowance for shelter. The reason for multiplying by 10 is this: As I explained before, to arrive at what a home really costs to live in on an annual basis, you simply take one-tenth of the home's market value. Here we are doing just that in reverse, multiplying our "ability to spend" by 10 in order to obtain the price or market value of what we can afford to purchase.

Let's try another example. Suppose you earn $12,000 a year. Twenty-five per cent of that is $3000, which multiplied by 10 turns out to be $30,000. And chances are, you could swing that expensive a home on $12,000 a year. But in the higher-income ranges, some other factors creep in. If you earn $12,000 a year, you may not *need* or *want* to spend the full 25 per cent of your income for housing. A $25,000 home might do very well indeed, which in the case of the $12,000 income would mean spending only a little more than 20 per cent for housing.

Or, on such an income, you could be virtually strapped financially, because of seven or eight children. Or you could have money to burn, being childless.

With many children, you naturally would want to spend as little for housing as possible; also you would need several bedrooms and lots of space.

With no children, on the other hand, you might go for the tops in elegance—a one-bedroom palace, with the emphasis mostly on convenience and styling. You might even stretch your housing budget up to a $35,000 house, even if you didn't need to.

This should prove that there is nothing sacred or absolute about the 25 per cent rule, for one thing; but that in addition, it makes a great deal of difference *how* the housing dollar is spent. No two families have exactly the same situation, or the same preferences.

Lower-income families have even more of a problem. For most families on modest incomes—those with children—25 per cent is probably too much to spend on housing. But so far, private builders have difficulty making a profit on low-cost homes. This results in many families with children spending too much on housing from lack of choice.

Nevertheless, unless there are extenuating circumstances, most families should try to keep housing costs within 25 per cent of their incomes. Otherwise there comes a day of reckoning, when other important phases of living take a beating.

Home-financing agencies approach the housing percentage figures in a slightly different manner. Most of them limit home buyers with substantial mortgages to homes worth not over 2½ times the buyer's annual salary. But the figure for housing comes out to about the same as in my method. Take the $8000 income example I used, in which, according to my method, you have the ability to buy a $20,000 home. Under the finance agency system, 2½ times $8000 comes out to $20,000, too. It's just a different way to arrive at the same answer in most cases.

However, an independent study group came to the conclusion a few years ago that most home buyers should limit themselves to homes worth only 2 times annual salary. The group cited these reasons, among others: property taxes are going up; interest costs have been rising; and modern homes, with all the built-in conveniences, take a great deal of maintenance. The higher the home price, generally speaking, the more the taxes, the more the maintenance, and the more the interest cost.

In my opinion, 2½ times annual income is stretching things to the very limit, even if the home can be purchased for cash. You can be conservative and go along with the independent study group, or you can gamble a little and use the 2½ times income rule.

About now you may be wondering where the mortgage payments fit into all this. Don't the monthly payments really determine how much home you can buy?

The answer is yes, the payments do determine how much you can *buy*; unfortunately, they *don't* measure your ability to keep the house insured, the taxes paid, or the home in good repair. And the payments on a home, as I stated before, bear no real relationship to the cost of living in a home.

Mortgage companies recognize this fact. That is why few such firms will allow a person to pledge more than 20 per cent of his income on home payments.

The real costs of living in a home—depreciation, upkeep, taxes, insurance, and the cost of tying up cash in equity—have nothing to do with the payments on the debt. Although some mortgage companies do require buyers to pay into an escrow fund to see that taxes and fire insurance premiums are kept up, to my knowledge no mortgage companies have prepayment plans for upkeep and depreciation. But it proves why mortgage companies should, and usually do, insist on the monthly payment being well below the 25 per cent of income marked for total housing costs —unless, of course, the home involved is priced considerably below the buyer's ability to support it.

Those persons owning homes in the booming, land-inflated West may laugh at such a thing as home depreciation. "Land prices and homes always go up in value, not down," they might logically answer. And for many years this has been true in the West. But families in less booming spots in the East and Middle West know homes can lose value. They've experienced it.

Actually, homes do lose value everywhere. This is often disguised because the land inflates in value, and the dollar itself loses value. Even in the West, Uncle Sam lets building owners and landlords depreciate their properties under our income tax laws.

And remember, there are different types of depreciation. There's the kind caused by age and use, the common kind. And there's the kind called functional depreciation, which is caused mostly by changes in the neighborhood brought about by decay, neglect, and unsightly commercialism. But it can also be caused by changes in tastes. One house may lose value much faster than a home of the same age and original price next door to it. The style and architecture of one home may be out of popularity, whereas a home next door may have a style just coming into vogue. A two-bedroom home is harder to sell today than a three-bedroom home. A home buyer wanting to hold his investment together has to keep abreast of the trends, and avoid the offbeat. We may not like it, but the tastes of the masses have a great bearing on how products, including homes, hold their resale value.

There is one aspect of home ownership that confuses even the experts in real estate. It has to do with the rising cost of land in relation to the total "package price" you pay for a homestead. Not too many years ago, if you paid $10,000 for a home and lot, the land itself would be worth about $1000—10 per cent of the entire price, in other words.

But in recent years, the land price percentage has increased to 30, 40, or even 50 per cent. If land continues to rise in value, the person with a $20,000 home sitting on $20,000 worth of land gets a good deal. He may be able to unload his $40,000 unit at a profit.

But if land holds steady in price, or actually goes down in value, millions of families will get hurt. After all, living above $20,000 worth of dirt can be pretty costly at 6 per cent a year, plus taxes. You might compare it to clipping the coupons off $20,000 worth of gilt-edge bonds and making a meal of them. My advice is, build your dream home on sensibly priced land. If the total package price of a home and lot is over 25 per cent sod, you really aren't a homeowner—you've become a real estate speculator.

One more warning as to how much housing you can afford. Don't include your wife's salary in your salary-housing measurements, unless her job is steady, and unless more children are a distinct improbability. Few mortgage men would allow you to get away with this anyway, unless you fibbed to them. But some persons aren't above a little fibbing when some particular house catches their fancy.

Of course, we've been discussing pure "housing costs" so far. The broader term SHELTER includes utilities and such. A home requiring a great deal of money for heating, cooling, and cooking would be more expensive to own than a home with fewer, low-cost utilities.

To sum up:

1. Try to keep your housing costs within a sensible percentage of your total budget, say about 25 per cent.

2. Make certain you know how to figure your true housing costs.

3. Think like a landlord would think if you have delusions about the low cost of owning your own home.

4. Don't confuse the mortgage payments with the real expenses of homes—notably depreciation and upkeep.

5. Be a bit of a conformist in what you buy, unless you can afford to take a financial shellacking when you sell out.

6. Unless you want to be in the real estate business, avoid high-priced land.

7. Don't include uncertain income in your housing budget.

8. Watch the overhead, the cost of the various utilities.

Since most families must finance their homes, the mortgage is an important factor. We'll discuss that next.

Obtaining the best mortgage

Mortgages can be deadly. This truth was recognized when the word "mortgage" was first used to describe a lien on property.

Because, like the word "amortize," the word "mortgage" has a Latin origin relating to death. Apparently, in the old days, mortgages were settled after funerals. It's the "mort" part, which is found in "mortuary," which has the deadly meaning.

But let's be fair—there are good mortgages and bad ones, even though any mortgage is a lien or plaster against one's property.

Here are some of the features to look for in a good mortgage:

1. Low interest.

2. Low closing costs.

3. Little or no penalty if you pay off ahead of schedule.

4. Modest and clearly-defined late charges if you are slow in making a payment.

5. Enough time and leeway to protect you if you get behind in your contract.

6. A fair treatment of funds you pay in advance to meet taxes and insurance.

7. The right to furnish your own fire and comprehensive insurance if you choose.

There are two other mortgage features which may or may not be advantageous to you. It depends on how you use them. They are:

1. Long, stretched-out terms.

2. An open-end arrangement, whereby you can repeatedly borrow against the equity you build up, with a minimum of time and red tape.

Before I discuss each of these nine features in more detail, I want to point out there are three basic types of liens against real property. One is the regular, familiar mortgage. Another type of lien is the contract, or installment sale device whereby title (legal ownership) to the property doesn't pass until the final payment. And a third is the "trust deed," which really isn't a deed at all, but a type of lien. Sometimes the three types are more or less combined under a trust deed arrangement.

A deed is simply a legal written instrument of conveyance or sale. But a trust deed, especially the kind used in California, becomes more of a lien than a conveyance of title. Words can be confusing. I will describe the three types later in this section.

INTEREST

Taking the interest factor first, it is hard to exaggerate the importance of keeping interest costs down.

Two factors influence the general trend of interest rates: supply and demand. While much has been said about the supply of money, very little has been said about demand—the price consumers are willing to pay. Because no matter how much lenders want for the use of their money, it takes two to make a bargain. The truth is, few home buyers really understand the difference one percentage point makes in the overall cost of owning a home. Here is an example of how interest does matter. I've used a $20,000 mortgage to be repaid in equal (amortized) monthly payments over a *twenty-five-year* period, a common enough transaction in today's home market. And I've used three interest rates, 5, 6 and 6.5 per cent.

INTEREST RATE	MONTHLY PAYMENT	TOTAL INTEREST IN 25 *Years*
5	$116.92	$15,076
6	$128.84	$18,652
6.5	$135.05	$20,515

So, 6 per cent costs you $3,576 more than 5 per cent, and 6.5 per cent costs $5439 more than 5 per cent, on the $20,000 mortgage spread over twenty-five years. The difference would be even greater on a thirty-year mortgage.

You can see, for instance, that at 6.5 per cent you pay more interest over twenty-five years than you borrowed in the first place. Believe it or not, in some parts or the United States, 7 and 8 per cent rates are common. In fact, the problem compounds itself, for this reason. The longer the time persons ask for in which to repay, and the less they pay down, the higher the interest rates. That is because longer terms and higher mortgage balances make for greater risk to the lender. And the greater his risk, the more interest he wants for assuming that risk.

There is another way to show the impact of interest on a mortgaged home, by showing how much extra interest you would pay at 6 per cent for each additional $1000 borrowed over a *twenty-five-year* period.

AMOUNT BORROWED	25-YEAR COST	ADDITIONAL INTEREST
$11,000	$10,261	
$12,000	$11,196	$ 935
$13,000	$12,128	$1867

At 6 per cent, for every additional $1000 you carry back on a twenty-five-year mortgage, you pay back in interest almost as much as you originally borrowed. The moral is: Pay down as much as you can.

There is another way to reduce the punishing effect of high interest rates on a long, drawn-out mortgage. Accept the extended twenty-five-year term with low amortized payments, if you feel at all worried about keeping up the contract. But whenever possible, double up on the payments. "Double up" is not quite the way to put it. You simply add to your regularly scheduled payment the amount by which your principal balance would be reduced by the *following* month's payment. Let's suppose your regular home payment is $95.34. Next month it would be the same, of course, but on the amortization chart kept by the financial institution, the second $95.34 might be broken down this way: $70 to interest, $25.34 to principal. So you ask for that breakdown and add the $25.34 to your $95.34. You simply give the cashier $120.68. And believe it or not, you save that extra $70 forever.

How else could you buy $70 for $25.34? If you do that sort of thing often enough, you might surprise yourself and end up actually owning your home, at a reasonable interest cost.

You may wonder how such savings are possible—the whole thing sounds unbelievable. It comes about because of the amortized mortgage, which has been held up as a boon to home buyers. And to some extent it is. It makes home financing much easier. But the amortized mortgage, where the principal and interest are homogenized into even, smooth payments, can be extremely expensive.

You see, back in the old days, mortgages came due in big chunks. If a man borrowed $10,000, he would be expected to pay back $1000 each and every year, plus the interest due. It was up to him to save the annual payment. While this took planning and sacrifice, interest costs were relatively low compared to today.

Now that mortgages are amortized, we pay on them each month, but the point is this: In order to make the payments nice and easy, very little of the payment is applied on the principal balance for some time. By adding the small sum of $25.34 to your regular payment, in the example given, you not only saved the interest that would have been paid on that sum of money over many years, but you actually accelerated the liquidation of the entire mortgage.

You now can see how costly each additional 1 per cent in interest is—even .5 per cent. And you've been shown how it affects each additional $1000 you borrow. And while I've given the amortized mortgage all the credit I feel it deserves, I've also tried to show the thorns on the rose. It should be clear now that it is worth a little shopping around and haggling to obtain the best rates you can.

It is simply a matter of learning the "going" rate in your community and playing one lender against another. You often can get lower interest rates by paying a little more down on your purchase, by shortening the repayment terms, or both. Generally speaking, you can get a lower interest rate on a twenty-year than on a thirty-year mortgage.

If you are a veteran, you should check with the Veterans Administration to see if you are eligible for a loan guarantee. On a VA loan you get fairly low rates and extended terms. Under a loan guaranteed by the Federal Housing Administration (FHA) you usually can do better on interest rates than on the regular "conventional" loans made by bankers, savings and loan firms, and insurance companies.

Under both VA and FHA loan arrangements, you also get a certain amount of protection as to the quality of the home you buy. The federal agencies have standards of construction which must be met; mostly they are to protect the lender and the insuring agency, of course, but they also protect you, the buyer.

A few states have their own plans to help veterans purchase homes. California, for instance, has the Cal-Vet program, which provides very low interest rates. You should check into your own state plan, if it has one.

As of this writing, about 80 per cent of all home financing is done without the aid of federal or state agencies, which means that 80 per cent of today's home loans are conventionally financed. The big three in private financing are (1) savings and loan firms, (2) commercial banks, and (3) insurance companies, especially life insurance companies.

Savings and loan firms handle the most home loan business. They are also the most lenient on terms and financing requirements. But because of this, they also charge higher interest rates, as a rule, than banks or insurance companies. If you consider yourself a top-drawer credit risk, have a sizable down payment, and don't want to pay "forever," start checking with insurance companies and banks. Or, if you belong to a credit union engaged in home lending, try that source first. It might be the best of all.

But wherever you get the money, watch those closing costs.

CLOSING COSTS

Closing costs include many expenses. One is the "discount" some finance agencies require from the seller of a home. Some call those costs "points," since they usually are expressed in terms of one or two points off the mortgage. Thus one point off a $20,000 mortgage would be $200 or 1 per cent.

Getting points is just another way for a financing agency to net a higher rate of return (interest) on its loan. Theoretically, the *seller* of a home pays the points, but in one way or another, the cost is usually assumed by the buyer-borrower. If a seller suspects he will have to discount his home a few hundred dollars, he usually ups the price somewhat.

As a buyer seeking a mortgage, you should inquire about this from the real estate broker before you even look for the money. Is the price padded for points? You may avoid them at your own finance firm. In that way you may protect yourself from having to pay the extra toll.

Another expense involved in the closing costs may be a survey charge, supposedly for having an engineer check the lot lines, making sure the property is as represented. If the financing agency actually has the survey performed, you have no just complaint. But if you are paying for something that isn't even contemplated, you have every right to object to or question the charge.

Then there is the abstract fee and the title search for bringing the history of your prospective home up to date. After all, you don't want the title to the home clouded by some carelessly handled divorce, an unpaid judgment, or a poorly drawn will. But if the lawyer making the title search is working *only* for the finance company, to protect just the company's equity, it's a fair question as to who should pay the lawyer. A safe bet is to get your own lawyer, in order to protect *your* percentage of equity in the real estate; or you may ask the finance firm's lawyer to represent you, too. It won't be any extra work for him.

Some states don't use the abstract and title search system. These states have title insurance, which is many times as costly, but which gives the buyer rather complete and simple protection. Originally held out to be less costly than abstracts and lawyers, title insurance has become rather expensive protection. But there is little you can do but pay.

Since the funds put up to buy a home must be kept safe until the transaction is checked out and completed, the funds often go to professional escrow services. An escrow agent is a third party who holds the funds for the benefit and protection of both parties to the sale. For instance, property taxes must be brought current. Charges vary around the country, but the fees usually are nominal.

There are other small charges connected with the sale of a home, all of which are deducted from the amount the seller puts into escrow. There is a credit report fee and a recording charge. You should read the list of charges carefully to see what it contains.

PENALTIES

Next you should inquire about the right to pay your mortgage in advance. Most mortgages today penalize the borrower if he tries to clear his debt in full before it reaches maturity. The penalty commonly is 6 months' interest on the balance owing. You may be able to cut that penalty to three months, or if there is stiff competition between lenders for your mortgage, you may be able to eliminate the penalty entirely. Aside from that, ask how much additional you can pay on your mortgage in any one year, without extra charges.

LATE FEES

Then there's the matter of "late charges." Some lenders assess a 5 per cent late charge for each missed payment. Not only that, the 5 per cent charge goes on month after month, year after year, until the payment is brought up to date. You can pay for a missed payment several times over in late fees. Make sure you know what you are getting into.

Before you sign any important document, especially a mortgage, which you will have to live with for years, read it carefully. Better yet, you read it and then have your lawyer read it. While a mortgage serves mainly to protect either the financing agency or the seller of the property or both, a mortgage is a contract. Any contract has two parties. So be certain your interests are protected too.

PROTECTION

Here is where the type of lien instrument you sign becomes very important. Trouble can strike anyone, in the form of loss of income, sickness, or just plain financial emergencies. So the question is: How many payments can you miss without being tossed out into the street—evicted or foreclosed, in other words?

Under a regular mortgage, you usually have one year to redeem your home, once foreclosure proceedings have been started. So a mortgage gives the most protection to home buyers.

Under the installment sales "contract," used in many states, the buyer has very little protection if he gets behind. In most cases, contracts are used because the financing arrangements in general do not meet the requirements of regular mortgage lenders. But since the seller retains the real ownership rights under a sales contract, he can get a delinquent home buyer out of his property in a hurry, sometimes within a few days after proper service by a court official.

Moreover, homes sold on contract usually are priced much higher than they would be if sold on a mortgage arrangement. The person who has to buy on contract not only assumes a great deal of risk, but he also pays a high price on the home itself, as well as in interest charges. Contract buyers should switch their financing arrangements to mortgages as soon as they are eligible to. Holders of contracts will often discount the balance if it's paid in full.

A "trust deed," as I said before, is a peculiar California arrangement. But as financing gets more lenient and risky, other states may come to use it, under pressure from financing agencies.

A trust deed is really a sort of mortgage contract. A seller deeds his property to a buyer, who then immediately deeds it over to a third party who holds it, acting as trustee. If the buyer gets behind in his payments, the trustee can quickly deed the property over to the finance company, and within four months (120 days) of proper notice and filing, the property can be foreclosed.

It's about that quick and simple. This system originated because of the land and housing boom in the West, where terms and financing requirements were stretched to the ultimate limits. The necessity arose to enable financing firms to recover their security fast, and the trust deed fills the bill admirably.

But as you can see, this system is a far cry from the old mortgage system, which gave homesteaders a great deal of protection against adversity and the loss of their homes.

Since many homes in California are purchased by speculators, status seekers, footloose folks, and marginal credit risks (rather than by families seeking cozy retreats and blue heavens), it is easy to justify the rise of the trust deed. But if you want more security and are eligible for it, you have every right to ask for a mortgage. What's more, you can get one, if you try, even in California.

FUNDS IN TRUST

If you are asked to include money for taxes and insurance in your monthly payments, it may help smooth your budget, but remember this: You will have idle funds on deposit most of the time at the financing agency, not drawing any interest. Furthermore, such a prepayment plan can slow the liquidation of your mortgage.

You could ask the finance firm to pay interest on your money it holds, or you could pay your own property taxes and insurance on the side. These expenses could be included in that second checking account I mentioned in the first section of this book.

Some savings and loan firms hold many millions of dollars on hand for home buyers, to pay taxes and insurance premiums. But the money draws no interest and constitutes a free type of investment for such companies. You have a right to question the advantages of such a plan.

INSURANCE

That is especially true if the finance firm wants to handle your home insurance, perhaps through one of its affiliate companies.

The wisest thing in such a case is to talk to your own insurance man to compare rates and benefits. The finance company should demand insurance protection on the home it has under mortgage, but it may not have the right to make a profit on the insurance, or demand the right to place your policy.

STRETCHED TERMS

Most home seekers want the longest terms possible. Thirty- and forty-year mortgages are fairly common today. But the longer the terms, the more costly the interest. It makes sense to extend your terms enough to keep the payments within your budget. But the truth is, if you need to stretch the payments beyond a sensible period, say twenty to twenty-five years, you probably can't afford the home! An exception would be if your income is high enough so that you derive some genuine advantages from the tax and interest deductions.

On thirty-year and longer terms, hardly any money from the payments goes to reduce the debt. Such buyers really are renting or leasing, not buying. If you don't intend to own your home, the time element probably doesn't matter. But if you wish to say, "It's mine," or intend to toss a mortgage-burning barbecue, shorten the terms. Or if you go for a thirty-year deal, double up on the payments now and then in the manner I illustrated before.

OPEN-END MORTGAGE

A new development in home financing has aroused much interest (no pun intended), the open-end mortgage. Under this plan, a mortgage can be added to regularly without high closing costs or red tape. For the fellow who always needs cash, this is most attractive. But it's also an open invitation to perpetual debt. If, of course, you can keep borrowing against your mortgage at 6 per cent, investing the cash at 7 per cent, you'd be a fool not to. But if your constant borrowing comes from your own mismanagement, including the amassing of consumer debts, give some thought to revising your budget. No one gets ahead by staying heavily in debt. This brings up one controversial point. You may have heard that it is wise to keep a huge mortgage on your place, in order to be able to sell it in a hurry. The idea is that persons short of cash will be able to assume your old mortgage. There is some merit in the theory, but there are plenty of disadvantages too. For one thing, the added interest cost of staying heavily in debt is a high price to pay for instant home liquidation potential. Then there is the matter of never having much equity in your homestead, a sort of debt brinkmanship.

The truth is, if your home is desirable, you should be able to sell it fairly quickly even if it's paid for. There are quite a few families with cash in the bank looking for homes. Then too, if your mortgage company is willing to extend you so much credit, chances are plenty of other folks will be able to arrange similar terms. Don't fall for the "stay in debt" theory simply because it's popular with lenders and the live-it-up crowd.

Pitfalls in home buying

AREA

An experienced real estate man once said, "There are three things to consider when buying a home—neighborhood, neighborhood, and neighborhood." There is much truth in that statement, even though it seems to be a little too pat. The homes around you, and the people around you, affect not only the resale value of your home; they also affect your enjoyment of the home while you remain there.

There is another angle to consider from the standpoint of location. Most real estate men say it is wiser to own a modest home in an expensive neighborhood than to own a plush home in a modest neighborhood. A small home may gain in value by being surrounded by fine houses, but a fine home may lose value nestled among a number of so-so residences.

DISTANCE

Many families are tempted to move far out from town to escape high real estate values. There is some merit in this unless the driving distance to and from work eats up the savings in land costs. Saving $5000 in the "price" of a home could be wiped out, almost exactly, from having to drive an extra 5000 miles a year.

Using the rule-of-thumb measurement we used to measure housing costs (10 per cent per year of home valuation), a family would save about $500 per year in housing costs by paying $5000 less for a home. But at 10 cents a mile (a low estimate for the cost of operating a private automobile) 5000 more miles of driving would come to $500. This could wipe out the savings from economizing on a home.

So before you move way out, use your pencil to measure any abnormal expenses in transportation against the saving you make in land cost. Also, time is money, so extra time spent in driving may subtract from your earning power. At the very least, it will reduce your energy.

FREAKS

I previously touched on the matter of buying unusual and off-beat types of houses, under Functional Depreciation. In almost every major city in the United States you will find strange-looking homes in the middle of a group of conventionally built structures. Usually the unusual houses are selling below the market.

Sometimes these now unpopular homes are made of metal. Sometimes they have odd shapes and outside decorations. But the point is, few persons are interested in these homes for the simple reason of "difference." Most persons today are conformists, and they put their money where their prejudices are.

The moral is, if money matters, stay a conformist in your major purchases. The more conventional you are, the better you will be able to hold your money together. You may obtain a smug satisfaction from being different, and the truth is, I'm all in favor of preserving individualism. But it can be quite expensive.

HOUSING SCHLOCK

As every developer knows, a new house sells faster with a few attractive gimmicks in it. By spending $1000 on a kitchen arrangement, indoor planters, and striking wallpaper murals, a developer can add $2000 to $3000 to the price of a home. That is just good showmanship and creative merchandising. You can't add genuine charm to a home with a shotgun or a brush, however. Charm is built-in, not stuck-on.

A home buyer ought to measure the cost of the special features no matter how much they appeal to his or her fancies. Many gimmicks can be added later at less cost than by being included in the package price of a home.

THE EXTRAS

As you enter a model home, you may be impressed by the landscaping. But is the price of the greenery and rocks included in the package deal? If not, how much will it cost to make your home look the same?

You may sink to your ankles in carpeting as you walk through the door. Will you get that same type of carpeting in your home, or does it cost extra? Do you really want carpeting all over the home? How much will it cost to replace the stuff when it gets a little threadbare?

What about all those appliances and conveniences built into the home? Are they the ones you really want? How long will they last before you must replace them? Remember this: You'll be paying for the mechanical units now in the home as long as the mortgage is outstanding, even while you are buying new ones.

The point is, keep your eyes on the main thing, the home

itself. Visit the place several times before you sign any papers. You'll be surprised how many things you'll discover—and question—the second or third time around. There is something as seductive about an attractively furnished new home as the smell of a new car. But as every new-car buyer knows, the scent soon fades.

THE VIEW

View is becoming the big thing in homes today. Many a new home has been sold, and quickly, because of what a prospective buyer sees from the patio, or as he looks out the windows or the sliding glass doors. Only a boor or a Babbitt could knock the importance of visual satisfaction. The only question is: What price the view? Because of all the modern-day home features, *view* has become the most expensive.

A good view overlooking the bright lights of a city, or one within sight of a mountain, lake, or ocean, can raise the price of land by $10,000 or more per lot. Yet in these busy days, both wife and husband should ask themselves, "How much view can I consume during the course of a week? Will I eventually take the view for granted anyway?"

To sum up, watch out for the offbeat housing trends, don't buy too much schlock, remember it costs a great deal to replace certain extras, and place a realistic price on the view.

Above all, consider the neighborhood, and accept the fact that your neighbors will have more to say about the resale value of your home than you will.

New trends in housing

Most of us find it hard to give up the Great American Dream— a piece of land entirely our own. That dream was one of the main reasons our forefathers came to this country. Yet land in or near our major cities is becoming too expensive to be cut up into private parks for every family.

As a result, more of us in the future will be living in leased apartments, leased town houses, or variations of those in the form of co-ops and condominiums. In other words, we will be sharing the use of the land, and in many cases sharing the ownership of the land too.

RENTED APARTMENTS

The two-year lease, with the first and last month's rent paid in advance, is becoming the accepted contract between landlord and tenant in many parts of the country. It might be foolish to sign such a lease without having an attorney look it over. All leases are drawn to protect landlords rather than tenants, although landlords rarely feel they are fully protected. No lease can completely insure a lessor, the owner of property, against careless, financially irresponsible tenants.

On the other hand, a conscientious tenant should make certain he has freedom of action to live the kind of life he desires, and he should make sure just what maintenance is up to him.

Most of the arguments against apartment living are psychological and sociological in nature, not economic. It is sometimes hard to find apartments if you have small children. In an apartment you will be close to other persons, closer than you might like to be. You may not have ready access to outdoor living and recreation. There are smells, noises, and human frustrations to contend with.

Nevertheless, people all over the world have accepted apartment living as the norm rather than as a punishment. Such living frees families from all the time, expenses, and irritations associated with keeping up a homestead and a small estate.

As I discussed under Renting Versus Buying, there is little financial loss, if any, from renting an apartment. If this were not true, there would be far fewer rich (and investment-conscious) persons living in rented units.

The profit to be made in owning land comes from buying

and selling it, not from living on it. So don't worry about the drain on your resources if you decide to rent for a while. The main thing is to shop carefully when apartment hunting. Consider the square footage, the room arrangements, the sound insulation, and the proximity to schools, shopping facilities, and your job.

If you are attracted to a unit, go back in the evening when the present occupants of the building are doing their laundry, entertaining, and even fighting. That's when you'll get the flavor (and smell) of the place. That's when you'll know how easy and safe it is to park your car in the dark, too. If you get a chance, ask some of the tenants how happy they are. Ask where their children play.

What about your pet or pets? How much of the redecorating will you have to pay for? Is the water pressure good? (Run the faucets and flush the toilets, preferably at the same time.) In other words, shop for an apartment as you would a house.

TOWN HOUSES

A town house is a sort of a compromise between an apartment and a private home. Originally the town house was called a row house. It more or less originated in the East, especially in Philadelphia.

The special virtue of the town house is economy, land economy. Regular-tract homes take up about one-sixth of an acre each, provided they have the full 60- by 120-foot lots. But a row house (town house) takes up much less land, because it has common walls with the houses on either side. Yet, provided the walls are of decent thickness, privacy is assured, and each family has its own, but enclosed, piece of ground. There are other economies that can be achieved in construction of town houses too, which makes them worthy of consideration by any family.

The row house had a bad reputation for some time, primarily because of poor planning and unimaginative construction. But now the principle of living very close to one's neighbor has been used in attractive design in many parts of the country, and it should have a bright future.

CO-OPERATIVE APARTMENTS AND TOWN HOUSES

Both town houses and apartments are being featured in joint ownership arrangements. In a regular co-op, each tenant owns a share in the entire building and development. So far, most co-ops are aimed at older people who have tired of the chores and responsibilities associated with home ownership.

Many of the co-ops offer jointly-owned work and recreational facilities. There may be swimming pools, play areas for children, and just green grass to enjoy, all of which belong to the co-operative. Some co-ops have indoor recreation centers for the adults, too.

The advantages of such joint ownership are: (1) less costly special facilities through sharing, (2) control over new tenants, and (3) larger tax deductions. The latter point seems to be the big attraction for older people; by owning shares in the co-op, they usually can deduct from gross income their share of the interest, property taxes, upkeep, and depreciation that go with any kind of home ownership.

The disadvantages relate to the responsibilities a co-op shareholder must assume. He must take an active interest in the upkeep of the entire building, and must keep all the units filled in order to keep his share of the costs down.

He must, in other words, think as both tenant and landlord, in order to obtain the advantages of both such parties to a contract. But living in a co-op does allow an apartment or town house dweller to have his cake and eat it too. He avoids most of the direct maintenance obligations associated with owning a private home, but he does get the tax advantages.

Not many years ago, co-ops were praised from the standpoint of eliminating the contractors' profits. People got together to cut building costs and high markups. Now most co-ops are built first and later sold to the shareholders, sacrificing some of the possible economies.

CONDOMINIUMS

The main difference between a co-op and a condominium is that in the latter the tenant-owner gets a deed to his individual unit, rather than getting a share of stock in a jointly owned venture. But even in a condominium, about one-third of the entire project is jointly owned. The owner of a condominium unit must take some responsibility for the community areas and recreational facilities.

He can sell his own unit if he chooses, provided the buyer meets with the standards set up by the group. And he can be taxed only on his own unit, plus his share of the mutually held land and improvements.

A condominium dweller cannot ignore his neighbors, however. In order to keep his overall maintenance costs down, and in order to hold the value of his unit up, he must take an interest in the entire project and keep vacancies to a minimum.

But, like the co-op dweller, he does save on income taxes. And if he buys wisely, he gets economy from land sharing and facility sharing. The savings on income taxes should be carefully weighed, however. As in the case of private home-ownership, being able to subtract interest and property taxes from gross income helps those with big incomes more than those with modest ones. Take this example: On a just-built condominium were these words, "Total monthly payment $270. $170 tax-deductible according to legal counsel."

According to the ad, possibly $2040 a year could be deducted from gross income as a housing expense. For a family in a 50 per cent bracket, the deduction would save on net taxes by $1020, effectively reducing the costs of housing.

But to a $10,000 income family, where the $2040 would fall more in the 14 per cent bracket, the net tax savings might be only $285 a year. This explains why older persons, and people with high incomes are more interested than younger persons in co-ops and condominiums.

SUMMARY ON HOUSING

There are many choices in housing today. Most of us still face mental blocks regarding how we want to live. And as long as you can afford the way of your choice, no one can criticize you. Just don't fall prey to the old economic myths about saving the waste from rent receipts as you rush into home ownership.

The home-building industry is a big one, and so is the home-financing business. Both have the right to toot their own horns. But it's your money, so compare the economies of all the alternatives I mentioned before you make a final decision.

FOOD—THE BIG INDULGENCE

Four approaches to the supermarket

It usually is easier to cut down on the food budget than on any other area of spending. For one thing, there is far more waste in food buying than in most spending habits. Many Americans use food as a sort of therapy to heal their frustrations. In addition, the entire subject of food is full of propaganda, myths, and mystery.

Let's try to approach the subject of the food budget from a realistic point of view. We'll do it from the standpoint of what food does for your health (nutrition), how much food energy you really need (calories), how much you can afford to spend (the budget), and what enjoyment you should seek (personal satisfaction).

NUTRITION

This is not a book on vitamins and minerals, so we won't get technical. But I will say this: No wife should serve food to her family without a reasonable knowledge of the health factors. She could go to adult education classes to learn more. She could contact a county extension agent working through the United States Department of Agriculture to get information. Or she could buy or borrow a number of good books on the subject of food and health.

But I've yet to hear of a respected nutritionist taking issue with a statement released by the Department of Agriculture a few years ago. That statement said, in effect, that the average family can rely on a proper balance of natural foods to give it all the nutrients it needs. Those foods fall into four classes: (1) Milk and milk products, (2) meats, eggs, and dried peas and beans, (3) fresh fruits and vegetables, and (4) breads and cereals.

So it is possible, with only a minimum knowledge about nutrients, to keep a family in good health through a well-balanced diet. There are, of course, two classes of food extremists, those who think most modern foods are poisoned and lacking in nutrition, and those who ignore food values completely.

The gullible and overly fearful spend millions of dollars every year on food fads and outright rackets. They consume gobs of yogurt, exotic grasses, and "tiger's milk" to ward off the shakes and the shingles. Maybe they are on the right track—I don't really know. The whole subject is being constantly debated. But I do know many, many healthy persons who have never eaten anything but standard commercial foods, and who show no signs of undernutrition.

Those who ignore food health completely seem to pay for it in more ways than one. It shows up in fat, lack of energy, and just plain poor health. So give some thought to what you eat and to what your family should be fed. Nutrition should be the first consideration in planning menus.

CALORIES

It's been said that our ancestors of several hundred years ago consumed as many as 6500 calories a day without running to fat. The point is, your ancestors worked hard—physically. The easy life of today isn't geared to that sort of food consumption. A male clerk with no off-duty exercise might have trouble handling 2000 calories a day, and his soft-living spouse could probably do with less than 1600.

A calorie is a measurement of the energy (or heat) contained in a food source, while a vitamin is an organic substance needed by the body to balance various functions; consequently, you could be eating too many calories and still be short on vitamins.

So you have two problems. You need to have a rough idea how many calories you are consuming by learning the caloric content of common foods. And you must also determine the energy needs of the various members of your family. Those needs would depend on sex, youth, and physical activity. But you needn't sit with a calorie book in front of you every day.

Study the charts a little first, then use your memory. And finally, watch for signs of fat or fatigue. If fat develops, either adjust the calories down, or the exercises up, or both. If members of your family show undue fatigue, they may not be getting enough vitamins and minerals, as well as calories.

FOOD COSTS

In 1958 a single person could have fed himself on about $110 a year without loss of vitamins, minerals, or calories. The diet might have lacked a little zest and imagination, but the nutrients would have been adequate. The diet mentioned would have consisted almost entirely of pure flour, kidneys, cabbage, and lima beans, with a few inexpensive seasonings and nutrients tossed in.

This proves how little you really need to spend in order to stay healthy. It goes without saying that the above diet would have required considerable cooking, peeling, and preparing, not to mention will power. Now we pay to have much of that done for us.

Upton Sinclair, the crusader, got so tired of pampering his stomach that he finally settled on a "rice pudding" for every meal, although the pudding did contain fruits, raisins, corn oil, and dried milk. But he claimed he lived happily, healthily, and economically on his diet, keeping his weight and his spirits under control.

You can spend about as little as you wish on food and stay healthy. It takes will power and knowledge to do it, though. I mention all this because if you wish to control your food budget, you should be exposed to the truth before being allowed to whimper about the size of the grocery bills.

You needn't, and probably shouldn't, spend over 20 per cent of your budget on food, no matter how little you earn. During 1963, the average family spent less than 19 per cent for pure eating at home. And that included many services not actually needed.

SATISFACTION

Not to be ignored is the fun and satisfaction we get from eating. You might break those satisfactions down this way: Taste, eye appeal, and experimentation.

A good cook can make almost any food taste excellent. It takes knowledge, desire, and practice. They say the French have the ability to rescue any food from the humdrum and turn it into a gourmet dish. But the English, say the critics, have the ingenuity to ruin even the finest of foods. Unfair comment, of course, but it helps to illustrate my point. Taste in food is not a matter of money—it is a matter of skill.

As to how foods look on the plate, that aspect is very important, too, but not necessarily costly. A good cook arranges food interestingly on the plate or platter. She mixes colors to achieve interest. She avoids oversize helpings at once, because the look of glut can ruin an appetite. And finally, she knows the value of browning certain foods and not overcooking others— vegetables, for instance.

The woman who swears she needs a larger food budget to serve interesting meals probably hasn't much imagination. Unless she has tried inexpensive, uncommon dishes, she can't make much of a case for her lack of cash. It may be time for her to invest in an economy cookbook. Experimentation can be fun.

Modern shopping hazards

Supermarkets are in business to make money. You can't blame them for trying to step up sales. However, a great deal of the food store promotion these days is pure medicine show stuff. Let's consider "giveaways" first.

GIVEAWAYS

A great many grocers, large and small, wish they could go back to merchandising and get out of the prize and lottery business. The chance for this seems a little remote, since so many Americans love to get something for nothing. The trouble is, few things are really free.

It hasn't been definitely proved to everyone's satisfaction that consumers pay higher prices for food because of trading stamps, coupons, bingo cards, and other giveaways, but there are costs associated with these practices and someone has to pick up the bill. It's not just the dollar cost of the prizes and gifts; the real expenses come from handling the paperwork and the details.

If it's fun, games, and prizes you're after, patronize the store with the most gimmicks. But if you prefer to save money on the grocery bill, give a nod to the market offering good solid values.

DISCOUNT STORES

A few supermarkets, catering to a popular revolt against questionable giveaways, are going into a type of discount operation. These stores feature actual cash reductions on food items. The hooker is that not all of the merchandise is reduced. You may save a few nickels on soapsuds and pay a few dollars more for meat. The only way to save money on food these days is to compare prices on all the items you shop for, not just the featured ones. Read the newspaper ads after making out a shopping list, but don't spend fifty cents in gasoline to save a dime on a rump roast.

PACKAGING

Packages these days are designed mostly to catch your eye. The size of a box has little to do with the amount of the contents. The size rating—for instance Jumbo or Giant—means nothing. And the adjectives used to describe the quality of the contents are meaningless.

When you shop for some particular product—boxed, canned, or in a jar—learn about the better brands in advance. You can only know about those from experience, consumer publications, or friends. Then compare the actual weights and volumes specified on the various containers to obtain a fair value. This isn't easy with products coming in three-quarter-ounce sizes and so on, but it's worth a try.

The best advice I can give on shopping for food is to pick reputable stores, those which concentrate on value, and then to insist on getting your money's worth. If you feel you've been shorted, cheated, or misled, let the store manager know about it. That doesn't mean quibbling at the cash register and holding up the line; it means being unafraid to register justified complaints where it counts, at the head office. All retailers are conscious of public relations and do not hesitate to relay gripes to manufacturers and distributors.

DISTRACTIONS

It has been said that the average female shopper walks through a supermarket in a sort of trance, almost mesmerized by the bright lights, music, and wealth of goodies. She's half-looking for food and half-looking for friends. Being preoccupied, she rarely stoops to find bargains on the lower shelves, or reaches up to the higher ones.

In other words, she shops only at eye level, thus rewarding the salesman with enough influence to get his products in the popular spots. To put it bluntly, the bargains aren't always within easy reach. It pays to look around and stay fully awake.

Whether a shopper knows it or not, she develops habit patterns as she strolls through the store. Too often she walks right by the genuine money savers to get to the first item on her shopping list. Yet the average female foodshopper spends money at the rate of $25 an hour, far faster than her husband can earn it.

Hundreds of thousands of motivation researchers and advertising men are working overtime to help us spend our money. Therefore it becomes necessary to stay clever, clear-eyed, and dedicated as we tackle our supermarket chores.

The grading mystery

The United States Department of Agriculture grades all sorts of foods as to quality. But I would be wasting my time urging you to remember all the grading systems. There are too many of them and the words are too confusing.

Here are a few examples: Top grade cheddar cheese is marked AA. But the best Swiss cheese is simply marked A. The best fruits are called FANCY, while the best vegetables are termed EXTRA STANDARD. Butter ratings go like this: 93, 92, and 90. Super Colossal is the largest olive rating. The point is, not many persons can remember all those ratings. But when it comes to meats, the food which takes most of our money, it pays to remember the rating system. In fact, it's a must.

The largest meat packers have their own grading systems, but we'll discuss the United States Government method first. Our Department of Agriculture grades beef according to three properties—conformation, quality, and finish.

The best grade is PRIME. Then comes CHOICE, followed by GOOD, COMMERCIAL, UTILITY, CUTTER, and CANNER. Few of us can afford PRIME, and little of the last three grades is sold in supermarkets.

Most of the steak and roast meats we buy are CHOICE and GOOD. But here is where the trouble develops. A meat department may be featuring prime ribs, which is just a general term for that cut of meat. The ribs may not be graded United States Prime.

Or you may see an ad offering top sirloin at $2 a pound. "Top" doesn't mean anything in relation to grading or quality—it simply means that the meat comes from the top part of the loin.

Had the prime ribs been PRIME BEEF, the price would have been staggering. Or had the top sirloin special been really "tops," in the sense of PRIME, $2 a pound might have been a steal.

There is more razzle-dazzle in the merchandising of meat than in any other food item. Less than one-half the shoppers in this country know their meat gradings, which means that you may be paying top price for third- or fourth-grade meats without knowing it.

You could take the butcher's word for the grading if you can't find the grade marking on the meat, but that is a bit risky. So to be on the safe side, look for firm, compact meat, with fine texture and a soft red bone. And if it's tenderness you're after, look for a good coat of fat, with the meat well marbled throughout.

As I said, the big packers prefer their own grading systems. Armour's *Star* is its best. Swift calls its top grade *Premium*. And Wilson's number one quality is called *Certified*.

You may prefer the lesser-quality meats for stews, burgers, and boiled dinners. Nothing is wrong with that. Just don't pay for PRIME or CHOICE when you're getting GOOD.

If you shop where meats are prepackaged, don't be afraid to call an attendant for help. Many meat labels fail to show any grade whatsoever. In other cases the printing is so faint as to be unreadable. You have every right to know what grade of meat you are buying.

General food hints

Experienced shoppers soon learn to avoid frequent and costly trips to the store. They shop once a week for the main things, and pick up bread and milk as needed, or they have those items delivered to the door. But here are some thoughts on how to cut the cost of eating in general, from experts on the subject.

(a) Make out a shopping list in advance, taking particular note of things you reminded yourself to buy during the week. A blackboard is good for this. Do a quick research on your supply of staples and toiletries. Leave some leeway in the list in case you discover some excellent bargains while shopping. Sticking too adamantly to a list is almost as bad as no list at all.

(b) Keep your food budget in mind as you shop. If you ration yourself to $30 a week, stay within that figure. Purchase the necessities before you indulge in the nice extras. You can buy a small hand computer at office supply and specialties stores which keeps a running total of your purchases; by using it you can save yourself the embarrassment of taking things back after you reach the checkout counter.

(c) Go easy on volume buying. Foods spoil, you know, and it's not an economy to fill up the garbage pail. In many cases, small-size cans, even though more costly on a per-ounce basis, really save money. There is no waste. While it's popular advice to plan for leftovers, make certain you really consume what's left. Otherwise, you're simply feeding the garbage disposal unit.

(d) When you serve economy meals—meat loaf, stews, etc.—don't ruin a noble effort with too many costly condiments and supplementary dishes. Porterhouse steak served with only salad and rolls can be less costly than hamburger heavily doctored with mushrooms, sauces, and several side dishes.

(e) Don't get in a food rut. Prove your courage now and then, and save money while you're at it, by tackling baked heart, kidneys, liver, and sweetbreads. And don't forget fish, a really economical dish and a tasty one. But obtain good recipes and stick to the print until you know enough to cut corners.

(f) Once a week, have a clean-out-the-refrigerator dinner. Use those leftovers to good advantage. It can amount to a free meal. Do it regularly, at least once a week, before the foods spoil. The husband who growls over leftovers should be reminded about the savings.

In summing up, the grocery bill is the easiest to reduce. That statement won't please the farmers, the food processors, the retailers, or the United States Department of Agriculture. But it is a fact.

Food has been America's greatest achievement, although at somewhat of a price—the subsidies and so on. But as the farmer's share of the food dollar declined, we began to spend more on packaging, promotion, and built-in "maid service" (peeling, cooking, and preparing).

It now takes a sharp shopper indeed to make the most of America's bounty. And if you really want to save money on food, do some of the maid service yourself. That would depend, of course, on how much time you can spare.

CLOTHING OR FASHION?

How much to stay dressed?

We Americans have been steadily spending less on clothing for several years. The reason is simple. Clothing is no longer the popular status symbol it used to be. Because even expensive lines can be copied and mass-produced, it's difficult to identify extravagance when we see it. We now prefer to impress our friends with homes, automobiles, and boats.

As a result, the average family now spends only 11 to 12 per cent of its income for clothing, including dry cleaning, laundry, and repair. A few years ago, we spent about 15 per cent of our budgets for the overall costs of clothing.

We dress more casually than we used to, and a greater percentage of us now live in warm climates, where heavy dress is not needed. Nevertheless, the clothing part of the family budget can be a real problem to two types of families—ones with many

children, and ones in which either husband or wife is extremely
clothing-conscious.

There are ways to keep the clothing budget well in hand, and
we'll discuss them under the headings of (1) Planning, (2) Where
to Shop, (3) When to Shop, (4) Care of Clothing, and (5) How
Quality Counts.

Five ways to control the clothing budget

PLANNING

If you earn $10,000 per year and decide 11 per cent of your
budget should go toward clothing, start with the maintenance
costs first. Eleven per cent, of course, would be $1100 a year. Be-
fore you plan to spend the entire sum on dresses, suits, shirts, and
socks, subtract what you have been paying, or expect to pay, for
dry cleaning, laundry, and repair. If that comes to $25 a month
—$300 a year—that leaves you $800 for clothing items themselves.

The next step is to agree on how to divide the $800 among
the various family members. A white-collar husband, needing an
average of one suit a year and a topcoat every four years, might
get by on $250 per annum, including what he spends for shirts,
underwear, shoes, ties, and socks. That is just an example. Take
into consideration the social and economic needs of each member of the family. Once each adult member of the family understands and agrees on his or her share, it becomes a simple matter
of how to spend the allowance. In this realistic world, it may become necessary to patch and mend more frequently to stay
within a budget. A wife may have to wear a dress an extra year.
A husband, now and then, may need to postpone buying a new
suit. Children may have to wear hand-me-downs, and so it goes.
But just remember this: If you exceed your clothing budget, the
money spent has to come from some other part of the budget.
Either that, or you stay in debt most of your life. And with the
popularity of the new revolving-type charge accounts, staying in
debt is easy to arrange.

WHERE TO SHOP

Because of the revolving charge accounts, which allow buyers to pay only about 10 per cent of the balance owing each month, persons today tend to buy most of their clothing at one store. That way they avoid too many payments. This does make for easy budgeting, although it also detracts from comparative shopping. And, of course, the revolving plan accounts carry an average interest rate of 1½ per cent per month, a true rate of 18 per cent annual interest. This cost really comes out of the clothing budget in most cases.

Those who intend to buy most of their clothing on such extended credit terms should pick their main store with care. The store should carry a rather complete line of men's, women's, and children's clothing. The items should be competitively priced and of good quality. The store should have a decent "exchange and return" policy, too.

So rather than shop for credit terms, shop the stores themselves first, before you tie yourself too tightly to any one retail establishment. The revolving plan does cement customers to a store; most customers with budget problems have little other choice, once in hock. Before you get thoroughly cemented, compare a number of stores on pricing, quality, customer relations, and selection of merchandise.

If you possibly can, keep your monthly payment account low enough to enable you to buy some clothing with cash. In that way you can take advantage of sales at other stores. Best of all, buy all your clothing by cash or check from a special budgeted-in-advance account. You'll not only save on interest charges, but you will be in a position to take advantage of sales and specials offered by *all* the stores in your area.

Women especially should cultivate one sales clerk at their number one store. Salespersons know genuine sales when they see one, and if friendly enough they will phone you in advance when real bargains are to be had. Even men can profit from this approach.

WHEN TO SHOP

Men usually are less thrilled by sales than are women. For one thing, men hate to stand in line and paw over merchandise. For that reason, most sales promotions are beamed at women. Since most sales are genuine, there are many times when the lady of the house should prod her husband into taking time off from work to pick up some savings on his clothing budget. We won't go into detail, but here is a rundown on sales in general.

Bankruptcy sales are few and far between, but when one happens, great savings can be had. Quite often a bankrupt concern sells its entire stock to another firm, but not always. So if a trustee decides to liquidate through the general public, it's worth a look.

In most cities, a retailer has to apply for a permit to advertise "going out of business." Here again, if the sale is legitimate, you can save a lot of money; unless, of course, the company was below par in the first place. Shoddy merchandise is never much of a bargain, even at half price.

Clearance sales, sample days, and close-out sales are quite common. But remember, such sales aren't necessarily storewide. If only the high-priced fashion items are on sale, you won't save by rushing down to buy children's shoes. But clearance sales, in particular, do offer some real bargains to selective shoppers.

You can save some money on annual sales too, but the savings may not be spectacular. These sales, such as "white sales," come around once a year at least, and aren't intended to clear out inventory. They are basically sales promotions.

Now and then the very large stores get into really rough competition in our major cities. At such times you can get certain items actually below cost, which means 40 to 50 per cent off the regular price. And as a rule, "dollar days" and anniversary sales give careful consumers a chance to pick up some bargains.

In general, remember that women's clothing is marked down after Easter and sometimes in February. Men's clothing takes a drop in price right after the first of the year. And January is also a good time to buy children's clothing, especially outer garments.

The whole point is, if you shop for clothing whenever the mood strikes and the wear shows, you'll pay at least one-third more than by using the sales and buying off season. To put it another way, sharp buying habits and techniques can stretch that $800 clothing allowance into about $1000 or more worth of retail purchases. Or you can get $800 worth of clothing for only $600 and spend the difference on a vacation.

CARE OF CLOTHING

Wear shows more quickly without care. Just hanging clothing properly can save money. Cleanliness in wearing apparel is more than pure sanitation. Dirty clothing wears out sooner than clean clothing, because dirt is an abrasive.

Too much starch in shirts and other clothing will harm the fibers, shortening the lives of the goods. All clothing should be protected from moths and other insects when not in frequent use. Mothproof bags or closets are good one-time investments.

Regular dry cleaning can be costly. In some cities, dry cleaners are forced into agreements not to cut prices. This is especially true of the small cleaners who farm out the actual cleaning to big establishments. But to offset this, the new do-it-yourself dry cleaning machines can be a boon to the thrifty family. One trip a week with several items to be cleaned can cut cleaning costs in half.

HOW QUALITY COUNTS

As a rule, the better the quality, the more the savings. But the word "quality" has several meanings in relation to clothing. High style is a form of quality, but high style doesn't mean durability. Until a family can afford more, it should concentrate its search for quality in clothing by comparing wearability, stitching, and general resistance to soil, creasing, shrinking, and fading.

However, in children's clothing, the goods should not outlast the fit of the child, unless there are younger members of the family able to wear the too-small items. Quality should be tempered by time. And in shoes, which are quickly outgrown, high price should be avoided, unless it takes high price to obtain a good healthy fit.

Both men and women are quite "label conscious" today. Some persons even remove labels from common stores and replace them with the labels from clothing purchased at prestige stores. That is one way to salvage status, although the idea doesn't appeal to me. Instead of that, I would suggest buying where you choose and being man or woman enough to admit you aren't worth a million.

THE FAMILY AUTOMOBILE

What is a car?

Most persons are willing to cut expenses on the dull essentials. But the family car really isn't an essential, not all $3000 worth of it anyway. Today's automobile can be many things—a status symbol, an outlet for aggression, a means of escape (like Thoreau's Walden Pond), and even a substitute for a thwarted love life.

Let's face it: Owning an expensive auto may be cheaper than hiring a press agent, getting in alley fights, running away, or heading for the divorce courts. However, you may be one of those persons willing and able to satisfy their emotional needs with less mechanical means, so from here on in, we'll treat the family car as if it were purely a matter of economics.

How much car can you afford?

The average family spends about 17 per cent of its income for transportation. But many families can't afford a car; so they walk or use public conveyances. This means that those who do own private automobiles usually spend much *more* than 17 per cent of their budgets on them.

The fact is, the average car-owning family spends almost as much for the car and feeding of its auto as it does for housing —about 20 per cent of income. Take your own case. If you are planning to spend 30 per cent of your salary for total shelter costs (housing and utilities) and 20 per cent for food, you've already budgeted one-half your income. If you want to go along with the masses and spend about 20 per cent for transportation, you've accounted for a whopping 70 per cent of your income. That leaves only 30 per cent of your gross salary for taxes, insurance, clothing, health, recreation, savings, and miscellaneous.

Name just one of those items you are willing to do without. To be sure, you could cut down drastically on housing and food in order to wheel around in a new Goliath 8, running the risk of chronic pneumonia and malnutrition. Some persons do just that. But except for the real car buffs, the "balanced life" is becoming more popular in America, meaning that even automotive costs must be controlled.

First you should decide what percentage of your budget should go for driving. You can only do that by making up your mind how much you want to spend for other phases of living—housing, food, and so on. Juggle the figures around, staying within 100 per cent, until you are reasonably satisfied, giving preference to the most important things in your life. Once you've agreed upon a percentage to be allocated to transportation costs, perhaps 15 per cent, the next step is to identify the various car expenses.

How to identify expenses

As of this writing, it costs about 12 cents a mile to drive a medium-priced American car of standard size. But the costs keep rising year after year. If you own a new car costing $2500 to $3000 and drive it an average of 10,000 miles a year, here is the way to split up those costs (12 cents a mile), based on 1963 figures.

These percentages had not changed much by 1966, except that in some parts of the nation, insurance costs were moving up rapidly.

Depreciation	6.5 cents
Insurance	1.4 cents
License fees	.2 cent
Gasoline and oil	2.6 cents
Maintenance	.8 cent
Tires	.5 cent
Miscellaneous	.1 cent

That is a rough estimate, and it comes to a fraction over 12 cents a mile. But it should prove one thing to you: Depreciation (replacement cost) takes over one-half of the 12 cents. To put it another way, over 50 per cent of the cost of driving private automobiles comes from their losing resale value as you drive them. Unfortunately, you can't reduce your automobile costs to 6 cents a mile by driving only one-half as much, say 5000 miles a year. Your car gets older and therefore loses value just sitting in a garage. But you may be able to trim the other expenses, except for license fees, by reducing your driving. Even most auto insurance is based on mileage these days.

Actually, depreciation on a new car drops a little each year for the first three years. Then it tends to level off. On a $3000 car, the first year's value loss would be close to $900 (30 per cent). The second year it would be about $500 (17 per cent of the new price). And the third year, depending on the make of car and how it had been taken care of, and assuming steady market conditions, the loss from depreciation might drop to only $300 or 10 per cent.

From then on, with normal usage, the car probably would lose about two hundred dollars in value each year. By the start of the fourth year, of course, the car would be worth only $1300 or so.

What about those catchy ads urging you to trade your car in right this very minute, before it depreciates further? Well, the best time to trade a car in is just before the salesman hands you the keys. It will not have depreciated much in a short time. If you fall for one of those urgent "trade now" messages, you will likely be trading in a car with a *low rate* of depreciation for a newer car with a *faster rate*.

Anyway, you can see where your 12 cents a mile goes. But if you are a sharp reader you will notice the list did not include garage rent. Garage costs, if you have them, vary a great deal, so the control is up to each individual. But the list ignored one other factor, an even more important one. And that is finance charges and interest.

Financing costs

About 80 per cent of the cars on the streets are financed these days. Few people indeed really "own" their cars. Nor do they ever intend to. After all, the mortgage doesn't show.

But show or not, mortgages are an important cost item in owning a private car. However, let me make two almost—but not quite—contradictory statements: (1) You don't save as much paying cash for a car as most persons think; and (2) car financing costs much more than it appears to, because of various ways of expressing interest.

Taking the matter of a cash purchase first, the same principle applies to owning cars outright as it does to houses. There is an implicit cost in owning anything free and clear, and that is the loss of income from the money you have invested. You may think of this as hair-splitting, but it isn't. If you own a car free and clear which had an average value over one year of $3000, you lost the income from $3000. Even at 4 per cent, that comes to $120 a year.

The point is, if you tie up $3000 in an automobile, you are consuming the earnings of that $3000. So much for that. Now we'll see how much extra you pay when you *finance* the purchase of a car.

Most new, and near-new, automobiles are financed at a true

rate of 12 per cent per year. The charges may be expressed in several different ways, and we'll deal more with that matter in the section on debt management, but the real rate usually is 12 per cent on the average amount owed. As a rule, it costs 8 per cent more, in terms of simple, annual interest, to finance a car than to pay cash. If you paid cash from your savings, you'd be losing the 4 per cent. This 8 per cent is the finance agency profit—gross profit. If the average amount owed on your car is $1000, you would have to add $120 per year to your car costs.

Let's pretend you are a rather typical car owner. Your car cost $3000 new, you drive 10,000 miles a year, you intend to keep it three years, on an average you owe $1000 on the mortgage, and your average equity is the same $500 as above. Under those conditions, your personal car expense sheet would average something like this over each of the three years:

Depreciation	$570
Insurance	$115
License	$ 30
Gasoline and oil	$350
Maintenance	$ 60
Tires	$ 75
Finance cost	$120
Equity cost	$ 20
Miscellaneous	$ 15
Total Annual	$1355

I did not include garage rental. And if you traded cars every two years rather than three, your total expenses would be nearer $1500, because you would not be getting the benefit of the low third year's depreciation. But by trading sooner you might offset the higher depreciation a little from lower maintenance and tire costs.

If you earn $9000 per year, and decided on 15 per cent of your income for private transportation costs, the example above would be right on the nose. But that's assuming you didn't have any accidents where you would have to pay the deductible amount. And it's also assuming no traffic fines.

Now, you may look at the above set of figures and wince a little. After all, $1355 is a lot of money just to own your own taxicab, when that sum goes out year after year. You can cut down on automotive costs if you really want to, without losing much face or satisfaction.

Ways to reduce expenses

DEPRECIATION

Since depreciation is the largest expense in car ownership, we'll start with that. There are several ways to reduce that cost. (1) You can buy secondhand cars which have already taken the big first- and second-year value losses. If you buy carefully from a reputable dealer, and get a decent warranty, the repair costs won't eat you up. They would rarely approach the depreciation costs of newer cars, propaganda notwithstanding.

(2) You could buy new "economy" cars, which cost less to begin with and therefore have less value to lose. Compact cars aren't necessarily "economy cars," however. But a car costing $2000 new can't lose more value than that sum, no matter how you drive it.

(3) The simplest way to cut depreciation costs is to drive a car longer. Driving a new $3000 car 8 years can cut depreciation costs down to around $250 a year, a great deal less than the $570 shown in the example. And it would take some pretty rough driving to make your other costs, including repair and maintenance, offset the saving in value loss. As a matter of fact, license and insurance costs drop on older cars.

INSURANCE

The best way to keep auto insurance costs down is to shop around and compare premiums. Ask the agents what you can do to keep your costs down. Sometimes the automobile clubs offer insurance at bargain rates. And as I said before, the longer you drive your car, other things being equal, the more the premiums drop.

LICENSE FEES

You can't control the fees, of course, but again, fees drop in most states on older cars. And the higher-priced your car, the higher the license fee in most states.

GASOLINE AND OIL

Driving a car less is the easiest way to save on the fluids. Driving only 8000 miles a year instead of 10,000 might save you $70 a year, the price of a new Easter outfit. Much of the driving we do today comes from boredom and restlessness, which might be cured just as easily by walking a little.

Then, too, economy cars take less gasoline and cheaper gasoline to boot. You can use regular gasoline rather than higher-priced premium gasoline in most compact cars. If you save only three cents a gallon by using regular gasoline, you can cut your expenses almost 10 per cent, or about $30 each year. And if you use less gasoline in addition, because of owning a car with less horsepower, you can easily save another $30.

MAINTENANCE

With careful driving, maintenance costs come to about the same figure for most cars. But rough driving can shoot the repair and service bills out of sight. And, generally speaking, the costlier cars have the highest maintenance bills. To be sure, quality cars are well-built, but each little part is expensive to service and replace. You can keep maintenance costs under control by purchasing lower-priced cars and treating them with respect.

TIRES

Even on lower-priced cars, whitewall tires cost from $30 to $40 extra for a set. And with the white strip getting slimmer all the time, it isn't much of a sacrifice to be caught with black shoes. One should never sacrifice safety for false economy, so buy good tires with good guarantees.

Small wheels wear out tires fast, so consider that angle. And never forget that fast stops and starts really shred rubber. High speed on highways means quick replacement of tires, if for the "heat" wear alone.

Retreading tires is an accepted practice these days, so before you toss out those $150 tires, give some thought to having them rejuvenated for tread. If you do decide to replace your old tires, pick the most reliable dealer you can find. The "quality" names on tires mean almost nothing. Today's top line may be tomorrow's third line, and vice versa. To play it safe, replace your old tires with exactly the same type, if the old ones were satisfactory. Don't be overly impressed with tire warranties. You won't get the full price refunded if the tires go bad; the original price will be used as a base for depreciation according to miles used.

MISCELLANEOUS

The other costs of operating a car include money for parking meters, extra decorations or accessories, and washing. You can spend about as much, or as little, for these things as you care to. The control is entirely up to you.

But you can see that it is possible to control almost every expense of owning and driving a private automobile. You needn't accept national averages as your own. And I should once again remind the skeptics that payments on a car have little to do with the real expenses. Payments are a means of retiring your mortgage, thereby reducing the cost of the interest. Other than that, they simply represent "outgo," not expense.

But payments can be an important part of your overall budget picture, because it matters what interest rate you pay, which lending agency you choose, and what type of instrument is used to finance your purchase. These will be discussed in detail when we get to the section on credit.

THE TWO-CAR FAMILY

When two cars gang up to own a family, the results can be disastrous. The point is not to let the cars own you. As shown in the breakdown of expenses, a family trying to operate two autos would be paying out $2710 a year. That would take at least an $18,000 yearly income to handle comfortably.

However, many families really need two automobiles, one for work and one for shopping and chauffeuring children. Many families accomplish this without undue expenses. At least one of the autos must be rather elderly, too old to suffer much in depreciation. In the case of quite modest incomes, having two cars usually involves both of them being several years old. But two cars or one, the trick is to keep total expenses down, depreciation and mileage in particular.

Since all cars, regardless of age, must be licensed, insured, gassed, and oiled, it is next to impossible to operate even a twenty-year-old jalopy for less than $300—at 1964 rates.

One last observation: It used to be considered a sign of affluence for a family to own several cars. Today it is more likely a sign of poverty. As every referee in bankruptcy can attest, most bankrupt families have a wealth of iron in their backyards—clunkers too expensive to fix and too worthless to sell for junk.

What about leasing?

There is nothing very mysterious about leasing a car. In most cases, leasing on the usual two-year contract is just a substitute for financing.

There are only two important factors to consider when debating buying versus leasing. One is the depreciation and the other is the financing cost. And in "financing cost" you should include what it costs you to divert money from other investments when you pay cash for a car, just as I explained before.

Almost all leased cars are new, so we'll go back to my $3000 example. I showed that your depreciation would come to about

$900 the first year and $500 the second. Thus your two-year depreciation would come to $1400 if you actually owned the car.

If you financed the entire $3000, you would pay about $360 in finance charges (6 per cent added on for two years). By adding the two-year depreciation to the two-year finance charges, you get a total cost of $1760, or about $73 a month for twenty-four months. If you can lease that $3000 car for two years for close to that figure, go ahead. You'll be breaking about even unless you intended to pay cash for the car. In such a case you would substitute the old 4 per cent simple interest, or whatever you can safely earn on your money, for the regular finance cost of 12 per cent (6 per cent added to the original balance rather than the declining balance). Thus, to compare leasing with paying cash for a car is different from the comparison you would make had you planned to finance.

The depreciation would be the same over two years—$1400—but your interest loss would be less: only $120, or one-third as much. To pay cash for the $3000 auto and keep it for two years could cost you about $1520, or only about $63 a month.

Moral: It is cheaper in most cases to pay cash than to lease, but it's also cheaper to pay cash than to finance. In most instances the charge for leasing is about the same as the cost under financing. Or, to put it another way, you are foolish to pay more for leasing a car than you would expect to pay if you financed it. Figure as closely as you can what it would cost to finance a car (depreciation plus finance charges); then hunt for a lease by which you can do as well or better. No one can estimate future depreciation on a car right down to the dollar, but you can come close enough to avoid paying too much for leasing.

Of course, if a leasing firm, either a regular auto dealer or a company specializing in leasing, offers to pay your sales tax and license, you should include those savings in making the comparisons. Don't worry about major repair. Most new cars are under two-year warranties. That aspect doesn't enter into leasing.

To strengthen my point that leasing and financing are equally costly to the careful shopper, most leasing contracts end up being sold to finance companies anyway. Both car dealers engaged in leasing and finance companies are just as happy to handle a good lease as they are to handle a normal finance deal.

But you do have to shop around to make certain you aren't charged too much. Just signing the first lease offered is very foolish. You should never pay much more on a lease than it would cost to finance the identical car, unless there are other considerations involved.

Saving on income taxes is *not* one of those angles. Leasing does not mean an automatic tax deduction. It depends on how you use the automobile. You can charge off in taxes exactly the same amount on financed and entirely owned cars as you can by leasing them. All leasing accomplishes is easy record-keeping.

For certain businessmen, leasing has one big advantage. Some businessmen can put their capital to work at higher rates than they would pay to lease or finance a car. Few ordinary consumers can, however. Most persons who lease cars pretend they are saving on income taxes when they really aren't. The main reason they lease is to avoid the stigma of "having to finance." In some cities, even the most expensive cars are leased more often than sold, which proves what some persons will do to impress others.

One final word on leasing. There are two basic types of lease used today on automobiles. One is the "firm" lease, under which a person leasing the car knows exactly what his costs will be.

The other is the "open end" lease, which provides for a payment adjustment at the end of the lease term. The adjustment will depend on the market value of the returned car, as determined by the leasing firm. Payments on "open end" leases are usually lower than on "firm" leases, up to the time of final settlement. The best way to protect yourself on the adjustment-type lease is to demand (in writing) the right to buy the car when you return it, if you think the appraisal is too low.

A gambler will pick the "open end" lease, happy about the low original payments, and hoping he gets a fair appraisal. A conservative will stick to a firm lease, after comparing costs.

But regardless of which lease you choose, if you choose any, read the contract, making certain you aren't limited to a fixed number of miles per year and held responsible for minor scratches.

Leasing makes sense for consumers. When you buy on time payments you are mostly leasing anyway. In fact, the original finance contracts were called "bailment leases." A few such contracts still go by that name. But the point is, an automobile doesn't stay with a family very long, and it is just one form of consumer goods. In other words, we consume automobiles just as we consume bread and butter.

Whether we own cars or lease them doesn't really matter in the long run.

SUMMARY

A friend of mine, after looking over the original of this discussion of automobiles, contended I had ignored some very real expenses. He listed them in this order:

1. The income we lose from not using car pools to share expenses.

2. The tax cost of highways and freeways.

3. The army of traffic policemen we employ to keep from killing one another.

4. The illness and discomfort we suffer from exhaust-provoked smog and air pollution.

5. The high cost of land for homes, resulting from the use of so much space for roads, parking lots, and garages.

6. The medical bills we pay from highway accidents.

I mention these to be all-inclusive, although I know from experience that few Americans really want to know what it costs to drive their own cars. I realize also that many families depend for their living on the manufacture of automobiles. But by mentioning all the costs associated with autos, I may be able to stir up more interest in efficient public transportation, including rapid transit systems for our major cities.

At the very least, perhaps more families will investigate public transportation thoroughly before indulging in second, and even third, cars.

HOUSEHOLD FURNISHINGS AND
EQUIPMENT

How much to spend

Most American families now spend about 9 per cent of their incomes for home furnishings and equipment. That is not an average; it is a typical percentage for middle-income persons. And it is becoming more difficult to know just what we are spending for such items now that many new homes include built-in appliances, carpeting, and draperies. But the cost is there, whether it is included in the package price of a new home or not.

Furthermore, the cost of furnishings and equipment is rising faster than the cost of many other budget items, especially for families with above-average incomes. The decorator has now entered the picture in a big way. The result in too many cases is that persons buy primarily for reasons of fashion, ignoring the other important aspects of furnishing a home.

The items you buy to furnish and equip a home fall into three main categories: the "hard" pieces of furniture (case goods), the "soft" furnishings, and the mechanical conveniences (appliances). Let's discuss them in that order.

Furniture

Most young families take one of these two paths when they set up housekeeping: either they buy everything needed to fill up the rooms (generally on credit) and then take years to pay for the items, or they buy just what is essential and add to their stock as needed, and as they are financially able. In this way they stay out of debt, or at least keep their debts well under control.

I prefer the last-mentioned system, if for no other reason than this: Being in a hurry to fill up a home doesn't give one time to be selective. Furthermore, one's own tastes change, sometimes within a few years after marriage, and quite often before the bulk purchase is paid for. Being in too big a hurry to appear affluent doesn't allow time to consider the following points in acquiring furniture.

USEFULNESS

You could get by for a while with something to eat on, something to sit on, and something to sleep on—the bare essentials, in other words. Young persons from substantial backgrounds will accept this practical approach to living more willingly than young persons from modest homes.

Working-class persons striving hard to improve themselves will do anything to avoid the look of poverty or enforced sacrifice, with which they are only too familiar. Those who have known a degree of financial well-being accept temporary hardship and frugality more cheerfully. As a banker friend of mine once said to his nephew, "If you wish to stay out of debt and get ahead in the world, marry a girl from an expensive Eastern college. She may challenge and frustrate you, but at least she won't bankrupt you trying to impress your friends with a lot of household trivia."

The banker was being a bit sweeping in his generalization, but it is true that people trying to move up in the world often concentrate on volume instead of quality.

So if money matters, and it usually does, buy furniture first from the standpoint of need. You can't impress the people you *want* to impress with sheer volume anyway. Buy what you really need and add the extras later.

COMFORT

A bed of good quality may be your most important purchase. The most important elements of a bed are the springs and mattress. So don't skimp on those.

Chairs and sofas should be tested several times for seating comfort before being purchased. Furniture shoppers often are so tired from walking around that any seat feels great, so test several pieces before making a final selection. This is particularly true of lounge chairs, where reading, watching television, and general relaxing takes place. It is far more important that they match your contours than that they match room styling and color schemes.

So aside from being useful and needed, each item of furniture should be tailored to your comfort.

DURABILITY AND MAINTENANCE

You do want things to last. Soft coverings should have some degree of resistance to soil, stain, and wear. And while you may be impressed with the economy of certain leather substitutes, consider how they would feel in very hot and very cold weather.

At one time persons were advised to buy solid wood furniture rather than veneered woods. But today much of the pressed veneer is of excellent quality and is less likely to warp or crack. And tough plastic laminate tops are not uncommon on best-quality furniture pieces.

Buying "brand name" merchandise isn't as safe a bet as it was a few years ago. Makers of top-quality lines like to cash in on the "borax" trade too—the shoddy, in other words. It is safer to bank on the reputation of the retailer than that of the manufacturer these days. Explain to the salesman that you want quality as well as economy.

Compare prices and merchandise at several reputable stores, keeping the sales in mind. February and August are good furniture bargain months, although summer furniture often goes on sale in July in many parts of the country.

One thing you should especially beware of: Even the best furniture stores take advantage of our fondness for volume. So they toss in ashtrays, lamps, and footstools to make up a "bargain" grouping. In too many instances the free knickknacks only camouflage the high markup on the big pieces. Buy and price one or two things at a time. In that way you'll be certain how much you are paying.

Another important point to remember is that small children mix poorly with dainty furnishings. Keep your furniture rugged enough to ward off daily mistreatment. In time you'll be able to replace the sturdy stuff with more delicate, stylish merchandise, if your taste runs that way.

FASHION AND STYLE

You have every right to be confused about furniture terminology. For one thing, the types more or less overlap. There is Modern, Contemporary, Provincial (Italian and French), Danish, Mediterranean, and Regency, plus modifications and amalgamations of all of them.

But it isn't really necessary to be able to identify the various furniture styles if you have a decent flair for color, form, and compatibility. A chair may not answer to the tag of French Provincial or Country French, but if it fits you and suits you, that's enough.

And it is quite possible to mix the various stylings without making your home look like a secondhand store. In fact, a good mix may be more sophisticated and have more interest than a perfect reproduction of a bygone era. This is important to remember, because it gives you greater leeway in buying secondhand merchandise from auctions, thrift shops, ads in the newspaper, and just plain friends.

One of the finest homes I've ever visited has not a stick of new furniture in it—all are second-hand, and many of the pieces were refinished or reupholstered. A nice thing to remember about our mass-production, "throwaway" economy is that persons tire of even the finest things quickly, making it easy for less affluent persons to pick up bargains.

There are so many items of living to buy today that we have to cut corners on most things. You can cut a lot of corners in furniture buying if you don't mind trying.

Soft furnishings and carpeting

We've now come to the point in our society where we spend more money on wall-to-wall carpeting and draperies than we do on highly functional furniture. Few things will attract a home buyer faster than overall carpeting and lush draperies. Those are almost "musts" if a home is to be sold.

To be sure, if these elegant things come with the home, the new owner won't have to spend extra cash to buy them. That is a convenience. But the question is: Why are people so in love with carpeting and huge draperies in the first place?

Carpeting is expensive. It can't be reversed or turned to spread the wear. You can't send it out for cleaning. It often covers places better covered with sturdier material.

To make my point more strongly, take the case of the family with two small children. The parents invested heavily in fine wall-to-wall carpeting throughout most of the home. Beneath the soft underfooting, of course, was a beautiful hardwood floor. Over that was an expensive padding. And over that went the floral carpeting. To ward off wear, the mother invested in a plastic spray. And to guard the spots with the most traffic, she tossed around a few throw rugs. But that isn't all. She finally issued an ultimatum—no shoes to be worn in the living room.

I can only say, "What living room?" Let's face it, the home belongs to the carpeting, not to the people. But it's persons like that who keep the old economy humming.

To take a positive stand: Plain carpet, used only where it matters, might be a wise investment for families starting out in life. Some rooms other than the living room and bedrooms could be covered with cork, linoleum, or just plain wood.

As to draperies, they do give a room a finished look. And they are also great for catching dirt, holding cats, and hiding the view. If you can make a good case for expensive draperies, by all means buy them. But if you intend to invest in them simply because it's the trend, pause for thought. There are plenty of ways to keep the sun out and give you privacy, far less expensive ones than fabric draperies. There are regular blinds, screens, shutters, and inexpensive curtains.

If it's fashion you're after, bear in mind that everybody has draperies—just everybody. Sometimes it pays to be different.

I really don't mean to knock the things most of us take for granted in home furnishings. My point is to show how easy it is to do without some things, at least temporarily—because that is exactly what most families starting out in life will have to do.

Buying all the things it takes to completely furnish a new home today, in the modern manner, takes at least $10,000. How many young people have that much money when they set up housekeeping? And even if they could plunge into debt that far, who would encourage it? By the time the debt was one-half paid, many of the items would be worn out—or out of favor. Timing is the key to better living.

Appliances and conveniences

During 1964, you could buy all of the basic home appliances for a little over $800, provided you shopped carefully and settled for the economy models. If you bought reconditioned secondhand appliances, the sum spent would be closer to $400.

It has been claimed often enough that electrical appliances are a substitute for human servants, which few of us can afford these days. There is much truth in that claim, and the beautiful part is that electrical gadgets don't require social security contributions or unemployment insurance. But they do wear out and need replacement.

A refrigerator may last fifteen years or more. A fully automatic washer, however, may last only eight years. How long your electrical and mechanical servants last depends on their quality and construction, how hard you use them, and how well you care for them. Original price is not the only real expense factor.

You won't go far wrong in computing the real "cost" of owning appliances and conveniences by adding the sum of money you are spending to buy the whole lot—refrigerator, range, washer, drier, vacuum cleaner, air conditioner, water heater, and so on— and then divide that total by 10 to average out your "per year" cost of owning them. As an example, suppose you paid $1500 for all your little "helpers." While some of them might last fifteen years before needing replacement, others might fold up in five. Fifteen hundred dollars' worth of these goodies would average out to a "per year" replacement cost of about $150. That is the sum you should set aside each year, possibly in that second checking account, to keep your family in servants.

Replacement, however, is only part of the cost. Maintenance and service are big factors. That will come to another 3 or 4 per cent per year of the total sum originally spent. So be prepared to spend another $50 a year for upkeep on your appliances if they originally cost about $1500.

Another expense is the feeding of the machines. They take water, gas, electricity, and soapsuds. Even robots have appetites. So the more helpers you employ, the higher the feed bills.

Here are the things to consider as you go shopping for the "big ticket" items—the appliances, conveniences, and luxuries.

1. How much can I afford in the way of all the costs listed above?

2. How badly do I need each appliance? (Small batches of wash should eliminate the need for an expensive washer-drier combination.)

3. How can I be assured of good quality? (*Consumer Reports*, published by Consumers Union of Mount Vernon, New York, can be of real help, even if you have to seek out the old issues.)

4. Are there places where I can buy some of the items second-hand?

5. Would I be wiser to use public self-help services for a time?

(It is about as inexpensive to use coin-operated washers, driers, and cleaners as it is to own your own equipment.)

6. Wouldn't it be wiser to rent some equipment, such as a floor polisher, a sander, a rug shampooer, or other seldom-used items, than to buy them? (It usually is much less expensive to rent these things when you need them than to invest in them.)

Whatever you decide to buy in the way of appliances, read the instructions, ask questions about operation, and save the warranties. You should have a folder in your file to hold all the guarantees. And to save costs from having to replace what you buy too soon, treat your servants with care and respect. Overuse and overloading will come right out of your own budget.

One final warning about the purchasing of appliances. You may see an advertisement featuring a very low price on, for instance, a refrigerator. Even after studying some consumer publications and visiting the store for a demonstration, you can get taken. The unit shipped to your home may be a slightly different model, somewhat less expensive than the one you ordered. Insist that the model number be on your sales slip, and then compare that number with the model you receive.

THE PHONEY PITCHES

Why so many unethical practices?

There's an old legal term, *caveat emptor*, which in Latin means "let the buyer beware." This has been the guiding principle behind our entire commercial system for many years. To put it in another way, in a free enterprise society such as ours, the burden is on the buyer to protect himself. Certainly this theory is not uniquely American. Street selling in many lands is a weird mixture of haggling, bickering, lying, and cheating. But in such areas buyers expect to be "taken" unless they examine all merchandise closely and argue at the top of their lungs.

Several factors, which have entered into the American attitude toward merchandising, have removed *some* of the burden from the consumer-buyer.

First, we have witnessed the rise of consumer groups, often labor-backed, which are pressing for more consumer protection. Consumer groups view the commercial scene from moral, social, and economic grounds.

Second, as a basically religious nation, we have attempted to inject ethics into commerce. This isn't easy, though. As a professor friend of mine likes to say (mainly to raise eyebrows), "The only thing that gives dignity to the profit system is the commercial ethic, but unfortunately, there isn't any such animal." Nevertheless, others disagree with him, and we try to temper our commerce with ethical considerations.

Third, many of us come from societies that traditionally frowned on "buying cheap and selling dear." Deep in our hearts many of us despise merchandising. We distrust it and want to limit its effects on our culture to a minimum. As a result of this, we encourage laws restraining bad business practices.

Fourth, even the most influential of businessmen realize that unfettered profiteering will react against the status quo. As long as profits aren't seriously affected, these businessmen go along with a reasonable amount of government policing.

Nevertheless, most businessmen would prefer to police themselves, through such agencies as the Better Business Bureau. Many of these bureaus are managed by dedicated, conscientious men, but we must be realistic. Such agencies are set up to protect the more influential and reputable businesses against the less scrupulous ones, especially in the matter of advertising. The public interest is a secondary concern, as it probably should be, since the general public does not support the better business bureaus. Furthermore, the bureaus have no law enforcement powers. Now and then, even some well-established business enterprises engage in questionable practices, and in many cases, these same firms are well-represented in Better Business Bureau circles. When that happens, bureau managers may look the other way.

Most large cities have racket squads as part of their police setups. But racket squads concentrate on outright frauds and bunco games; they haven't the manpower, the mandate, or the authority to tackle either ethical problems or the delicate matter of commercial fakery.

At state levels, genuine consumer protection is almost non-existent. Some states have consumer counsels with limited powers, or create committees to investigate specific problems. But most states rely on a hodgepodge of regulatory bodies to keep commercial abuses at a minimum. As any observer of the political scene will surely agree, most so-called regulatory authorities soon come to serve those industries they are supposed to regulate and police. The regulators are wined, dined, and sometimes persuaded in less savory ways to dilute their militancy.

Federal attempts to protect the public meet with great resistance on the part of both lobbyists and legislators. And at the national level, many legislators appear to be both lawmakers and lobbyists, especially since we don't require our congressmen to declare their sources of outside income, and don't seem particularly concerned about "conflict of interest."

I am forced to make these rather cynical observations to put you on guard, and to answer in advance in case you are shocked enough by some practices to say, "There ought to be a law."

We Americans apparently have not yet made up our minds as to what is "good" and what is "bad" in the commercial arena. Until we do, it's every man for himself.

But before I begin warning you against what I consider "bad" in the way of selling, advertising, and general merchandising, let me sum up what I have just said.

1. The legal attitude toward commerce is still "buyer beware." Unless you can actually prove fraud, going to court won't help.

2. There is very little consumer protection in the true sense of the word, despite a number of attempts to regulate commercial practices.

3. While businessmen do set up agencies to keep competition clean and respectable, consumer protection is only incidental to the main goal.

As ex-President Coolidge said, "The business of America is business." There is little doubt in my mind that our vigorous economy results from a general hands-off policy on the part of our lawmakers. It is highly debatable how many protective laws we should have in this country.

But I do feel business itself should do more, much more, to eliminate bad practices that hurt wage earners. Businessmen spend millions of dollars every year in image-making, hoping to create confidence in consumers. So far it has worked. The American consumer is the most trusting the world has ever invented. He believes—he really believes.

How long that will last, I don't know, with more giant industries being indicted every month for antitrust violations, price-fixing, and general questionable practices.

My aim is not to create hostility toward business. My aim is to open the eyes of young consumers to the realities of today's commercial world.

The most common skin games

HOME IMPROVEMENT RACKETS

There are two big reasons why so many quick-buck schemes are aimed at homeowners. For one thing, we love our homes and take pride in them. The other reason has to do with the Federal Housing Administration, a federal agency set up to stimulate home building and home improving many years ago. The FHA was created to guarantee the home loans made by financial institutions when lenders began to get cold feet.

The loan guarantees extended by the FHA made it easy for home improvement firms, good ones and bad ones, to sell their finance contracts to banks and savings and loan firms. Since most of these finance contracts ran into thousands of dollars, many unscrupulous operators jumped into the home improvement field. As long as the loans were guaranteed by the FHA, too many lending institutions didn't bother, enough anyway, to screen the contracts, the workmanship, or the integrity of the outfits performing the work.

To make the situation even worse, many homeowners thought the FHA "guarantees" (on the loans) meant that the FHA approved both the work and the firms involved. The unscrupulous operators didn't try to correct that misunderstanding. They capitalized on it.

Actually, the FHA guarantees nothing except that the lending institution will get its money back if a buyer-borrower defaults, as long as the papers were in order when the loan was made. One of those papers, the "completion certificate," caused much of the trouble. Too many persons signed these certificates even before the work had started, saying the work had been satisfactorily completed. Once that paper was signed, a buyer had no further recourse, even if he had been badly bilked.

Metal siding was the number one problem, and it still plagues many parts of the country. There is nothing wrong with metal siding, or most other kinds of siding for that matter. The trouble is, in too many cases the siding is way overpriced, poorly installed, and greatly overrated. Hordes of suede-shoe salesmen will descend on a community and "hard sell" homeowners on the virtues of siding, leaving town with hundreds of thousands of dollars the easy way.

The finance contracts, along with the signed completion certificates, may be sold to financial firms miles away from where the work was performed.

The FHA has cracked down somewhat on these practices, mailing out the names of firms not eligible for loan guarantees, and placing the names of other questionable firms on a "precautionary list." But bad practices still exist, with or without FHA approval. Some banks and savings and loan firms have set up their private financing arrangements, without FHA backing, but with even higher interest rates to persons improving their homes. The business is too lucrative to let a federal agency pull out the rug.

Siding is just one example of how you can get rooked fixing up your home. Additions, remodelings, and other improvements are subject to the same abuses, even today. So heed these warnings if you would improve your home, outside or in:

1. Deal only with reputable firms.

2. Get several estimates.

3. Don't sign the completion certificate or a similar paper until the work is satisfactorily completed.

Even if you heed those warnings, you should question what any major improvements will do toward raising the value of your home or toward saving you money on paint or heating. Sometimes the economic advantages of home improvements are exaggerated by the most respectable concerns. Demand a little proof of claims made. Ask to talk to satisfied customers and phone the utility companies.

WORK-AT-HOME SCHEMES

The number one offenders in the work-at-home rackets are the sewing machine salesmen. They often sell good machines, but by misrepresenting the facts. Naturally women like to help their husbands meet the monthly bills, so why not invest in a sewing machine if it will pay for itself several times over?

The pitch on sewing machines goes something like this: The lady of the house is told there is a big demand for certain home-sewn products. If she will just sign the credit contract for the sewing machine, she will be taught to sew. Then she will be furnished enough work to perform at home so that the sewing machine will actually be free.

So she signs up, learns to sew, and tackles the work assignments. But before long her products come back with a note saying, "Sorry, your quality of work is not up to our standards." End of drama, except for the payments, which go on and on.

If a sewing machine can be used profitably to make things

for your family, it can be a wise investment. Sewing can be an interesting challenge. But if a person expects the machine to pay for itself commercially, he'll likely be disappointed.

One should always be skeptical about buying a high-priced machine for sewing, typing, or whatnot, with the pitch that money can be made using the machine at home. It just doesn't figure.

THE FLATTERY PITCH

"Because of your standing in the community and your excellent reputation, we would like to give you, absolutely free, our new set of encyclopedia books." That's how the pitch starts, and who could resist it? After all, you are well thought of and popular. And why pass up a little payola as a reward for helping sell your friends? Oh, you aren't dumb. You know the book company is using you, but why not?

So you get ready to accept the books, barely hearing the salesman mention the "annual supplements" which will cost you a nominal fee each month. You sign some papers, supposed to signify your acceptance of the gift, and then you thank the sales representative.

Well, by the time the books arrive, so does a copy of that contract you signed so hastily, along with a letter. The letter makes it clear that the price of the annual supplements is large enough to include the price of the books themselves. And, as the letter says, you signed a noncancelable agreement. So for years you pay and you pay, now and then glancing at the fine set of encyclopedias.

In time you try to sell them, at one-half the price you paid originally. And now you know why so many such books are for sale at bargain prices in the newspapers.

Some persons have squealed long enough and loud enough, with the aid of an attorney, to get their money back. Most persons are too embarrassed to complain.

There is another variation of the book pitch. This one works particularly well on parents who dropped out of school early and who wish their children to get the best education. The general idea is that if the parents will buy an expensive set of educational books, the children will read them (as they get older) and get all A's in school. The truth is, the children might well become fine scholars—if they would read the books. But when parents themselves don't read, children tend to follow suit. The books in many cases are never cracked or are out-of-date by the time they are.

It must give a book salesman a fine feeling of contributing to the betterment of society, knowing he is selling "knowledge." But I wonder how he feels going back to homes of people having a hard time making ends meet when he tries to collect the past-due payments.

Both encyclopedias and children's educational books are excellent products, of more potential value than most consumer products we buy today. Then why do they have to be sold in such devious ways?

Does the "potential" end justify the means? The point is: I would definitely encourage the buying of such books, provided they compare well with other similar books on the market, are priced right, and provided you or your children are quite likely and ready to use them. Those are big "provideds."

EAT-BETTER PLANS

The television commercial begins with the pitchman saying, "If it costs you over $12 a week to eat, you should investigate our frozen food plan." Since just about every family spends more than $12 a week for meats and groceries, the ad has great appeal.

What the commercial announcer meant, but didn't say, is this: You can buy all those frozen goodies, all four hundred pounds or so of them, for $12 a week all right, but you'll likely eat them up at the rate of about $30 a week. In time you'll be out of the frozen food, the best cuts of meat anyway, and heading back to the old supermarket, but you'll be paying for the food you consumed on credit for many, many months.

Not only that, but you may have to buy a freezer to hold

all the food. That means several hundred dollars more expense. Even if you bought the food at a bargain price, say 20 per cent off retail, it would take a lot of savings on food to pay for the freezer, not to mention the finance charges.

Then there's the way the pitchman in the commercial describes those four hundred pounds of food—"steaks, roasts, chops," and then his voice trails off as he mentions vegetables and less glamorous foods.

For all but farm families and those growing a great deal of their own food, the freezing compartment of a regular refrigerator is fully adequate for storage. And even for farm families, renting a freezer locker in town will suffice. A home freezer is mostly a luxury today, that and a "security symbol." Having lots of fine food on hand does make a person feel quite secure.

As to buying large quantities of frozen foods all at once, it takes excellent management to avoid spoilage and waste. Even if you pay for the foods and leave them with the frozen-food merchant, just what are you accomplishing? There are food markets all over town willing to sell you food whenever you need it, and at prices which compare well with those offered by the bulk plan merchants.

And if it's atomic war you are worried about, where will you get the electricity to keep the freezer cold?

REFERRAL SCHEMES

Referral schemes are related to the chain letter hoax. The general idea is to be instrumental in selling some product to a number of your friends and acquaintances. As an example, let's say you want to buy a new car for $3000. So you pay a little cash down and sign a finance contract for the balance.

Then, for every friend you help sell a similar car to, you may get a $100 credit on your contract. All you have to do is "bird dog" about thirty friends and the car you bought is free.

In the first place, the "credits" usually apply to the tail end of your contract, so even if you manage to sew up a few referrals, you must make the regular monthly payments promptly.

Second, even with the population explosion going on, it's amazing how fast you run out of people, especially people who want a new car, have good credit, and will agree to talk to your salesman friend. Also, there are many other persons running around trying to point out their friends to auto dealers and thereby get free cars. As I say, the whole scheme is much like the chain letter racket. Some states have outlawed referral schemes entirely. But the practice goes on and on, all over the country, involving every product imaginable.

CURES FOR SOCIAL OUTCASTS

Almost every person wants to be healthy, beautiful, talented, and popular. We want to be trim and be able to dance skillfully in order to mix well at social functions.

When there is a demand or a need for something, American ingenuity will find an answer. Some persons will try to help; others will try to profiteer. And when it comes to loneliness, it seems that the angle-shooters have more cures than the social agencies.

It is one thing to make frequent trips to a gymnasium or "health club," paying as you go, or on a year-to-year basis. The YMCA and YWCA offer excellent and reasonably priced facilities to keep fit and slim. At least, these nonprofit associations have facilities in most big cities.

But it is another thing to sign a long-term contract with a promotional "health club," committing yourself to pay hundreds, even thousands, of dollars. Such contracts are fairly foolproof from the promoter's standpoint, except where they are outlawed.

The same goes for the contract-type dance studios, where you are assured of instant popularity if you will just pledge a good part of your earnings for the rest of your life. Some persons have committed themselves to pay thousands of dollars, and these were not just elderly persons either. Loneliness is not restricted to senior citizens in our large cities.

Few persons can buy popularity on the installment plan, except that type of popularity coming from professional "friends" who don't mind fawning over their clients. To be sure, you may meet some other clients of those commercial establishments selling social aids, but you might also meet them at church, genuine social clubs, or just anywhere.

Bait advertising

As most merchants contend, to make a sale they must grab your interest, enough to get you into their places of business. Maybe it doesn't matter how they get your attention, short of hitting you over the head. The real concern may be over what happens to you once you are at the point of sale.

But in case you dislike being razzle-dazzled into wasting your time, here are some of the commonly used "baits."

NO DOWN PAYMENT

The ad featuring "no down payment" may be factual when used to sell certain products such as furniture and appliances. But even then, you must have "qualified credit." Most newspapers and other ad media now insist that advertisers stress the "good credit" qualification when offering merchandise at "nothing down" terms.

But when auto dealers advertise "no down payment," they usually mean something else. In most cases they mean they will help you "borrow" the down payment, usually through a loan company charging rather high rates for the money.

In such cases you will end up paying two financial firms, sometimes several, one for the down payment and at least one for the balance on the car contract itself. This often involves payments that are higher than usual, high interest charges, and in many cases, paying for a "dead horse." Should the car be repossessed, you'll have to go on paying the loan company that lent you the money for the down payment. And sometimes, in order to borrow the money for the down payment on a car you knowingly or unknowingly pledge your furniture and your salary as security.

So know what you are getting into when answering a "no

down payment" ad, read what you sign, and try to avoid making two payments for one piece of merchandise. Such unorthodox financing should be a warning to you. You probably don't need the merchandise that seriously.

GENERAL PUFFING

It seems generally agreed that advertisers should have enough leeway to exaggerate a little. That is known in the trade as "puffing." Just be aware that many ads stretch the facts somewhat. You particularly have to watch the "weasel words," those which give an impression without actually saying as much.

If we were to remove all puffing from advertising, it might reduce commercial activity to a crawl and take the challenge out of life. We couldn't regulate advertising to that extent even if we wished to do so. Man is much too ingenious to be controlled in such a manner. After all, most of our English adjectives have several meanings, and it would tax the abilities of our courts to set up arbitrary meanings to all words used in commerce. Just be a realist and don't expect every new household cleaner to perform better than the old ones without the aid of human hands.

WHAT THEY REALLY ARE SELLING

It has been said many times before that American consumers rarely buy products for purely functional purposes. The use of any item sold today is often less important than the psychological message it conveys to buyers. We all desire to be loved, respected, protected, and envied.

As I mentioned briefly under the section on automobiles, pure transportation often is the least important of considerations to those who purchase cars. We buy a certain car because it fits in with the image we wish to create in the minds of others.

We buy certain household products because, if we use these products, our lives will be happier, our wives or husbands will love us more, and our neighbors will be jealous of our abilities. Washings can be only so white, but washings on the line may be viewed by others. White, white laundry today is a status symbol, rarely a matter of hygiene.

This is an age of anxiety and loss of security. Therefore many of us buy products from huge concerns holding themselves up as father images and pillars of strength. If the man around the house is too domesticated, insecure, and overcivilized, perhaps a wife can't be blamed for patronizing the company that "holds her in its hands," or the one "guarding her against all trouble."

And perhaps she can't be blamed for buying the product with the packaged genie who does all the nasty cleaning around the house, even though she realizes she'll need to do the real work herself.

Most firms making and selling consumer products hire psychologists who study our hidden wants and frustrations. They try to learn our motivations and subconscious needs. And from such research comes the advertising and packaging which influence our buying habits.

It may be too much to ask that we dig into our own subconscious thoughts in order to analyze all the commercial messages aimed at us. But we at least can ask ourselves, "Why am I so interested in buying this particular product?"

If enough of us approached the problem with more concern and analysis, we might bring some reality back to the world of advertising.

Why spending attitudes are so important

It may be unkind and unjust to lump motivational research techniques in with rackets and phoney pitches. The market researchers relying on psychology can make a good case that they serve the economy well. But it would be harder, much harder, to prove they serve humanity well, for the simple reason that a good underarm deodorant doesn't really make a person more popular. It may make him *less unpopular*, but not really more popular. The lady with the whitest wash in town won't likely be named as club president. Or will that neuter of a genie substitute for a strong male in the family.

We consumers live sufficiently vicarious lives as it is without relying on mass-produced merchandise for fulfillment. It also seems too much to ask that we spend our money lavishly and frivolously just to keep other persons employed. Because unless most of us, as individuals, obtain genuine satisfaction from what we earn and spend, what have we achieved for our society as a whole? Already there is evidence of rebellion against the ersatz "good life" on the part of young people. I, for one, shall not discourage that rebellion.

A lie is a lie. It is just as big a lie to hint that we will be the envy of the neighborhood if we buy a certain detergent as it is to tell us that Brooklyn Bridge is for sale. Surely we don't need commercial psychologists to run our lives. Some persons may question my concern, even as they gulp tranquilizer pills and hark back to the good old days. But it is my contention that we have a clear choice ahead. We can stoically accept our role as consumers, hoping for inspiration from each new bauble tossed our way, or we can prove that human beings have enough capacity to determine their own needs.

There is one more important point to remember about spending in general. If we still operated on a cash basis, we would have problems enough, but at least we couldn't lose more than we have in savings. We might fritter away our money on baldness cures and other patented potions, just as our great-grandparents did, but we wouldn't have to run to the bankruptcy courts every few years.

This is the age of installment buying—the "credit revolution," some call it. And it enables the swindlers and gyp artists to operate on a grand scale. Without consumer credit, the professional con men would have to go back to matching pennies with innocent travelers and selling dandruff cures.

This is the age when even an insolvent day laborer can spend thousands of dollars foolishly, and instantly, by signing a credit contract and pledging his future income.

It would be grossly unfair to blame the credit system for becoming the tool of the swindler. Nevertheless, every young person should have a firm understanding of today's credit fundamentals—what makes credit tick, in other words. That is the subject of Part III.

SPECIAL SITUATION:
THE YOUNG MAN ON THE WAY UP

The young married man with a good education and specialized training is certainly entitled to dream in full color. The world can be his oyster, provided he uses common sense and plans ahead. We are living in an age of great change and great promise, technologically speaking. Yet we are also living in an age of computers and general automation, with machines drooling enviously at jobs now held by brainy, young decision-makers. All this makes for insecurity among young people, even among those chosen "Most likely to succeed" by their peers. When a man is insecure, he is not given to planning far into the future; he is more apt to respond emotionally to daily pressures and threats to his way of life. But let me get this off my chest before we go on. Granted that mankind faces its greatest challenge in history from the creations of our own brains, and granted that anyone now reading this book could be automated out of his paycheck before he finishes reading the next chapter, the future doesn't seem that dark to me. Machines cannot vote and we'd be fools to let them try. Even if you and I turn out to be totally inefficient, as compared to the electronic brains, we'll still be running the show, and we'll still be drawing "spending power" of some kind, far into the foreseeable future.

Aside from lacking the power to elect or influence politicians, machines don't spend money on consumer products. These two factors alone combine to keep humanity in the driver's seat. Our world will change, provided we don't destroy it out of our own frustrations, but it likely will go on, and men with ability and foresight will get the most from it. They will also contribute the most to it. If you have much on the ball, you'd be a fool not to think and plan ahead. If upheavals in our way of life upset your plans, then adjust as best you can and make the necessary changes. But merely having a plan for your financial future can relieve some of the insecurity which may be plaguing you. The important thing is to be flexible, philosophical, and reasonably hopeful. When you come right down to it, is there any workable alternative to this? The husband who refuses to plan for the future, preferring to just drift along, may be compounding his problems. Dr. Joshua Bierer, editor of the *International Journal of Social Psychiatry*, called Americans "the most worried people in the world." Men worry about the loss of male status and lack of money. Women worry because some men aren't dominant enough, and women also worry about lack of money.

So, it may be possible to kill two birds with one stone, or at least wound them. While I have already covered the controversy over who should manage the money, the husband or the wife, now I am aiming at the man on his way up. It is only fair to concede that many a man who works primarily with his hands is often married to a woman with a better education and a better skill with finances. And this is sometimes true of the bright young organization man as well, but not as typically.

The typical young corporation man is married to a woman with grand ideas about moving up in the world, too fast and too furiously. Without the husband realizing it (after all, he wants to be fair and reasonable), such a wife can quickly ruin a husband's career, even bankrupt him.

Steer with a firm hand

By letting it be known early in the marriage, before the dew is off the romance, that he is, after all, the main provider and therefore the boss, a young husband may be able to bolster his male image and preserve his solvency. Charge accounts should be carefully controlled and checked. Definite limits should be set on spending.

A wife, of course, may be overexposed to neighborhood women who say they run the whole show, and perhaps they do. But this is your marriage, not the guy's next door. Perhaps your wife will read some of the popular garbage about how much she is worth to you in dollars, because she performs so many chores and works so many hours. O.K., pay her half of what you earn, and then insist that she kick back the entire sum to the family spending pool, just as you have to do.

Far be it from me to try to establish a male dictatorship in any home: it is only that you consult with your wife on financial decisions. You should encourage her to handle as much money as is prudent. She should know the most intimate details of the family financial status, such as how much you earn, where the records are kept, how much is in savings, and how much you owe. But stay at the helm.

There is no guarantee that by following this advice you will cease worrying and become rich. A certain amount of nervous twitching is probably part of our Darwinian make-up. And as to getting rich, not many of us will make it. But just plain getting ahead and staying ahead is not to be sneezed at, nor is the good feeling of having some control over where you are going. Your charming co-pilot may gripe now and then at the austerity program, but this will be offset in time as you pass the wheeler-dealer types, and acquire a solid base. Then she'll respect you more.

On the other hand, if you can't stay away from bars and have a tendency toward profligacy, maybe you should be the co-pilot. I can only assure you that from the moment you turn over the financial controls, matriarchy will no longer be just a word in the dictionary. You may have to drink even more, just to tolerate the shame of it all.

If marriage were merely a sprint to the altar, there'd be little need to gaze far into the future. But it isn't a sprint; it's a long-distance affair with lots of barriers and hurdles. If you know what's ahead, you can learn to step high at the proper times and pace yourself. That's why a look at the typical "family financial cycle" is more than an academic exercise; it's a matter of studying the maps before you take off.

What to expect for the first 25 years

While he was teaching financial management at the University of Southern California, Rodney G. Klein, who is a friend of mine, would break down the stages of the family life cycle. The subject matter was discussed in classes, and then a chart was furnished to each student. The students were asked to estimate the various expenses associated with each stage of family development and growth. Needless to say, the cost figures varied considerably from student to student, even though most of the young persons were remarkably stereotyped in estimating their future incomes. Based in part on the general outline used by Mr. Klein, here's what the young family man usually has to face up to in the way of financial planning. And for that matter, most every person reading this book will be presently going through one of these phases.

Newly married, or want-fulfillment

Since it is taken for granted that each American generation should begin married life more comfortably than the last, the basic requirements of a plunge into wedlock are beginning to resemble the unrequited dreams of a nineteenth-century banker. And far be it from me to criticize this trend, as long as the money is available without too much of a subsidy from parents. Wanting and striving for more than we've been accustomed to has been called "THE REACH." In its advanced stages it often turns into "INSOLVENCY," and in its ultimate stage, it sometimes evolves into "BANKRUPTCY." But before this financial metamorphosis is complete, it feeds hungrily on credit, mass advertising, status-seeking, and just plain foolishness.

At any rate, newly marrieds are immediately faced with buying a car (or two), purchasing things for the home, including all the soft goods, and beginning their security programs. Since most young couples have a decent amount of clothing, and since the stars in their eyes keep them home more than older couples, neither dress nor recreation is too big a factor for a while. In fact, this last point leads many young families into overextending themselves on installment payments for hard goods and automobiles. Moral: If you feel reasonably certain you'll be content at home in the evenings for quite a while, without making the "spots" or entertaining, then take on some credit payments of limited maturity if you need to. And as to clothing, most of what we buy today has a short life span. If you buy hard goods on credit payments which last over a year to eighteen months, you may find yourselves in rags and tatters, also lacking the means to dine out once in a while or socialize.

Most credit payments for durable goods come from robbing the clothing and recreation budgets, not to mention savings. While you realistically may plan to cut down on savings while you are building up your physical assets, it is a very serious matter to reduce your family life to forever watching television in old clothing. Life is not made of that stuff, and romance is often a fragile thing. Even a sure-to-succeed organization man might find it prudent to begin married life with a serviceable second-hand car and some good quality used furniture. Just a thought. After all, any used item you buy can be replaced later, one piece at a time, and under less pressing circumstances. The "Acquisition Period" is a tough hurdle to clear otherwise.

The first year of married life also brings the frightening (to some men) awareness of having a dependent—a wife. Thus the need for life insurance. (The types of life insurance will be covered later.) And with this sudden recognition of financial responsibility to some other person comes the urge to save, to get ahead financially. In other words, once the honeymoon is over, conflicting forces set to work on the family budget. There is the incentive to spend and go in debt for durable goods, offset by the need for protection and thrift. And as I said, the only redeeming factor is less need for new clothing and a temporary willingness to sacrifice socializing and the bright lights. However, these conflicting forces can tear a man apart, especially if his wife is demanding and short-sighted.

Birth of children and pre-school, or we're not alone any more

Unless the young marrieds have been reasonably frugal in their spending, or awfully lucky in inheriting some money, the arrival of the first child may be all but overwhelming. Life can become pretty grim all at once, balanced, of course, by the joys of parenthood. In the first place, apartment life may no longer suffice, at least not psychologically, even if the landlord is willing. Suddenly there comes the desire to be a homeowner, so that baby and the parents can play in the yard. There's usually the pressing problem of an extra bedroom. There's even the psychological need to take roots and become a part of a baby-oriented suburbia. It seems very important what type of friends Bobby or Susie acquires. So, it is suddenly necessary to come up with a down payment for a home, and money for moving expenses. Not to mention all the baby paraphernalia.

Since this change in attitude comes about the time Daddy owes the doctor for delivery and has to pay for baby medicines, there's usually only one way out, a loan from some financial institution. And since Mother takes a while to get back on her feet, there's possibly the cost of a day nurse, plus some temporary domestic help. When you add all the costs of the baby, including the need for a new and larger home, it usually comes to $4000 or more. Aside from the urgent cash needs, the basic budget takes a beating too. Father probably should increase his life insurance coverage, has to pay for baby foods and medical checkups, and must foot the bill for baby-sitters now and then. These are the days when marriages come apart at the seams, when young mothers experience deep-seated depressions and when fathers run to the neighborhood pub, or even another woman, rather than face reality.

Yet these situations are all a part of living, and they must be faced. Getting prepared to meet them is an obvious answer, along with a sense of humor. It also helps enormously to keep one's perspective, and to recognize that one can too easily be trapped by conformity. There are desirable apartments which accept children, which would eliminate the need for the down payment you don't have. Medical bills can be amortized over future months, if proper arrangements are made with doctors and hospitals. The grandparents often can, and should, help occasionally with the baby-sitting. And instead of Father avoiding his somewhat suffocating home-life, he could give more thought to what his wife is going through. Now may be the time to spend a few dollars entertaining or going out, to be paid for partly out of money *not spent* on psychologists, marriage counselors, and even lawyers. But even as Father dreams of getting the doctor paid, Mother is dreaming of the time Junior will be ready for expensive pre-school.

To be brutally frank, the cost of pre-school usually is too high for the typical family budget. Yet it is almost an essential for many families. I personally think the lack of adequate, supervised, low-cost child care centers is one of the greatest criticisms one can level at our affluent society. Yet the Italian Government was toppled over just such an issue not long ago. There is a great deal of organized hostility to government-sponsored child care centers. As Faith Prior, Extension Family Economist at the University of Vermont, recently said: "The United States in the midtwentieth century was a nation with great respect for the dead. At the same time these people did not consider the care of young children important." She was, of course, thinking about what future historians might report on our culture. So I say to young mothers and fathers, instead of lamenting the lack of decent child care centers, along with the cost of those now functioning, you would be wiser to get behind organizations which are striving for improvement in the field. The present lack hits working mothers the hardest, especially those with low incomes. But there is no reason why a rich society cannot also come to the financial aid of young, struggling members of a future leadership level. At present, pre-schools are generally either a luxury or a gamble, which require careful consideration.

Elementary school

Once the young child gets more into the world at large, his own wants begin to multiply. He desires what other children have, and at such times the parents need to rationalize their financial limitations. Phrases such as "We can't afford it" are sometimes avoided out of pure pride and embarrassment. Junior really doesn't know what things cost, from the standpoint of money or sacrifice; he only knows what he wants when he wants it. In addition, parents are afraid a child may be scarred for life unless he has everything other children have. This is pure nonsense, of course, but nevertheless, the very backbone of our economy.

Even swing sets and tricycles can be purchased second-hand, assuming a mother has enough common sense to save money that way. And while it is obvious that children need exercise, there's no health rule that I know of saying that price is the main ingredient. There is this to consider, even though the baby days are over, health and medicine costs remain fairly high during the elementary school days. As the child advances in school, there are other expenses to consider, including dancing, swimming, music lessons, and summer camp. What you save on early-age gadgetry can pay for more essential things later on.

Perhaps, and hopefully, Father has increased his income since those nip-and-tuck days of diapers and pins. Perhaps even more hopefully, he has managed to salt away a few bonuses and windfalls. Maybe Mother is back in the work force adding to the family income. If so, the elementary school years can be quite happy ones. The family may be over the hump, financially speaking, with a modest net worth, including an equity in a home. There may be several children by now, each slightly less expensive to raise than the first one. If so, the next big hurdle can be faced without flinching. Let's hope so, because aside from the obvious teen-age complications, high school can be the most financially demanding time of all. It comes, as unkind fate wills it, just as many parents stretch their resources to join clubs, lodges, and more swinging groups. And usually just before high school, a dentist has convinced you that Bobby or Alice's "bite" ought to be improved. Whether you call it orthodontia or cosmetology is unimportant. There goes 1000 bucks.

High school

Even before Junior gets to high school, he may be going on dates, demanding a substantial allowance, and very conscious of what he wears. He's been covetous of the family automobile for some time, and probably has been allowed limited use of it. But suddenly he wants one of his own—an old clunker perhaps, but readily available when he wants it. Who knows, a few years from now, Junior may be insisting on his own spacemobile.

Well, maybe Junior will have to earn his own private transportation by working after school, over the weekends, or during vacation. It depends on the family resources at this period, and on how seriously Junior is about it all. The same goes for his dating money, if it exceeds the limits of his regular allowance. High school girls also have unlimited wants which require substantial outlays of money, but they too should be governed by the income capabilities of their parents. It would be possible to fill a page with things teen-age boys and girls want, including such items as surfboards, musical instruments, hi-fi sets, records, and sports equipment. A Sears catalogue would be a simpler way to itemize them because teen-age spending has become a multibillion-dollar market.

The mode of living most people reach for is that temptingly displayed by mass-market advertising. But these value standards are often a far cry from reality, and for a family of modest means to accept them as the "norm" would be fatal. It is one thing for young people to reach for more than their parents began with; it is another thing for parents to subsidize the "reaching" to the point of ruining themselves.

Children should receive an allowance, if possible, once they reach the point of understanding money. That allowance should be as much in line with the allowances received by a child's play group as feasible, provided the group is of a somewhat similar economic background. In my opinion, it is never too early to point up economic differences, because that is an essential part of any education. The parent who lacks the tact and ability to communicate on this point is in for serious trouble sooner or later. An allowance, in its finer definition, is simply a system for providing a child with enough cash to cover his essential needs, mostly things the parents would pay for directly otherwise—plus a relatively small amount for personal-choice spending. The actual "need" part of any allowance is fairly easy to break down—school expenses, lunches, transportation, and perhaps clothing, depending upon the age of the child. What is doled out over and above actual needs should correspond roughly, and on a seniority basis, with the "extra" monies parents allow themselves, which is often very little.

If Junior or his sister insist the allowance money is too meager, it's time to go over it again, item by item. Perhaps some important essentials have been overlooked. What usually develops, however, is that a youngster has succumbed to some personal indulgence which requires an above-average subsidy. If such is the case, and the indulgences are acceptable, parents might allow the youngster to perform some essential chores around the house— not "make-work," but jobs which really need to be done. Junior shouldn't have to account over and over again for his regular allowance, once it has been fairly determined. Neither should he be forced to work for it. His allowance is his fair share of the family income. On the other hand, it is only common sense that he be required to earn money above and beyond the definition of normal requirements.

The common problem with allowances comes from the parents themselves, who think they would lose caste by saying "no" to a child. No one likes to plead poverty to a youngster, but admitting to financial limitations is something we all do every day. Furthermore, the fancies of young people change with the winds and with the times. As a young person enters the senior year of high school he begins to wonder if Dad has saved enough money for those expensive college years. And Dad is wondering the same thing. The "soft-touch" dad begins to lose his image, whereas the tight-fisted father acquires more respect from his suddenly grown-up son.

The college years

Since this is directed at the young man on his way up, the treatment so far may have aged him considerably. Having perhaps recently graduated from college himself, it appears that I've suddenly handed his unborn child an IBM card for enrollment at a university. Not so, really. I'm mainly trying to map out the various hurdles to be cleared. A four-year college education today can cost from virtually nothing up to $15,000 per year. It depends on where one goes to college, how lavishly one lives, and on such unknowns as scholarships and student loans. And, quite frankly, I can only guess at what the future holds twenty years from now.

We adults have frightened ourselves almost unto death over college, both as to what it means and as to what it costs. It seems to "mean" a sure ticket to economic success and social respectability. And it seems to cost a fortune. Perhaps college ought to mean improving the talents and awareness one already has, rather then being the minor leagues for the Chamber of Commerce.

And instead of depleting the modest savings of parents, perhaps our institutions of higher learning are more worthy of outright support from government than already rich farmers. To some extent, our colleges and universities are already being subsidized.

The truth is, almost any eligible youngster can go to a good college without much undue strain on his parents, provided he is willing to live at home and attend a local school. Many thousands of students do this every year, and most of them suffer very little from it. That is one choice open to all parents and children. There are also many cases of bright, but poor students being subsidized by the prestige universities themselves. If at this stage I seem to reverse my field a bit, by saying that parents needn't sacrifice "too much" in seeing that their children get a college degree, it is because I don't believe too much of the burden should fall on parents. I still urge thrift, planning ahead, and all that sort of thing, but there are some costs beyond the reach of most parents. One of those is a top-drawer education for a youngster at a private university or college, along with board and room. Junior may have his heart set on Harvard, and perhaps Betsy won't settle for less than Vassar, but the "how" of it all is important too. If you didn't have the courage to deny Junior his new bike when the bill collectors were after you, you will find it even more difficult to deny him his educational status symbol. But if you can swing it, more power to you.

If you can't, there's no very good reason why Junior can't attend State U., perhaps working a little for his board and room. If and when he graduates, he can go on for an advanced degree at a status-type school, if he chooses to. There are all sorts of alternatives and compromises available these days, and while a parent certainly ought to make some personal sacrifices to assure a decent education for his offspring, there are limitations. It's one thing to drop a country club to pay for college tuition; it's another thing to go so far in debt that you sacrifice your own security.

Even since the Russians lofted their first satellite into space, the heat has been on both parents and students to measure up to the challenge. Unfortunately, most of this heat was generated out of a "cold war" philosophy. We wanted better technicians to man our armament and space laboratories, not necessarily better people per se. And if we really expected already overtaxed middle-income families to pick up the entire tab for this crash program of technology, we were simply engaging in a form of cruel taxation. Educators, for the most part, were of little help. Suddenly they were in the saddle, spurring youngsters on to greater and greater challenges. Perhaps without knowing it, many teachers were put in the position of co-conspirators in making Johnny a brilliant robot. It has never for one moment amazed me that so many bright students took to placards and dope. By and large, too many educators took the position that the modern-day curriculum, even in high school, was too demanding for youngsters to work at odd jobs. Study was the thing—study, study, and more study. The price was too high.

The point is, your youngster can get through college if he really wants to, even if your finances are in so-so shape, provided he has the ability and the inclination. But in my opinion it matters less where and how he goes to college than in what he wants and gets out of it. If he wants an advanced "trade school" education, that's what he'll get. But in an age when technology changes almost by the hour, trade school training never ceases. It goes on and on, long after a man is considered "middle management." Personally, I think it makes more sense to become an enlightened human being before becoming an engineer or an administrator. It at least makes a man better prepared and more amenable to changing occupations several times during his life, which even now an adult man must be prepared to do.

There are several redeeming developments to all these expenses related to getting married and raising a family from Cradle to Cum Laude. One is that we live longer and stay healthy longer than a few decades ago. Instead of being ready for the junkyard once our children get their degrees, most of us can look forward to many years of living, contributing, enjoying, and saving. So even if you are in your late forties by the time commencement exercises are over, it could be only the beginning. Furthermore, it is not then too late to begin your own retirement program, not even if you owe the bank a few thousand dollars borrowed to send your boy to college.

The big hurdles are past; now you and your wife can give almost undivided attention to planning for retirement. Not only retirement, but for the way you want to live long before you actually retire. Perhaps your wife will want to go back to work, now that the children are raised. Aside from higher taxes, extra income now could go almost entirely to extra savings. Maybe a smaller home, or even a modest apartment, will do nicely. If a man and woman enter the post-education phase of living with decent health and a zest for life, new horizons begin to appear. There is a chance to travel and make new friends, even while systematically saving for the day when work is over. It is a time to go more to the theater, to broaden interests, and perhaps to reminisce.

Those depressing financial problems of the past can now seem worth laughing about, rolling about in your memory. It is terribly important for young people to realize this, because if they know how the horror of a current money crisis can later become a worthwhile page out of life, they can more easily adjust and overcome. It is too bad that parents don't always tell their children about past adversities. Not that Father should bore Junior with how he carried newspapers at the age of ten, to make Junior ashamed or resentful. But the father who grins and says "You know, when you came into the world, your mother and I were two payments behind on the car and overdrawn at the bank" may establish a certain rapport. Maybe "grins" is the key word in that entire sentence. At any rate it might help a young man or a young woman realize that although life is hard, it is conquerable, and worthy of a smile.

In fact, the transformation these early financial problems go through in human memories can be quite astounding. Many a man and woman who struggled through the family financial cycle is impatient to try it again. Second families are becoming a phenomenon of the mid-twentieth century, sometimes accidentally to be sure, but rarely with regrets. It is partly because, as someone said, youth is wasted on the young. But it is certainly mostly attributable to the fact that we stay young longer these days. Not too many years ago parents of just-graduated collegians were already thinking of wheelchairs and rest homes. Now they are more apt to be toasting a sheepskin in Las Vegas or Palm Springs. So let me assure you there's a lot of living after the first brood has been raised and educated. And usually enough time to get started on plans for actual retirement. Since that phase of life has mostly to do with managing a limited income and rearranging one's assets, it will be covered in a later section.

PART III

MANAGING YOUR DEBTS,
or The Art of Using Credit

THE THEORY OF CONSUMER CREDIT

Does it pay to use credit?

A great number of American families aren't really interested in what credit does for them, or to them. They're already deeply involved in the credit system. Others use credit wisely without getting into serious trouble. Before you invite credit to be the domineering force in your life, know as much as you can about it—its history, theories, techniques, and alternatives.

For if you don't absorb most of what is in this section of the book, you needn't go on to the next section, Managing Your Assets. You may not have enough assets to manage.

The truth is, the business of extending credit to consumers is more than just a system today. It has become an institution, one which fought its way from serious disrepute to a position of strength and respectability. As an institution, it now has its own superstructure, public relations department, and mythology. It also has its own demonology, based on whoever gets in its way.

When you speak of the credit industry today, you are referring to a vast complex of bureaus, associations, foundations, and lobbies. A multibillion-dollar industry naturally will do whatever necessary to stay in business.

The most commonly used argument for consumer credit goes like this: Credit moves goods. The more goods we move, the lower will be the cost per item because of mass production, so theoretically credit pays for itself. And, of course, moving goods means jobs. To put this in a negative way, the wage earner who sticks to cash is being a little inconsiderate of his fellow man. Or so it would seem.

Certainly the constant barrage of propaganda has helped to mellow our attitudes toward going in debt. Credit has become a way of life to millions of American families, most of whom descended from thrifty stock. We now live from payday to payday and from payment to payment. As of early 1966, we owed some $90 billion in short-term debts. Since not all debts are reported, the figure more likely was closer to $100 billion. On the average we had pledged close to 15 per cent of our incomes toward monthly installment obligations alone, and over 20 per cent of our incomes to meet all our short-term debts including charge accounts.

We didn't change our attitudes toward debt overnight. As late as 1910 credit to consumers was generally frowned on as being immoral. But from about that time on, each succeeding generation of Americans has been handed down somewhat looser credit habits.

In general our public schools have accepted the changes graciously; for every schoolbook warning students against easy credit, there are several books pointing out its virtues. Many of the pro-credit books are supplied directly or indirectly by credit agencies themselves. One set of consumer education books, favorable to installment buying, cost credit agencies $400,000 to produce and publish. If this weren't enough, our school curriculums are for the most part too crowded to include the "domestic arts" in any comprehensive manner. It is enough of a challenge getting youngsters ready for college and preparing them to make a living. Furthermore, there aren't enough teachers with sufficient training in economics to fill the need.

We continue to send youngsters out into the world without any real grasp of budgets, buymanship, or credit. To put it bluntly, they become fair game for all the traps in the marketplace.

It has been said, over and over again, that our old feelings against going in debt were based on obsolete, puritanical standards. Maybe so. Times have changed, and so have our values. But just because most of us use credit liberally today doesn't mean that cash buying is obsolete or that debt holds no dangers. What is "modern" depends less upon its genuine virtues than upon how well it is being promoted. Any way of doing business, or any business for that matter, which succeeds in entrenching itself, will do all in its power to stay entrenched.

On the other hand, nothing will stay in vogue forever without *some* real merits. There are times when using credit, consumer credit, makes sense. We intend to be fair about the subject.

When using credit makes sense

Buying a home on credit usually makes sense, for those who want to own homes and who understand the costs. Borrowing to buy a home generally isn't considered using "consumer credit" because home mortgage terms are so extended. But a home really is just a form of consumer goods. We consume homes by using them, just as we consume automobiles, furniture, and bread. Houses simply last longer than most consumer goods.

It is primarily for that reason that borrowing to buy a home makes sense. The merchandise will outlive the debt. And homes cost so much that few of us could save enough money to pay cash for them. Then, too, the federal government has been kind enough—and realistic enough—to allow us to deduct interest costs from our income taxes. That reduces somewhat the expenses of staying in debt for housing that is essential to our survival. It is not really a luxury.

So far, at least, credit charges for home-buying have been based on easily understood, simple interest. And as long as home ownership on credit is kept decently priced and easily available, it will balance and compete with the cost of renting. All these factors make it worthwhile to buy homes on credit.

So whenever you consider using credit, apply those guides that I used to justify home mortgages. Ask yourself:

1. Will whatever you are buying on credit outlast the debt?

2. Could you comfortably save enough to pay cash for the item later on?

3. How much more costly will the credit charges make your purchase?

4. Do you really need the item or could you do without it? Is it a luxury or is it a necessity, by any reasonable definition?

5. Could you rent or lease the item at less expense?

6. Do you understand the credit terms and costs?

Using credit for everything would be just great, were it not for credit immediately turning into "debt." While credit has many advocates, debt has virtually none. Many persons cannot live comfortably under a load of debt, even in these days. Debt has a frightening sound to it. It smacks of being behind, being beholden, and living dangerously. However, as long as you stay solvent and have some net worth over and above the amount you owe, using credit need not be a traumatic experience. There are many examples which make debt worthwhile, even essential. Here are some of them:

1. Taking on a job which requires an automobile. Better to go into debt a reasonable amount for a car in order to accept a job than to stay unemployed or pass up a chance for advancement.

2. Buying home laundry equipment on credit, when such a purchase would save money as compared to using more costly commercial services.

3. Using credit to purchase books and musical instruments, when cash is short, to further the education of a talented child.

4. Buying any kind of an essential on credit when cash buying is impossible or inconvenient, as long as the essential is needed immediately.

5. Borrowing as much money as you can in order to invest it at a more profitable rate than you would pay the lender.

All of these examples involve the same principle: making credit pay for itself in a practical manner, whether sociological or purely economic. But in every single instance, paying cash would save you money, if you had it. None of the examples above would encourage borrowing just to live a little higher on the hog a little sooner. And unfortunately, providing that better living is the "magic ability" of credit, according to many credit agencies.

When using credit doesn't make sense

Far too many persons think of using credit in terms of increasing their spending power. Being able to use credit makes it possible to have things a little sooner than by waiting to pay cash, but that doesn't mean that your long-range purchasing power is increased. In fact, just the opposite happens; your long-range spending power will be reduced by the amount of the interest and credit charges.

That fact seems a little too obvious to harp on, yet many persons really believe that credit enhances their overall ability to buy the good things of life. One of the mottos of the credit industry is "The Good Things of Life on Credit." But the motto fails to mention the interest and carrying charges, a cost to the consumer.

Furthermore, the chronic user of credit often forgets to shop for price and quality. He begins to shop for terms, low downpayments, and a long time to repay. This may be even more costly than the interest charges. As he takes on more and more debt, he loses the ability to shop around and bargain. Because of all the debts he was encouraged to assume, he may become a bad credit risk and be turned down for credit by all but the most marginal credit houses. While credit firms urge you to use credit, the amount of debts you already have may be counted against you. That is one of the ironies you must face.

Even more of a paradox is the fact that it's often difficult to obtain credit if you've always stuck to cash. It may pay to use a *little* credit, just to establish yourself, even if you don't need the credit. Running a small charge account or two, at a time when cash is plentiful and you are assuming no risk, is one way to handle the problem. The point is, at some day in the future you may want to finance a home, go into business, or meet a financial emergency. Having a credit rating established would help you at such times. But borrowing money or using credit at a time when you aren't dependent upon it really puts you in the driver's seat. At such a time you can pick the best sources of credit, and borrow at the most favorable rates. Strange as it may seem, the best time to use credit is when you *don't really need it*.

Putting that statement in reverse, the worst time to seek credit is when you desperately need it. Everything is against you. The cost of credit is like the cost of everything else—it must be bargained for. A seller of credit will get the most for the use of his money as he can, within the legal limits. So stay in a good bargaining position.

That means holding your debts to a small figure, well within your ability to repay without strain. If you use credit whenever the impulse strikes you, chronic insolvency will be your way of life, not the happy-go-lucky existence pictured in the credit ads.

It never pays to go in debt without an emergency cash reserve, one that you can tap to meet payments if your income stops, or if expenses suddenly mount. It rarely pays to pledge future income you can't be fairly certain of receiving. Even on layaway plans you may not be able to get your deposits back if you change your mind. Be sure to inquire.

The truth is—and I learned it from being a court-appointed trustee for hundreds of insolvent families—most persons overuse credit because they are unhappy, bored, or confused. Credit shouldn't be a crutch for your morale; it simply won't support you. Credit is too demanding a beast to ride comfortably, if I may mix a metaphor to drive home a point.

I have tried to explain some of the theories behind consumer credit, showing when it can be used wisely and when it can be used unwisely. In some cases it depends upon the type of consumer credit you choose. There are several categories.

THERE ARE MANY KINDS OF DEBT

Credit as a convenience

You'll never go too far wrong using credit as the rich people do. They use credit as a means of increasing their incomes. One way is to borrow at 6 per cent, for instance, and to invest the money safely at 7 or 8 per cent. Another way is to borrow money for use in business. A third way is to buy items for family use on credit, items which substitute for more costly commercial services.

But even the rich shy away from credit and debt if they can more profitably put their own cash savings to work. Persons of means and reasonable intelligence never borrow money unless they know the cost of the money will be offset by the profit they will make from the proceeds of a loan. This should be quite clear, since wealthy people don't need to borrow money from future income just to live better. Only persons with modest incomes try that trick.

But persons with good incomes do use credit as a convenience. They run up charge accounts with great regularity. They do this because they don't want to carry large sums of cash or write checks every time they buy something. Furthermore, thirty-day charge accounts carry no interest.

You may think you don't use thirty-day charge accounts, but you probably are mistaken. If you have a telephone bill or a utility bill, you are using a charge account.

The point is, genuine convenience credit holds few dangers to those who use it wisely. It is not a matter of pledging income you don't have yet, in most cases. It is a matter of delaying drawing on funds you already have in the bank. Oil company credit cards are a fine example of convenience credit, and they hold no problems for careful users.

Some persons stretch this theory a little, by using charge accounts when they haven't the money to pay cash. In other words, they are relying on the next month's pay check. Even this isn't particularly foolish if charges are held down to reasonable amounts. Nevertheless, running up bills which are payable by the tenth of the following month isn't quite a matter of convenience; it is a matter of living on future income. When the total of all your charges exceeds much over 10 per cent of what you have coming in pay the following month, you are living dangerously.

Be sure to distinguish between true convenience credit and the kind that requires a little dipping into the future. To be sure, the future always comes around, and so do the billings, but pay checks are unpredictable, and they stretch only so far.

Paying a little each month

The department stores came to some logical conclusions a few years ago. They realized that (1) regular thirty-day charge accounts were a bit too tempting, but hard to keep current, for many consumers, and (2) if they, the stores, would just extend the payment plans a little, consumers would spend more money on soft goods, including clothing. The stores had been concerned with the decline of spending for clothing as a percentage of the family budget. More of our dollars had been going for the "big ticket" items—automobiles, furniture, and appliances. And the reason was easy credit.

BUDGET ACCOUNTS

So suddenly a number of installment credit plans became available to the average consumer at major stores. One feature was the so-called "budget account," or ninety-day charge plan. Actually, a number of stores have been using this credit device successfully for many years. Under the ninety-day plan, give or take a few months, a shopper could amortize the payments on his account over a longer time, in most cases without any carrying charges. He could mix the purchases too, by including both soft goods and the durable kind in his extended account. The ninety-day plan is not a type of convenience credit. It definitely means "buying now and paying later," from future income.

The only danger comes from overextending one's buying, not from paying high interest rates. In most instances, the goods are purchased on "open account," unsecured by a mortgage or sales contract, so repossession isn't a factor to worry about.

But here again the stores recognized they were tapping a very limited market. The person who can buy several hundred dollars worth of goods at one whack and then retire the debt at the rate of $100 or so a month has to be well-incomed. The stores were aiming at the big mass market, not just at the executives and junior executives. The ninety-day charge plan didn't interest the wiser families with modest incomes, nor should it interest you unless your income is sufficient to meet large monthly payments on top of all your other payments. To put it in more revealing terms, if you can clear a $300 debt in three rather sizable payments, why go into debt at all? Why not simply postpone your purchase for three months and then pay cash? Very few department store purchases are so urgent they can't be delayed for a few months.

The advantages of waiting to pay cash are: (1) You run no risk of being delinquent in your payments, thereby spoiling your credit rating; (2) with cash, you might get a better price and value on the identical goods at another store, one not relying heavily on credit sales; and (3) with cash in your hand, or in the bank, you may decide you really don't need such expensive merchandise. It is easy to sign a sales slip on credit. Parting with hard-earned cash is a painful thing; it reminds a person of his budget.

Partly for these reasons, the ninety-day account never boosted department store sales to any great extent. So the next step was to stretch the payment plans even more.

REVOLVING ACCOUNTS

The so-called "revolving account" turned the tide for our major stores. It not only boosted overall sales enormously, because of the extended payment plans, but soft goods began to come back into their own. The stores were correct—easy credit plans for buying durable goods had been cutting into our clothing budgets. Now we could buy suits, dresses, and even socks on long, easy payments too.

But the revolving plans, unlike most ninety-day accounts, weren't to be free to consumers. Most of these plans carry a rather high rate of interest, from 12 to 24 per cent. Eighteen per cent is typical, although the rate usually is expressed as "1½ per cent per month on the unpaid balance." (We'll cover that phase of the problem in more detail later.)

Bear in mind that revolving accounts are aimed primarily at the soft goods trade, not at the market for durable goods such as furniture and appliances. Sales on hard items, even to this day, usually require the signing of a separate installment sales contract, in which the merchandise bought on time is pledged as security for the delay in payments. The revolving plan account is geared to the sale of clothing, toiletries, soft household goods, and minor utensils of living.

As an example, if you already have a revolving account at a certain store, and wish to buy a $300 refrigerator there too, you probably would need to sign a separate contract, thereby assuming two monthly payments. If your credit were excellent, you might buy the appliance on a thirty-day charge, or even on a budget account of ninety days, but you wouldn't be allowed to add the bill to your revolving account under normal circumstances. Stores have differing policies, but as a rule what I just said is accurate enough.

Now even rapidly-consumed goods are being sold on extended terms. For instance, if you were to add a two-months' supply of beauty aids and toiletries to your revolving account, you might be paying for these niceties many months after they were used up. It is possible to buy clothing with a short life on "eighteen months to pay." However, most of the revolving plans are based on one year or less, and in some cases your monthly payment is exactly one-tenth of what you owe, plus interest of course.

Granted that revolving plans make it easy and convenient to buy all those things that make for more comfortable and more civilized living, they are far from being the type of "convenience credit" I mentioned earlier. The payments definitely come from the future, not from money already in the bank.

So while it has become easier to *buy*, it has become harder to *budget*, in the real sense of the word. You always know approximately what you must pay the following month, if you keep track of your charging, but it becomes much harder to know how fast you will have to replace the items you are buying. Soft goods have short lives, especially today, and suddenly many consumers are finding it easier to get into credit problems. Taking even ten months to pay for a thirty-day supply of cosmetics is like buying that frozen food for $12 a month and consuming it at the rate of $30 a month.

As credit houses stretch out their terms to make it easier for us to go into debt, they are forcing us into more realistic planning habits. Every purchase must be carefully considered as to cost, replacement, interest, and addition to the debt load.

Installment credit for durable goods

Most hard goods—autos, appliances, and furniture—are bought on credit. Few persons pay cash for these items today, and in some areas credit sales are 80 per cent of the total. There are two methods of financing the purchase of a piece of living equipment. One is "buying on time payments" directly from the seller. The other is borrowing the money in order to pay cash.

When you deal directly with a seller of goods in financing your purchase, you may obtain certain advantages. As long as he continues to hold the finance contract, you may be in a good position to demand service and to enforce the terms of your guarantee. Few merchants—car dealers or retail stores—want to repossess what they sold on credit. They usually can buy better merchandise at less cost on the open market. So they try to keep their credit customers reasonably happy. You can't get away with outrageous demands, but you can expect decent service.

Another advantage, sometimes, is the matter of negotiating for lower finance rates than you could get by borrowing the money to pay cash. It would depend on where you expected to borrow the money, and on how well you can drive a bargain. My point is, finance charges can be bargained for in the same manner as the merchandise itself. Many persons do not realize this. They may spend hours arguing over a $20 spare tire "thrown in" to their set, only to win the point at their own expense. The dealer simply adds $20 or so to the finance charges.

Remember these two things. If you expect to gain an advantage from financing where you buy, at the point of sale, be certain you'll actually obtain advantages such as better service and more attention. The credit seller may sell (discount) your contract to some third party, such as a bank or finance company, to get out from under the direct responsibility of keeping you happy. In fact, this is the rule rather than the exception. You have the duty to ask where you will make your payments, who will own the credit contract if you sign it. If a third party buys your contract, he will claim innocence of any promises made by the seller. So you'll have to keep paying whether the merchandise holds together or not. You could, of course, go back to the dealer or seller to make the proper demands, but you'll certainly have no club to hold over his head. You may have to hire a lawyer to get satisfaction. This is particularly true on used merchandise, since new items usually carry manufacturers' guarantees.

Therefore it makes a great deal of difference where you buy on time payments, whether it's a store or car dealer. And it makes a lot of difference where you eventually make the payments. Find out in advance.

As to saving on finance charges by borrowing cash to buy, it depends entirely on where you would expect to borrow. There are no fixed rates on finance charges. Most lending institutions, however, have more or less set rates. This ability to bargain can be an advantage, but there is one potential disadvantage to "buying on time" from the seller. Sellers of goods on credit usually use "installment sales contracts" to finance goods. On the other hand, firms that lend money directly, without selling goods in addition, use mortgages—chattel mortgages. And there is an important difference between a sales contract and a mortgage.

Under an installment sales contract (finance contract) you really don't own the merchandise until the final payment is made. Under the section on home financing, I mentioned "contract sales" and their possible dangers. The same holds true for installment sales contracts on consumer goods—autos and appliances. Financing a purchase from a seller doesn't give you real ownership for a long time. And that means that the seller or his finance company can reclaim the goods in a hurry if you get behind.

On the other hand, if you borrow to buy from a direct lending institution, you sign a "mortgage," not a sales contract. While it is true that some courts treat a "purchase money mortgage" (money loaned to buy something) just as if it were a sales contract, most mortgages involve "due process" and legal foreclosure proceedings. That gives a credit buyer more time, if necessary, to catch up his payments, refinance, or liquidate his property advantageously.

To sum up, it is safer in almost all instances to "borrow to buy—on mortgage" than to sign an installment sales agreement with the possibility of easy repossession.

You may think the matter would never arise, since *you* will always meet your payments promptly. Most persons think the same way. But thousands of autos and pieces of living equipment are repossessed every day, in many cases from well-meaning but careless credit buyers. The instrument you sign can be highly important.

When credit buyers do get behind on their installment payments, they soon get reminded of the fact. First a notice comes in the mail, then another notice. Next comes a phone call. And eventually there is a knock on the door. If the payment is caught up, fine until the next time. If not, the merchandise suddenly disappears—it is repossessed.

During this rather harrowing sequence of events, most past-due credit buyers soon come to thinking of borrowing more money to make up the payments. This can be called "panic credit."

Panic credit

Borrowing money under pressure usually means more trouble. Most panic borrowing arises from being behind on payments for some type of consumer goods, things the person is quite fond of and hates to lose.

BORROWING TO CATCH UP PAYMENTS

One thing you should be warned against in particular. Many finance companies—those which purchase credit contracts from sellers of goods—also have their own direct loan departments. If you get behind on a car payment in the amount of $100, you may be encouraged to borrow that sum from the finance company's lending department, or from an affiliate of the same outfit. Next month you must pay the regular $100, plus the payments on the $100 you borrowed, perhaps an additional $11 a month. So for a year or more you are paying $111 in total, not merely the agreed $100. Furthermore, you will be paying 24 to 36 per cent interest on the $100 you borrowed. That can be both expensive and budget-busting.

FLIPPING THE ENTIRE CONTRACT

Another variation of this is called "flipping." Under this arrangement you are asked, or encouraged, to refinance the entire past-due sales contract by taking out a new loan. Actually it is a form of refinancing, but a darned expensive kind. The high cost comes from getting only a fraction of the original finance charges refunded, or credited back, when you take out the new loan. What you'll actually be doing is paying interest on top of finance charges.

To show a typical case, if a $1000 balance is refinanced because it is past due, that $1000 could easily contain $100 in finance charges which originally amounted to a true rate of 12 per cent. The rates on the new loan would be at least 24 per cent, perhaps more, at a private loan firm. Paying 24 per cent interest on 12 per cent finance charges is a sure way to go broke, as many innocent buyers have learned. Refinancing is costly under the most favorable conditions. In almost every case a buyer ends up paying credit charges on top of credit charges.

If you do get behind, offer to pay a one-time-only late charge if you can't catch up the payments. Do everything possible to avoid additional borrowing or refinancing. Panic borrowing can arise from problems other than missed installment payments, but that is the common source of trouble. Panic can set in from just being short of money—money to eat, buy gasoline, or get into a hospital. At such times you should force yourself to sit down and think slowly.

Taking on another debt just complicates your problem in the long run. Instead, you should go over your budget, your spending habits, and your entire debt structure. You may consider refinancing the whole mess.

THE CONSOLIDATION LOAN

Wrapping up nasty debts in a nice fresh package is a great American pastime. Some naïve persons go so far as to describe a consolidation loan as "getting out of debt." It isn't, of course. Regrouping debts is simply that and nothing more. It can reduce total outgo. It can give you time to get a fresh start. And it can give you a psychological lift. At least the pressure is off for a month or so. But "getting out of debt" it isn't.

Perhaps the pressures and insecurities of these times force some persons to think in terms of weeks and months rather than in terms of their working careers. This must be so, otherwise fewer people would be willing to pay such fantastically high prices for a few weeks of bill freedom.

Of all the consumer credit inventions, the consolidation loan can be the most deadly. Yet it is the most popular. How much of the $90 billion we recorded in short-term debts during early 1966 was consolidation credit, we can't be sure. But a substantial portion of it was.

Most families who consolidate their bills do it over and over again, pyramiding their debt loads higher and higher. Each time there is some compounding of interest. Each time there is striking evidence of chronic mismanagement, yet most persons are reluctant to revise their spending habits to eliminate constant borrowing of the debt consolidation type.

I will discuss later what action should be taken if you are in over your head. First, I want to show you what different kinds of credit are available today.

Some credit may help you, but rarely as much as if you paid cash. And some types of credit are downright dangerous and foolish. As a rule, the higher the interest rate, the more foolish the credit—not just from the extra expense, but because high interest rates should be a warning not to borrow in the first place. So learn as much as you can about interest.

UNDERSTANDING INTEREST AND CREDIT CHARGES

Most persons have a vague idea that interest rates are limited by law. While this is true to an extent, the belief puts people off their guard.

Many of us think of our society as a "good" society, and of interest as being basically "bad." The feeling against interest comes from religious attitudes and from history itself. "Interest" and the word "usury" mean almost the same, but not quite. Actually usury means charging for the use of almost anything, in its oldest sense. In a way usury is closer to "profit" than to just "interest." And as you'll surely agree, profit isn't bad in itself.

Contrary to popular opinion, usury and moneylending did not originate with the Jews. To be sure, Jews took to moneylending because most other avenues of commerce were closed to them. But all races and creeds have been involved in lending of money. And in every society, high interest rates soon became the rule rather than the exception, resulting in oppression of the poor. Eventually most societies had to limit the amount of interest charged in order to avert revolution and serious unrest.

We Americans adopted the English and Roman restrictions on lending, limiting interest rates from about 10 per cent at the maximum, down to as low as 5 per cent in some states. Eight per cent simple interest is about the average limitation on interest. Each such limitation is called a "usury law," meaning a "law limiting the legal rate of interest."

Bear in mind, however, that our federal government does not limit interest rates; only the fifty states do that. All of which has resulted in a fascinating, unbelievable hodgepodge of usury laws.

If from curiosity alone, bear with me as I attempt to explain the various ways lenders express and extract their interest in America. I will try to keep my explanations basic. Don't forget, this is a credit economy, and without a basic knowledge of interest you are lost. So lower your resistance to learning about percentages and interest rates. The subject isn't that tough.

After that I will explain how our usury laws complicate the matter.

How interest rates are expressed

SIMPLE, ANNUAL INTEREST

In commerce, interest is almost always stated "per year" or "per annum," because a year is the standard unit of time on which to base interest. If you originally borrowed $1000 and kept the entire sum for a year, you would be charged $60—if the rate were 6 per cent, simple interest.

However, if you were repaying the $1000 in equal payments over the year, you might owe the lender only $500 on the average over the year, because you would be reducing your debt more each month. So, at 6 per cent simple interest, you would pay only $30 in interest. Homes are financed on just that basis, except that each year's interest is collected a little bit each month, as you make your payments.

Here is an example of how simple, annual interest *should* work on installment loans, repayable in equal monthly sums. Bear in mind that even though interest is computed on an *annual basis*, it may be collected each month (one-twelfth of the annual rate). Let's assume that $1000 is the amount borrowed, repayable in 12 installments of $83.33 a month. The first month's interest at 6 per cent would be $5 (one-twelfth of $60). But after the second month you would owe only $916.67, since you would have reduced the debt owed by $83.33, and paid the $5 in interest. Six per cent simple annual interest, for one year, on

$916.67 is $55, so for one month it amounts to only about $4.58. By the time you had reduced your loan to $500, the annual rate of interest would be only $30, or $2.50 a month.

So, if you were repaying the $1000 you borrowed in equal monthly payments, and still had to pay $60 in interest, your actual interest rate would be double what it appeared to be. You would be paying about 12 per cent on the *average* amount you owed over the year. The lender would be charging you $5 for each month, whereas you wouldn't owe that much. This is the way many lenders, including some banks and loan companies, obtain higher rates than they appear to advertise. I said "appear" to advertise because the ads never say "6 per cent *interest*"; they say just "6 per cent," meaning 6 per cent of what you originally asked for, not of what you will owe them on the average. Sometimes the ads specify "$6 per hundred."

DISCOUNT INTEREST

Some lenders use a variation of the simple interest method. They deduct in advance the estimated full year's interest from what is borrowed. In the example just given, you would sign a note for $1000 under the discount method, but you would *receive* only $940 to use for the twelve-month period. In such a case the lender really isn't charging 6 per cent interest; he would be getting closer to 6.5 per cent on the $940. True, he would be charging only 6 per cent on $1000, but you wouldn't have the use of the full $1000; you would have the use of only $940.

ADD-ON INTEREST

A slight variation of the discount method of charging interest is called the add-on method. Instead of deducting the interest in advance, they add it to your note. Thus, in the $1000 example, you would sign a note for $1060 at 6 per cent, on a one-year basis, but at least you would get the full $1000, not merely $940.

One trouble with this system, which is used by almost all banks in their consumer loan departments, is that most borrowers misunderstand the honest rates. When paying the loan back in equal monthly installments, they are reducing the amount they owe the banks without getting credit through reduced interest charges. The real simple interest rate is closer to 12 per cent than to 6 per cent. If you question a banker as to the "true" rate you are paying on what you owe, he may state the rate as about 11.6 per cent.

But if you don't question the rate, there will be no explanation forthcoming. Otherwise the banks would state their interest charges more revealingly in the first place.

PER MONTH INTEREST ON THE UNPAID BALANCE

Many lenders, including loan companies and credit unions, state their interest rates as "per month." Think of "per month" as "for a month," not as "collected by the month." That word "per" is a tricky one. Why do so many lenders state interest rates in terms of a month, rather than by the year? Because 1 per cent per month sounds better, less expensive, to a borrower than 12 per cent for a year. After all, a month is one-twelfth of a year, so to translate a monthly rate into annual interest, you simply multiply by 12.

Under that not-so-complicated translation, a loan company charging 3 per cent per (for a) month on the unpaid balance is really charging you 36 per cent simple annual interest. And a credit union offering the money at 1 per cent per month on the unpaid balance is really getting 12 per cent a year.

A department store charging 1½ per cent per month on your average balance would be getting 18 per cent simple interest. It really isn't hard to understand and compare rates when you learn and remember how to do it.

PER MONTH ON THE ORIGINAL BALANCE

Now and then some ingenious lender or merchant carries word trickery to the ultimate limit. He will advertise "2 per cent per month," realizing that on the surface that rate compares quite well with the 3 per cent charged by small loan companies in many states. But the licensed loan company, high as its rates are, at least charges its 3 per cent per month on the *unpaid balance*. Whereas that "2 per cent per month" ad by a sharpie could be on the *original balance*, without any credits given on the interest charges as payments are made.

As I showed, "3 per cent per month on the unpaid balance" would be 36 per cent simple interest. But "2 per cent per month" (if on the *original* balance) would figure out to a simple rate of 48 per cent.

Here's why. Suppose you borrowed $1000 (for one year on payments) from the lender or merchant using the devious "2 per cent" ad. Two per cent for each month on $1000 would come to a total for the year of $240. But since you would be paying back the $1000 in rather equal monthly installments, you would owe only about $500 on the average over the year's time. Well, $240 for the use of $500 is pretty high, 48 per cent to be exact. Try it with your own pencil.

So, whenever buying on credit or borrowing money, know the true interest rates, the simple annual rates. Translate all the rates advertised into yearly terms on the amount actually owed. You must ask:

1. Will the interest be deducted in advance, raising the true rate?

2. Will I get credit on the interest charges if I pay back the money in monthly payments?

3. Will the lender add the interest to my note at the start without giving me credit for reducing the principal?

4. Will the per month interest be based on the unpaid balance or on the original balance?

THE MYSTERY RATES

Sometimes interest rates aren't stated at all; they are just added to finance contracts without any percentage explanation. This is particularly true of auto finance contracts. If you ask a dealer what the rate is, he might answer with anything, orally of course, but not in writing. In such a case, you could do one of two things; go elsewhere for your credit, or try to determine the real rate you are being charged.

The formula is: $$I = \frac{2\,(YC)}{M\,(N+1)}$$

I means the true rate of interest, in simple annual terms.

Y means the number of payments in a year.

C means total interest you are being charged in dollars.

M means the amount you originally borrowed (carried back or financed)

N means the total number of payments in the contract.

Let's use this as an example. You decide to finance $1000 on an automobile purchase. The dealer offers you a contract on terms of 30 equal monthly payments of $55 each. He is vague about the true rate, but claims he is offering "bank rates." From reading this book, you realize that most banks offer consumer interest rates of about 6 per cent add-on, true rates of close to 12 per cent. So you decide to see how the dealer's rates compare with 12 per cent simple interest.

You have at a glance all the figures you need to use the formula for determining true interest except C, the dollar amount of interest you are to pay. To find this amount, multiply the amount of each payment ($55) by the number of payments (30) to determine the total sum you are to repay. Then subtract from this total the $1000 actually borrowed; the difference will be the finance charge, in this case $650.

Using the formula, you come up with these figures in place of the algebraic letters:

$$\text{True rate} = \frac{2 \times (12 \times \$650)}{\$1000 \times (30+1)} = \frac{\$15,600}{\$31,000}$$

The real rate, $15,600 divided by $31,000, comes out to about 50 per cent. That is far more than 12 per cent. So at least you know how to determine the real rate, even if you rarely use the formula.

THE COME-ON RATES

Some credit merchants advertise "no interest or carrying charges." There is a very real cost involved with consumer credit, a cost as real as any other cost of doing business. To say that credit is being given "free" is like saying, "We don't include the cost of transportation or warehousing in our retail prices." A merchant making that statement would be laughed out of the Chamber of Commerce.

You need to compare the *total* price on any article with the *total* price of an identical article at other stores. Total price would include delivery, installation, and credit charges. A refrigerator with a cash price of $265 may be offered for sale on credit at twelve payments of $25, with nothing down. That makes the total credit price $300.

So if another store offers the identical refrigerator for sale at a cash price of $310, no charge for credit, you aren't getting much of a bargain either way. You can beat the cash price, or the credit price, by purchasing the article at the first store, which is being more honest in its pricing.

Another misleading credit appeal offers "bank financing." Bank financing isn't the same as "bank rates." The dealer offering bank financing usually means he sells his credit contracts to a bank, but the dealer may still charge whatever the traffic—and the law—allows, pocketing some of the charges himself. When banks buy credit contracts from dealers, the banks don't set the rates. The dealers do that. So don't be conned by the car agency offering "bank financing" unless it also offers true "bank rates." Even so, get out your pencil and figure the rates yourself.

There is one more especially tricky bit of credit advertising. A dealer, or seller of some sort, may offer very low interest rates on financing. The ad may say "3 per cent interest." But the actual cash price of the article may be marked up to cover such low interest. Or in other cases, there will be a "finance charge" in addition to the interest. Many credit agencies refuse to concede that "interest" is quite the same thing as a "finance charge." So check your invoice and your sales contract very carefully.

Why they can charge so much

Usury laws were originally designed to protect businessmen, poor businessmen, to be sure, but businessmen nevertheless. When I referred to ancient societies passing usury laws to prevent unrest over oppressive lending practices, I didn't mean that wage earners were the victims. There weren't many real consumers using credit in olden times. The borrowers were mostly small merchants, artisans, and farmers, trying to make a living.

These businessmen knew what rates they were paying. It wasn't a matter of ignorance; it was a matter of lack of choice. Today we have an entirely different situation. Here is why rates are so high today.

(a) Few consumer borrowers understand how to compute interest.

(b) Consumer interest charges are expressed in so many ways that even lawmakers aren't aware of the true rates.

(c) Not many consumers care about the rates as long as they get the credit.

(d) A number of financial institutions have been able to get special laws passed allowing them to charge more than the usury limitations. Loan companies, credit unions, and other lenders operate under what amount to special exemptions from general usury laws.

(e) Most usurious charges are too small to take into court. It doesn't pay to hire a lawyer to have $25 or so refunded.

(f) In many states there are no real penalties for overcharging on interest. And sometimes the overcharge is cleverly hidden.

(g) Most state courts still take the attitude that credit charges on goods sold and financed directly by a seller are not really interest. Therefore, "finance charges" aren't supposed to be under the state usury laws. Federal courts have held the opposite, however, and in time all credit charges may come under the usury statutes. In 1963, the Nebraska Supreme Court held about one billion dollars' worth of credit contracts to be usurious and therefore unenforceable. The credit industry is still recovering from that shock.

My point in dwelling on usury is not to be a historian; I mainly want to impress you with the importance of being on guard against high interest rates. It is unrealistic to believe that government agencies are zealously guarding you against unlawful usury. It just isn't so.

You must be very careful where you borrow money. There are plenty of different sources available to you. And in this section we are dealing only with short-term cash loans, not home financing.

WHERE TO BORROW MONEY

The types of lenders

FRIENDS

Borrowing from friends and relatives can be the least expensive financially, but a fine way to alienate them. My personal feeling is that unless all other reasonable sources of money are refused you, don't borrow from friends, relatives, or your employer. Borrowing is best kept on a businesslike basis. Cost isn't everything.

LIFE INSURANCE

One of the least expensive ways to raise money is by borrowing against the cash value of life insurance policies. But don't get the impression you are borrowing back your own money. That isn't quite accurate. Your life insurance premiums are based on the insurance company's investing the cash value in your policies. If you borrow those funds, the company must charge you, just as it would charge any other borrower.

The rates on life insurance loans are "simple interest," the same as the rates businessmen pay for loans. You don't have to repay such loans in monthly installments. No other collateral is needed. So check life insurance loans before any other source.

BANKS—SINGLE PAYMENT

In some cases you can take your life insurance policy to a commercial bank and borrow against the cash value at a lower rate than the insurance company would charge. The reason is, life insurance companies really aren't in the consumer lending business, while the banks are. The rate differential may be small but worth considering.

Then too, some banks will lend you more than the cash value of your insurance, especially if you assign the death benefits of your policy. As long as the cash you borrow against your policy is not much greater than the cash value of your insurance, you shouldn't have to make monthly payments, or even repay the loan at all. The bank will be well-secured and ask only that you pay the interest when due, and perhaps rewrite the loan occasionally.

MUTUAL SAVINGS BANKS

These cooperative banks are found mostly in our New England states. But they are an excellent source of money when you need it. The rates vary, but 12 per cent simple interest is common. When making loans on good security, mutual banks often drop their rates well below 12 per cent.

SAVINGS AND LOAN ASSOCIATIONS

In most states, savings and loan firms can lend only for home financing and home improving. Most of the home improvement loans are made under FHA rules and guarantees, and the top rate is 10 per cent simple interest. It usually is expressed in the add-on manner we mentioned, as, for example, 5 per cent add-on. But when borrowing to improve your home, you should consider savings and loan firms, as well as banks of all kinds, before paying higher rates.

BANK INSTALLMENT LOAN DEPARTMENTS
(COMMERCIAL BANKS)

When you borrow directly from a commercial bank, you will pay about 12 per cent simple interest on smaller loans, which will be stated as "6 per cent" or "6 per cent add-on." On larger loans, those well-secured at least, the rate may drop to as low as 8 per cent, stated as "4 per cent add-on." Always remember, as I explained earlier, that the add-on method of stating interest can be misleading. Double the add-on rate to arrive at the approximate true rate.

In some cases, persons with excellent credit ratings and good incomes may be able to borrow from the commercial loan department of a bank. If so, they will pay commercial loan rates of 6 per cent simple interest, give or take a percentage point. But these loans come due all at once, not in monthly payments, so require some good planning.

CREDIT UNIONS

You must be a member in order to borrow from a credit union. A credit union is a "mutual," owned by its members; in other words, it is a cooperative lending agency. The rates charged borrowers compare well with rates charged by banks, except that credit unions express their rates by the "per month" or "for a month" method. Thus 1 per cent for a month becomes 12 per cent for an entire year.

Credit unions are competitive with banks, so when banks are offering low "4 per cent add-on" rates (8 per cent true simple interest) the credit unions may be offering .667 per cent a month. That also figures out to be a simple interest rate of 8 per cent.

In most cases it is easier to get a consolidation loan from a credit union than from a bank. Credit unions usually arrange to check off payments from the pay checks of borrowers. They collect through the employer. This gives them an edge in collecting their money. And credit unions still encourage consolidation loans, whereas banks, for the most part, have had bad experience with persons trying to wrap up their old mistakes in new packages.

Both credit unions and banks usually demand security of some kind on loans over a few hundred dollars. The security can be an auto, furniture, or cosigners at a credit union. Banks rarely accept furniture as collateral for a loan.

Some credit unions are chartered by the federal government; others are chartered by the various states. This makes a difference in their lending policies. As a borrower, you should treat credit unions just as you would other lending firms. If you can get better borrowing rates at a bank, there is no reason to borrow at your credit union. While credit unions do stress their "self-help," cooperative nature, they must pay their savers fairly high interest on their savings, often 4 per cent and better. So compare rates at credit unions with rates offered elsewhere.

INDUSTRIAL LOAN COMPANIES

At one time the industrial loan companies were called "industrial banks," but the commercial banks objected. The "industrial" part of the name is misleading; it was used because these lending firms dealt primarily with industrial workers, not because they loaned money to industry. Morris Plan firms are a type of industrial loan company.

As a rule, industrial loan companies make larger loans at lower rates than the small loan firms, but the industrial lenders usually charge more than the commercial banks. Think of them as a compromise between the consumer loan department of a bank and a small loan company.

Banks use the add-on method of stating interest rates, small loan firms and credit unions use the per month method, and

industrial loan companies often use still another system. That is
the "discount" method I explained earlier.

For instance, if you borrowed $100 from one of these lenders
for one year, you would sign a note for $100 but receive only
$93 or so, the exact amount depending upon the usury limits of
the state where you borrowed the money. The example above
would be a 7 per cent discounted rate.

Most industrial loan firms operate under a special amendment
to, or exemption from, usury laws. Instead of asking state legisla-
tures to grant them special privileges to loan money at rates in
excess of usury limitations, the industrial lenders came in the side
door, so to speak. They asked for only two favors: one, that they
be allowed an "investigation fee" of about 2 per cent of the loan
requested; and two, that they be allowed to hold the monies
borrowers repaid each month in a special trust fund. By not
crediting payments made each month to the unpaid balance of a
loan, the industrial loan companies manage to get a true interest
rate of double what it appears to be.

Here is an example. If you wanted to borrow that $100 shown
above, the firm would first deduct a $2 investigation fee, then
the $7 of interest. So you would likely get only $91, not $93. But
you would be required to sign a note for $100 and make pay-
ments each month of about $8.33. Since you received only $91 to
begin with, the average amount you would owe the firm, over
one year, would be about one-half of $91, or $45.50. Nine dollars in total charges for the use of $45.50 for one year amounts
to almost 20 per cent simple interest.

Yet even if the state usury law set the maximum chargeable
interest at 7 per cent, the industrial lender would be getting
about 20 per cent, apparently legally, and apparently without
much modification to the law. And to the lenders the beauty of
it is that most borrowers think they are borrowing at 7 per cent.

To be fair, 20 per cent is less than the legal rate allowed
small loan companies, which varies from 24 to 42 per cent a year,
depending upon the state. But 20 per cent is much more than
the 12 per cent most banks charge. You can see why it is im-

portant to reduce all rates to annual simple interest on the amount of money you actually owe over a certain period of time.

Industrial loan companies do fill an important gap. They deal with many persons unable to get money at lower rates from banks, but too proud and rate-conscious to borrow from small loan firms. Industrial loan firms can lend on almost anything in most states, from second mortgages on homes to bits of family equipment. Most of them, however, rely heavily on cosigners and guarantors. Their business began as a means of financing cars, but gradually evolved into relying on getting as many names as possible on a note. It is the unwillingness to involve friends as cosigners that leads many persons into paying higher rates at the small loan companies.

SMALL LOAN COMPANIES

These companies charge the highest rates of all lenders, except for the unlicensed loan sharks, who are rapidly disappearing. Small loan firms operate under a rich variety of names, such as consumer finance companies, personal property brokers, and personal finance companies. The small loan companies evolved out of a period when loan sharking was rampant, shortly after the turn of the century. In response to a cleanup campaign, the Russell Sage Foundation did some investigating and decided that 42 per cent interest was just about right on loans made to wage earners of that era. The loans would be limited to $300 and the rates would be expressed as 3½ per cent per month on the unpaid balance.

Since then, back in 1910, most all states have adopted the Sage Foundation recommendations, although the $300 limit has been raised and the interest rates dropped. But rates in most states remain high, running from 30 to 36 per cent per year on small amounts and dropping down to 18 per cent and less on larger sums. Even when rates are reduced, however, the rates stay high on the first $100 to $300 borrowed.

Because over the years small loan companies have been allowed to lend larger amounts, these companies have crowded the industrial loan firms almost out of existence. It is getting more difficult to define the various private lenders because they are merging into the same type of lending operation.

Small loan companies cannot lend on real estate, nor can they hold security in their offices, as pawnbrokers do. But they can lend on almost anything else. Most of the business today is done by a few giant chain operators, each with one thousand offices or more. Most of their business comes from relatively low-income families, especially those not good at arithmetic.

Three per cent a month sounds inexpensive, but as I have stated before, it comes to 36 per cent a year. How many persons would borrow at those rates, if they understood them, is a question.

But aside from the interest cost itself, there are other dangers to consider when you borrow from small loan companies. Many of these firms have developed the art of selling money to a fine degree. Even after three or four payments, most of which is applied to interest, borrowers are encouraged to renew their loans. Girl cashiers are trained to solicit renewals at the payment counter. Each month borrowers receive offers of more cash. All you need do is phone, and then come in for the money.

Another angle to consider is the "loan boosting" technique. You may be attracted by an ad offering to loan you $50 at nominal cost (in actual dollars) for a short time. But if you manage to get out of the loan company office only $50 in hock, you are a person of unusual will and determination. Once in the office, the manager can think of many reasons why you should borrow more money: to pick up some extra bills, take a vacation, or just to live more joyously.

When you stop to consider that even in states limiting small loans to $300, the average unpaid balance comes close to $250, the point is proved. Besides, there is no real rate competition. Almost all loan companies charge the maximum rates allowed by law on all loans made.

Borrowing money from loan companies at high rates can turn into the stickiest kind of debt imaginable. The fellow who renews his loan after every fourth or fifth payment, as many persons do, is practically borrowing back his interest. And then in effect he pays interest on the interest. Compounded 36 per cent interest is almost sure-fire bankruptcy to the person who pays it. Compounding interest on small loans is unlawful, to be sure, but the system of constantly renewing loans accomplishes about the same thing.

If you can borrow at less costly rates you would be wise to do so, even if you are afraid of losing some privacy. Loan companies stress the confidential angle. All lenders use credit bureaus today to check up on borrowers, so with the possible exception of credit unions, no loans are really confidential. And even credit unions have credit committees to approve loans.

If you do get involved with a licensed loan company, repay the money as fast as you can. Otherwise be prepared for a long and costly relationship. The average borrower stays in debt to a loan company for at least five years, without interruption. And of those who pay off sooner, many do it by patronizing a different loan company. Enough said, to the wise at least.

SECOND MORTGAGE COMPANIES

From the angle of pure interest alone, it can be less costly to borrow against your home, on a second mortgage, than to use the more common loan agencies. But interest isn't everything. When you answer an ad offering to lend money against your home to clean up all those unpaid bills, the offer may be misleading. The interest rate may be nominal, no more than that allowed by law, but it's those extra charges that will hurt.

Here is the way some of the second-mortgage companies operate. The law may allow them to charge a "brokerage fee" of up to 15 per cent of the loan. The escrow charges may come to another 15 per cent. Then there's the interest, which may go as high as 10 per cent, depending upon the state law. Under these circumstances, your first year's cost on a $1000 loan might amount to 40 per cent. Furthermore, a person borrowing on a second mortgage against his home usually takes many years to repay the loan. You run into the same problem of extra costs when you try to refinance an existing mortgage on your home. That is an expensive way to borrow money, unless you have an "open end" mortgage arrangement.

PAWNBROKER

Today the pawnbroker services the rich, or the pretenders, more than the poor. Those with expensive pieces of jewelry often prefer to place such things in pawn rather than borrow elsewhere. Rates charged by pawnbrokers are about the same as small-loan rates—36 per cent a year, or 3 per cent for a month.

One thing about dealing with a pawnshop: You do have complete privacy and don't have to lose "face" at the established financial centers. As long as the broker can be certain the merchandise isn't "hot," he doesn't care who you are. He'll lend you maybe 30 per cent of the value of what you pawn and therefore takes little risk. It is an expensive way to borrow, but you may lose far more than the sum you received. You may not be able to redeem your pledged merchandise in time.

Those with uncertain or unsteady incomes use pawnshops a great deal. That's why actors try to keep one or two items of pawnable jewelry on hand at all times. It's one way to be sure of eating. Persons have marital troubles use pawnshops a great deal too. They can get cash without involving the other half of the marriage partnership. But it's still a costly way to do business.

LOAN SHARKS

The loan shark is almost dead. Some hoodlum outfits still force shaky businesses to borrow at outlaw prices, but consumers can get enough high-rate money at licensed places without patronizing the back alleys.

The death of the loan shark is not without its mourners. The lender with sharp teeth was the very essence of the high-rate credit demonology. How better to justify your own 42 per cent rates than to point to the evil shyster who charges even more? And for a long time such comparisons were valid.

Back in 1910, there were loan shark outfits which boasted of fifty or more offices. The usurer of today is mostly on his own, picking up a few bucks from the guys at his factory who will repay $7.50 for $5 borrowed until payday. That comes to about 2600 per cent annual interest if the charge is for a week, but it's only $2.50 in cash.

And of course there are still a few grocers and corner merchants who aren't above lending a few dollars for a short time at usurious rates. The truth is, except for some strong-arm outfits in minority group areas, the loan shark is dead, killed by the legal rate lenders.

The credit problems of today, from the consumer standpoint, mostly stem from the amount of debt assumed, not just from the interest costs, high as they usually are. Consequently, the amount of debt you handle may be the real key to your future.

Even if you patronize the finest credit establishments, protect yourself by reading the contracts, and drive hard bargains on interest rates, there are three other factors to consider. You must watch the total amount of debt you assume, put a limit on the monthly payments, and always keep a way out, the ability to liquidate if necessary.

HOW MUCH DEBT IS TOO MUCH?

Amount of debt

There is only one kind of debt that can be measured intelligently from purely the amount of dollars you owe. And that is the "dead-horse" debt, the kind used to buy some item which has a short life, or an item which doesn't show up in your asset column to balance the debt. So, when measuring your ability to load up on debt, we will ignore home mortgages and automobile contracts. Total debt assumed for houses and cars is better measured by the monthly payments and by your ability to withstand the depreciation and other expenses of those two possessions.

Dead-horse debts include credit accounts for the following: medical bills, dental bills, charge accounts, soft-goods revolving accounts, loans for vacations, consolidation loans, and any debts run up for goods or services that quickly lose value, including furniture and in most cases appliances. Items for your home have relatively low resale values and can't be quickly sold to liquidate a pressing debt. My opinion, based on experiences with financially burdened families, is that you should think of retrenching when your total dead-horse debts exceed one month's income. If, for instance, you earn $600 a month, and owe that much in debts of various kinds, not counting your home and car mortgages, you are already living a month ahead of your income.

If the bulk of the debt had been assumed to buy appliances and furniture, you might be justified in not worrying. But if most of it arose from not being able to meet certain expenses in full as the bills came due, you are confessing to a certain degree of insolvency. Or, if you had borrowed money to pay past-due or burdensome bills, the insolvency should have been apparent at that time. Even if the debts came from vacation expenses, you have been living on future income.

On the other hand, if you owed $600 and had that sum in the bank, free to pay off the debts at any time, you certainly aren't in any trouble. But the question is: Why are you in debt at all under those circumstances? Are you asking some creditor to wait for his money just to keep you in a liquid condition?

List all the debts you now have other than for home and car. See how it compares to one month's salary. Then analyze your position. Why do you owe the money? Can you repay it now, most all of it, or are you just counting on future income? If in reality you are living off the uncertain future, how far into the future do you want to dip? If you use this analysis, you probably won't go further into debt for anything, until you get into a more solvent, liquid position.

MONTHLY PAYMENTS

While a dead-horse debt load equal to two months' income might
be disastrous—eventually, anyway—to some families, automobile
debt is best measured by the payments. To most families, payments on the family car usually substitute for depreciation expense. To know how much you can assume in car payments,
determine how much you can stand in total auto expense, including depreciation. As I showed earlier, few families can afford
to spend more than 15 per cent of their gross incomes for total
auto expense. On fairly new autos, depreciation alone comes to
about one-half of the 15 per cent.

So to measure how much auto debt you can afford, consider
the following points:

a. Are your payments keeping up with the depreciation of the
car?

b. Can you really stand that much depreciation expense?

c. If you get behind, could you sell the car and pay off the
debt in full?

To some extent you should measure all debts incurred from
purchasing durable goods by those questions. Those are the real
ways to measure and control the amount of credit you take on to
buy durable goods.

But remember this, too: While under normal conditions you
might comfortably carry a high payment on a car, if you have
much dead-horse debt, the picture changes. You may be constantly flipping a coin to decide whether to keep your old creditors happy or keep the car contract current. The total amount of
your debts influences how much you can bear in the way of payments for cars, furniture, and appliances.

CAN YOU LIQUIDATE?

Buying a savings bond on credit isn't one bit dangerous. You can
always sell the bond and get your money back. The same principle applies to buying certain other assets. A person can assume
tons of debt as long as he can sell what he's buying to pay off

the debt. Nobody wants to lose things by having them repossessed or having to sell out. But at least buying genuine assets on credit isn't consuming the future. It can be expensive, but there is always a way out.

When you measure your total debt load (dead-horse debts plus installment debts for durable goods) keep the balance between the two in mind. As long as your assets exceed your liabilities (debts) you aren't in serious trouble. If worst comes to worst, you can sell an expensive car to pay the mortgage. Then, if necessary, you could pay cash for a cheaper car, temporarily. The real measurement of how much debt you can assume is based on how much of the debt you have already consumed, or by how far past due it is.

The ideal amount of dead-horse debt is zero, none at all. Short of this ideal, keep your installment payments for the goodies and necessities in line with your ability to repay, your ability to stand the replacement expense, and your ability to liquidate in an emergency.

When to call a halt to credit buying

Of the 166,000 families filing bankruptcy proceedings of various kinds during 1966, almost all were "no asset" cases. Yet every one of these families had been using credit liberally and supposedly amassing the good things of life on easy payments.

They simply took on more debt than they could handle. They ignored the old bills, failed to compensate for replacement costs, and as a result, couldn't liquidate without resorting to the courts.

To be fair, a "no asset" case has a legal quirk to it. In almost every state, wage earners filing bankruptcy proceedings are allowed to keep essential pieces of furniture, as well as a car, just to hold their families together and keep earning a living. Certain items are exempt from general creditors of a bankrupt, although specific mortgages against any property must be paid. At any rate, most of the bankrupts had something left, a few hundred dollars' worth of cars and household equipment. But they had nothing to compare with the thousands of dollars they listed in debts or liabilities.

From talking to hundreds of these families, many of them with fairly good educations, a common pattern unfolds. They began to sniff their insolvency but didn't know what to do about it. They borrowed to catch up, resorted to consolidation loans, robbed Peter to pay Paul, and finally they just quit caring.

To accept bankruptcy, most persons must be in despair. Contrary to what you may have heard, our zooming bankruptcy statistics are not just a matter of moral decay—they can be laid at the door of the credit system itself. Most of us are a little weak-willed. Few of us are quick with figures. All of us would like to live better than our salaries afford. So we use credit, because credit is given the "hard sell" and because credit is always available. We may be foolish and impatient, but darned few of us start our credit careers as deadbeats.

The time to call a halt to credit buying is at the very moment you get behind. The first time you have trouble with a payment —even with a doctor bill—go over your entire budget, and if necessary, retrench. There are many things you can do before you get into serious trouble.

HOW TO PREVENT A LITTLE ILLNESS FROM BECOMING A MAJOR DISEASE

Refinance with safety

Refinancing can be both dangerous and costly. In most cases you will end up paying interest on top of finance charges, or interest on top of interest. So you must consider several factors when your total payments exceed your ability to pay.

Look for the real trouble spot. Usually it is a high car payment, or a high consolidation loan payment. Whichever it is, concentrate on that one thing. Don't be obsessed with the "clean broom" philosophy—that of sweeping all those nagging (but non-interest-bearing) accounts into a new loan. By including your little unpaid bills in a new interest-bearing loan, you add unnecessary costs, and in a sense you are simply sweeping them under the carpet. You really haven't cleared them up—you've transferred them to a new creditor.

Yet most persons with a high car payment, plus a number of small unpaid bills, will blame the little bills, saying, "I don't have any trouble making the car payment—it's those messy little ones that bother me." This is self-delusion and rationalization on the grand scale.

Refinance if you must, but concentrate on the larger payments. Don't add unnecessary interest charges to your already high debt structure. There are other ways of handling the smaller bills.

When you refinance a loan or car payment is order to reduce the monthly outgo, give yourself as long as possible to make the first installment on the new contract. Forty-five days is not out of line. Then you will have more time to make payments on the smaller bills.

Reschedule payments on small bills

The next step is to analyze those unpaid bills. The really small ones you might clear up from one pay check. Others you may have to spread out over several months, even a year. The way to do that is to call those creditors and explain your situation. Offer to pay some on each bill once a month—not more than you can easily meet, however. If the creditors agree, tell them you are sending them a letter to that effect, and will they please O.K. the letter in writing. Make sure you get a written reply to your propositions, for this reason: A doctor, dentist, or bookkeeper may consent to receiving delayed payments on a bill, but later the consent may be forgotten and the bill turned over to a collection agency. The professional bill collector, once the bill is in his possession, will want the money all at once—or else. If you have a letter in your file, showing the new payment agreement, the bill collector will have to go along. Otherwise both he and his client can get in serious trouble.

If you do this you may avoid high interest costs on old unpaid bills without seriously hurting your creditors. Not only that, you will be in a position to pay cash, for a time, to obtain some of the essential goods and services you need. A creditor is happy to keep your cash business during the time you are struggling to liquidate an old account with him. So tell each patient creditor that you plan to do business with him on a cash basis while you are repaying him.

Take another look at your spending plan

If it took much persuasion and negotiation to get yourself back on a current, re-amortized basis, your problem must have been more than a temporary one. Chances are your whole budget is out of whack. Try to find out why you got into such a mess. Is your medical insurance adequate? Are you setting aside money in advance to meet medical and dental bills not covered by insurance? Are you spending too much on food, entertainment, liquor, or clothing?

There has to be a reason, a traceable reason, why you are going in the hole. It may be because you haven't followed my advice to open a second checking account to accrue (set aside in advance) funds for those big expenses that arrive at irregular intervals.

You may be carrying too much cash on your person for what is called a "personal allowance" or "pocket money." Less cash to spend freely can mean great savings. You may elect to spend $1.25 for a lunch, rather than $2. You may skip the noon drinks.

You may even carry lunch once in a while. Even the biggest executives do that occasionally.

Another big leak in the family budget can be traced to the evening cocktail hour, stopping in at the favorite pub for a belt or two. It's great sport and quite a diversion for many up-and-coming persons, men and women alike, but it's pretty costly. Many highly paid persons in the entertainment business have their spending allowances doled out in small sums by their business agents just to avoid "cocktail hour insolvency."

If that aspect of living is your problem, count the drinks, carry less cash on your person, accept the fact that few important persons are impressed by "big spenders" anyway, and consider entertaining more at home. Above all, don't run a bar bill, and watch those checks you cash after work. I realize that some high-strung persons, alcoholics, and those who are exceedingly insecure won't accept this advice. But the advice can help those who innocently fall into dangerous habit patterns without considering the consequences.

Get rid of things you don't need

The horrible truth is that some persons refuse to face the facts when they learn about them. Deep down in your subconscious, you may realize you can't afford the home you are living in. You try to blame your insolvency on everything but the real culprit—your high-priced home. Go back over the section in this book on home ownership to check that phase of your spending. If your home seems to be out of line with your income, do one of two things.

a. Sell the home and purchase a less expensive one.

b. Keep the home, if it means that much to you, and cut back drastically on almost all your other expenses—and I do mean drastically.

If you do decide on less expensive living quarters, don't just

walk away from your house or let it "go back." That can ruin
you for life. List the place for sale and accept whatever price it
will bring. It should, at the very least, clear your mortgage. After
the sale, if you are too strapped to buy another home, one more
in line with your income, rent for a while. You can rent houses
as well as apartments.

Or suppose it is your automobile that cuts into your solvency.
No matter how much you think you love that car, get rid of it.
The odds are about ten to one you don't love the car at all. It
may be the status the car brings you. It may be the feeling of
power as you sit behind the wheel that keeps you fascinated.

Just remember: An inexpensive older car can bring a degree of
prestige too, especially in a society where everybody, just everybody, drives fancy cars. Try being a little unique, if money is a
problem, saving your budget and your credit rating in the process.

Getting rid of things you really can't afford and really don't
need is a genuine cure to chronic "red ink." Furthermore, it can
be very therapeutic. Don't despair when the bill collector calls;
get rid of some of the things you've been trying to consume on
credit.

As in the case of getting out from under a too-expensive home,
do your own liquidating. Repossession may seem like the easy
way out, but it is mainly a matter of laziness. Sell your own personal property; you'll get a better price that way. You may be
able to "trade down," exchanging your costly merchandise for
less expensive items.

If a merchant (or finance company) reclaims his goods from a
credit buyer, the agency will take the first offer in many cases. It
may just arbitrarily set a "wholesale price" on the repossessed
goods and hold you, the seller, responsible for any loss it takes.

You may be sued later under what is called a "deficiency
judgment," which makes you liable for any shortage arising from
a forced sale. Some persons erroneously think that a repossession
finalizes the credit transaction. This is not true, except in a few
states where "shortage-type" lawsuits are outlawed.

Seeking outside help

Analyzing one's own spending habits takes complete objectivity, something few people have when looking at themselves. So it might be wise, if you can't balance income with outgo, to visit a financial counselor for at least one interview. If you can't find one you trust, or can afford, ask help from a banker, life insurance man, accountant, social agency, or wise parent. The imperative thing is to get in balance, one way or another. That may take some sacrifice.

Some persons simply haven't the ability or self-discipline to bail themselves out of a serious debt situation. They often run to a lawyer whose advice is to "take bankruptcy." Bankruptcy is a legal right, open to all honest businesses and individuals. Ninety per cent of our bankruptcies are family-type rather than commercial.

However, bankruptcy costs money, often $300 to $400 (on the line) for an individual. Furthermore, not all debts are discharged in many cases. Then there is the matter of pride. Filing bankruptcy stays with you all through life. My advice is: Don't file bankruptcy unless all other avenues of escape are closed.

One such avenue is hiring a debt counselor, debt adjustor, or prorating firm. Many states outlaw private debt adjusting, or limit it to attorneys and nonprofit agencies. The general procedure, regardless of who does it, is to allocate a portion of your future income to each creditor, depending upon the size of each debt, and upon how well the debt is secured. The value of the adjustor, or counselor, comes from his knowledge in the field and from his being an impartial third party. He can get the creditors off your neck.

Before you hire a debt adjustor (counselor—prorater), make sure he is licensed under state law, or that he is highly spoken of by reputable persons. Many debt adjustors are incompetent or worse. On the average, you will pay about 10 to 12 per cent additional, over and above what you owe the creditors, for the services of a good adjustor or debt counselor.

Credit firms in general dislike debt adjustors. They dislike a third party coming into the creditor-debtor relationship. The whole idea infuriates some loan companies, which hate being separated from debtors. As a result, a few credit agencies offer to prorate your debts free, mainly to keep you from going bankrupt or hiring a commercial debt counselor. These credit firms aren't just being kind or altruistic; they are trying to bail themselves out, stay in business, and keep the good name of credit from coming into criticism.

As a person who has had much experience in both bankruptcy proceedings and private debt counseling, I have grave doubts about the idea of credit houses counseling debtors—free or for a fee. There is a serious conflict of interest in my opinion. It may be similar to asking the Tobacco Institute to help us curb our smoking. My advice is, if you absolutely cannot, or will not, handle your own debt tangle, hire a competent person who will work for you and you alone. That would be true even if you have to pay a fee. Those who helped you get into trouble in the first place qualify poorly as experts to help you get out. To repeat, that is just my opinion.

A *final* resort

Some readers of this book may justifiably feel they will have little need for my suggestions on getting out of debt. But there are few people today who don't *occasionally* encounter others with this problem. Wealthy families often have relatives who stay forever mired in debt. Personnel managers meet with the insolvency problem rather frequently. In fact, many a thrifty person will at some time in his life run afoul of the bill collectors.

Anyone in a position of authority ought to be informed on what to do about the problem of overwhelming, unmanageable debt. He can then be able to offer "first aid" if necessary, or to at least steer a troubled debtor in the right direction.

A number of reputable credit firms and organizations have rather belatedly recognized the need to set up "community debt counseling" services. And they also have faced up to the question of being honest with debtors and of presenting help on a truly objective basis. No debt counseling service staffed primarily by bill collectors or lenders will be believable.

In Chicago, Illinois, my friend Prince Patton helped to set up the Family Financial Counseling Service of Greater Chicago. It is a nonprofit institution, and on its board are representatives of industry, labor, credit institutions, and social agencies. The cost of the rehabilitation programs is shared by the debtors and the credit grantors, although the original cost of the endeavor was subsidized by various organizations. At latest report, this new community service was meeting with an excellent response from troubled families. As of this writing, a number of other cities are attempting to copy the Chicago experiment, although some are finding it difficult to raise the necessary capital to get things off the ground. This author has been approached to help set up a similar plan in Los Angeles, California, and if the community responds as hoped, debt problems in that city may be alleviated.

Industrial relations men, social workers, men of the church, and others in a position to offer advice should make every effort to check up on aid-to-debtor organizations in their areas. Debt problems can be so pressing as to lead to divorce, drugs, alcoholism, and even suicide. Many times only twenty-four hours can make the difference. It is disheartening to any man or woman who has been referred to an agency which is ill-equipped to be of help. It can be even worse to send such a person to an agency *professing* to want to help, when its *main* goal is that of collecting money and avoiding a loss in the bankruptcy courts. Far better to refer a debt-burdened person to a reputable, private debt adjustor, who operates under a state license. There are many good ones.

In certain other cities, attempts to aid debtors have been too closely tied to credit firms to be supported by all sections of the communities involved. During 1965, the U. S. Department of Defense refused to cooperate with debt-servicing agencies owned and operated by credit-granting firms, and I salute this move. Turning a serviceman over to his creditors under the guise of "rehabilitation" would be a questionable practice of our armed forces.

Even the best of the debt-rehabilitation agencies have their limitation. One cannot expect an indebted wage earner to be "re-educated" to any reasonable extent simply because he is getting help with his unpaid bills. Education in the use of money and credit is too enormous a chore to tackle on a one-by-one basis. No community organization can be expected to fill all the gaps in our basic school program. As George Crane said, money management is the blind spot in our educational system, and no careless debtor can be genuinely educated through casual meetings with his counselor and/or money manager.

The "typical" overindebted person in this country is quite young, under twenty-eight in fact. He is married, has two or three children, and attended high school for three years. He works at a semi-skilled job and has made many of the mistakes outlined in this book. In most cases, he is so insecure that he lets his often poorly equipped wife handle all the details of family spending. The reasons for his being insecure (and somewhat resentful) are: (1) his limited education, (2) lack of stability in his job, and (3) his television set, which depicts a way of life on the tube that he can never possess. But he tries, and so does his wife— by using too much easy credit. He is encouraged to do just that by hundreds of advertisements beamed at him every day. How much we should criticize him for all this is debatable.

When and if he reads his daily newspaper he may learn that Americans are saving more money than ever, that savings accounts are at the highest level since such-and-such a year. Perhaps he may feel a little better, knowing the country is so solvent. He may even feel vicariously thrifty, enough so to dash out and run up some more bills. In case you think I'm stretching a point, let me assure you that I am not. One of the greatest economic arts of today is that of arousing "consumer confidence."

But debt is far from confined to the young, the uneducated, and the unskilled. Carelessness with credit reaches into all levels of our society today. It hits executives, engineers, doctors, and professors. Your high-living next-door neighbor may be on the verge of filing for bankruptcy. Many sensitive persons would rather discuss sex openly than to talk about their money problems. They are even reluctant to admit to themselves that the brink is only a step away.

And while a man may laughingly admit to being a poor dancer or a duffer at golf, he'll fight against facing up to his lack of ability in handling money. Women will cloud the issue too, defending their debts by saying "We had to have this." The first step toward curing a seriously messed-up money situation is being honest with yourself. Stop pretending it's only temporary, or justified, or someone else's fault. Do something about it, through a self-help program or by seeking professional aid.

If it's simply that you won't, or can't live on what you earn, try to increase your income. As I said before, a wife can go to work and help considerably. A husband can work at two jobs if it's absolutely necessary. Or, if you think you are worth more money and stand a chance of getting it, ask for a raise. You can even switch firms, change your occupation entirely, or strike out on your own. The main idea is to somehow raise your income sufficiently to meet your minimum standard of living, while at the same time paying off your debts.

You may come to the logical conclusion that it's easier to live on what you earn now, and that the only solution is tightening your belt. As I said before, the American Standard of Living, as portrayed on television and in certain magazines, is beyond the financial reach of most young families. That standard of living is more or less a goal to shoot for—something to keep us striving and drooling. You'll never reach it through the liberal use of consumer credit. You'll more likely reach it by saving your dollars and paying cash whenever possible.

Some persons finally attain their dream standards in their later years, after their children are raised and educated. A few of us will attain it by luck or inheritance. Unfortunately, far too many of us reach it only temporarily, just before we file bankruptcy or go to jail.

SUMMARY ON CREDIT

Your credit rating

A credit rating is important to your future. A good credit rating can help you finance a home, go into business, and expand your investment opportunities. Too many credit-consumers think of a credit rating strictly in terms of helping them get more *short-term* credit, the same type of credit that already has them on the ropes.

Credit ratings are compiled by credit bureaus, which take their ratings from the information various credit firms send in to them. A credit bureau may be privately owned and operated at a profit; the profit comes from what credit firms will pay for reports. But it can also come from the collecting of past-due bills.

Some credit bureaus are set up on a nonprofit basis, owned and operated by associations of credit firms. Thus many credit bureaus have come to have a third function. Besides furnishing credit reports on consumers and collecting bills, the bureaus do promotional work for the credit industry. In fact, credit bureaus are part of the superstructure of credit I mentioned earlier. I stress this because if you have dealings of any sort with a credit bureau, you must realize it is part and parcel of the credit system. It is working for credit houses, nonprofit or not.

If you receive a bad credit mark, you have the right to trace it back. It may have been an error. Credit bureaus often refuse to divulge the name of a member credit firm giving a bad rating to a borrower. They insist on privacy. If you feel injustly rated and can't trace the source, get a lawyer to intercede for you. On the other hand, you may deserve the bad mark and should admit it, once you locate the trouble.

Another point to remember is this: If a credit bureau pressures you into paying one of your slow accounts it has for collection, look at your entire picture. The bureau may be subtly threatening you with a bad rating if you don't give preference to the bill it is collecting from you.

There are times when a slightly bad credit rating would be preferable to losing your car, your home, or your utilities. You can talk directly to the creditor involved if you feel you are being railroaded into messing up your finances. The creditor may call off the bill collector—for a while at least. Later on you can re-establish your credit rating. Do the fair thing—that is important—but don't be bluffed by unfair tactics.

Theoretically you aren't supposed to know your own bill-paying rating. That is supposed to be a closely-guarded commercial secret, available only to members of the credit club. But if a good "reputation" is as important as the credit firms make it out to be, you have a right to know your own rating. Some credit man will reveal it to you if you ask him. And after all, how much privacy have you had, with so many credit firms prying into your life?

As I said, these ratings *are* important in today's society for a number of reasons, so keep yours high. You can do that by using credit gingerly when you don't really need it, keeping your debts well under control, paying promptly, and following up on any bad marks, whether deserved or not. If you do get a "minus" on your "report card," try to have a little talk with the credit firm involved, and set things right. Most ratings come out on a year-to-year basis, so a minor black mark soon becomes ancient history. And even in cities where credit ratings are compiled on a continuous basis—going clear back to the beginning—you can wipe out a mistake by asking a creditor to "re-rate" you after you have re-established yourself with him.

Why you must buck the trend

This society is well-advanced economically. We have a surplus of goods and capital abundance. How logical it is to combine these two assets into a system! By lending consumers money to buy things, we not only put our extra capital to work, but we help to move the goods that would otherwise pile up in inventories.

Moreover, capital used to finance consumer "appetites" gets a higher rate of return than money put into factories and loaned to businesses. Consumer credit commands true interest rates of from 10 to 40 per cent. Commercial loans do well to earn 7 per cent. That explains why so much of our credit is channeled into consumer credit.

And while credit may help to keep goods from piling up in factories and warehouses, each citizen-consumer must look to his own immediate needs first. Show me just one business—or successful businessman—that spends money *primarily* to keep the economy rolling, and then I will concede the point that individuals on modest incomes should do the same. When economists, theorists, and Presidents of the United States plead with you to spend your money (just any old way) to keep the economy humming, then things have reached the ridiculous. Until someone in high places guarantees you future income enough to make payments on your debts, there is absolutely no obligation on your part to spend money for reasons other than your own needs.

Running in place

Running in place without getting anywhere is not conducive to mental health, not even if they change the artificial scenery now and then to produce the illusion of travel. Who doesn't aspire to live as the pretty people do in the movies and on television?

But if you try to live as they do in the fairy tales by using credit most of the time, be prepared for disenchantment. You will be racing on a treadmill with the apple just out of grasp. We live in a highly "mobile" society, speaking socially as well as geographically. Moving up to the next social strata is a pretty tricky business.

Easy credit for consumer goods is well on the road toward freezing the blue-shirted worker in his tracks. He runs and runs, mostly from bill collectors, but he gets nowhere. As a member of a group he is too often going backward. He ought to be doing better, thanks to new business equipment that increases his productivity. But the 3 to 4 per cent he gains from increased productivity won't begin to offset the 10 per cent of his income he loses from paying high interest charges, which in turn impairs his solvency and reduces his bargaining power.

The middle-income family, the white-collar crowd, which is also trying to move up, has essentially the same problem. Most young persons pouring out of our high schools and colleges will start at the middle-income level. They, too, will soon learn that they can't move up socially and economically by borrowing from the future to live better now. That may help the economy in a nebulous sort of way, but it doesn't do much for the individual.

The irony of it is that the sociologists keep warning us of the new leisure. That leisure is mainly for the rich, not for those who aspire to improve themselves. As a friend of mine said the other day, "Now that I look back, I can see that I had too much leisure. I managed to stay solvent and even save money. But I have three children to send to college now and that will cost me about $30,000. I haven't quite that much money, and even if I did, how could I afford to spend that much with my retirement staring me in the face? The truth is, I should have been working at two jobs for the past ten years."

It depends upon what you want out of life. Some people want and expect very little. But if you want to achieve a reasonable degree of comfort and security, plan now. You must acquire some assets and put them to work, safely and profitably. That will be the next subject.

PART IV

MANAGING YOUR ASSETS,
or How to Build Security

WHAT COMES FIRST?

The meaning of security

If you were an out-and-out gambler and single with no responsibilities, you might be willing to plunge into an investment program without laying proper groundwork. But most of us want to feel reasonably secure even while we are trying to get ahead. So let's see what security in these times really means.

The purpose of keeping control of your income and avoiding unnecessary debt, is to acquire some assets. By that I mean assets capable of working for you—earning you additional income to give you some degree of security. Most of us are literally surrounded by assets—consumer assets—that help us with our work and give us pleasure, but these consumer assets wear out quickly and aren't able to bring us either cash income or real security.

Of course, security itself is difficult to define. It depends upon what you want out of life. Some men are able to adjust to poverty and still enjoy life. Others are quite content with mediocrity. Still others amass great fortunes, sometimes quite ruthlessly, without ever attaining psychological security.

All of which leads me to two points: (1) Genuine security comes from within. It is possible to train a man to be a financial "mechanic," just as it is possible to teach a man to be a carpenter. But the man who follows a set of mechanical rules to build security won't necessarily find it. Nor will the house the carpenter builds automatically become a home. I can offer some rules and techniques relating to money, but I'm not selling happiness.

And, (2) this is not a book on "How I Made a Million in

the Opium Trade." There are a number of books on the market showing how to wheel and deal in the stock market, or how to evict needy tenants by raising the rents. This is a book outlining my views on how to stay on the "plus" side of life, financially speaking. You might say that I'm trying to make sense out of money. Some persons will be content doing just that. Others will want to drive on to bigger things.

I do feel certain most of us want security. Few of us know it when we see it, but we certainly crave it. Americans may seem carefree and daring to the rest of the world, but the taxes we pay give us away. During 1963, we paid the staggering total of $160 billion in taxes to various governmental agencies. That money was supposed to give us security, in the form of military might, police and fire protection, and welfare spending. Yet we seem to be more anxious and insecure than ever.

When you add all we pay for security, in the form of taxes, to what we pay in casualty insurance premiums, the average American family is spending over 30 per cent of its income to stay protected and secure.

The trouble is, we may be spending so much for collective security that we haven't enough left to provide for our own private security programs. This shows up in the many thousands of older persons who have to pinch pennies to survive, even though during their working years they too spent a sizable proportion of their earnings for security.

While I won't argue with the need for a reasonable amount of protection against our potential enemies and all the hazards of living, I think we have the right to question the *amount* of money being spent by governmental agencies, and to question the emphasis as well. Some hazards get top billing, others are ignored. Guns and bombs we have aplenty, but why so little concern with our food, air, and water?

We spend only piddling sums to keep our air free of smog and filth. Few persons seem concerned about the dangerous chemicals poured into our rivers and streams. Until recently the federal government spent next to nothing guarding us against deadly drugs, dangerous additives in our food, and outright deceit in the marketplace.

If all this sounds a little out of place in a section on saving and investing, let me explain further.

It embarrasses me that the average wage earner has so little left of his pay check to save and invest. It is my contention that every working person should save something. Saving is not just for the elite of a society, it is a must for almost everyone. But until we get our taxes reduced, substantially reduced, saving money will remain a real challenge.

Most of us save money so that we and our children can live the "good life." Until we demand that government agencies channel more of our tax dollars in the direction of guarding our air, water, food, and general health, all will be lost anyway. Who cares how rich he is if nature itself has disappeared, along with the real joy of living?

As it stands now, after almost 30 per cent of our money goes toward taxes, and after we have struggled to achieve the American Standard of Living, we still have to set aside money for old age, emergencies, and general adversity. In the meantime we must see that our overall plan is not ruined by major financial calamities, including premature death. We must insure our lives, our incomes, our assets, and our solvency.

Life insurance

You should look at life insurance from the standpoint of its main purpose—that is, its *original* purpose—to guard a family against severe economic suffering resulting from the death of the main breadwinner. If a man dies after he has retired, there might be no economic loss—mental and emotional suffering, yes, but not necessarily a money loss. Therefore, life insurance is a bit of a gamble. Furthermore, it is a measurable expense. There is a limit to what a family can afford. Most families spend about 3 per cent of their gross incomes for life insurance expense.

The average American family, during 1964, owned about $12,000 in life insurance. But since some families had no coverage at all, those families which did own life insurance apparently averaged closer to $14,000 each.

A fairly good rule regarding life insurance coverage is 2 to 3 times your annual income in "face value" coverage. Thus, a man earning $8000 a year might take out from $20,000 to $24,000 on himself. If his wife didn't work outside the home, he might take out $2000 or more on her life, and some small policies on his children. Perhaps the minimum protection on any life should be enough for burial expenses.

TYPES OF POLICIES

When life insurance first originated, there was only one type of policy. Now there are over two hundred life insurance plans available. Despite this profusion of policy plans, it seems to me that there are only three basic types of life insurance. These are: regular, term, and endowment. By combining these types and offering a wide selection of payment plans and options, the life insurance companies are able to tailor policies to individual needs and preferences.

In too many cases, however, prospects become confused by all the choices. And the very number of plans makes cost comparison more difficult. Here are some explanations of the three basic plans, with comments on each one.

a. *Regular life.* These policies also go by the names of "whole life," "ordinary life," and "straight life." Insurance men may quibble as to the correct terminology; but whatever it is called, regular life protection is the most common type of coverage sold today. It is the original life insurance plan, and many unbiased experts feel it is the only type of protection the average family need consider; or that, at least, it should be the primary coverage purchased.

Regular life insurance offers these benefits:

1. The premium stays fixed, based on the age of the insured at time of purchase.

2. The policy builds up a cash value, or cash reserve. This can be borrowed against, cashed in, or used to convert the policy into paid-up lifetime insurance.

Limited-payment plans are a variation of the regular life plans, but they can be fairly expensive to a young wage earner, since the premiums are higher than on regular life. They must be higher because premiums stop after a certain number of years, usually twenty or thirty, whereas ordinary life policies require premium payments for much longer periods.

It can be a great feeling when a thirty-year limited-pay policy matures. Not having to pay any more frees income for other purposes. The catch is that an insured person is usually fifty years old or more when his limited-pay policy matures. He may be in his top earning years. He scarcely notices his little windfall then. But he certainly could have used any extra income when he first took out the policy. Every extra dollar counts early in life. That is why regular life policies may be the better bargain at the start of a marriage.

b. *Term life*. Term insurance is written for a limited number of years. It accumulates no cash value. For that reason it doesn't appeal to many people. But it is relatively inexpensive, and it accomplishes the main purpose of life insurance. It provides cash immediately upon the death of the insured. In other words, it is pure protection. There are two factors to consider if you take out term insurance: insist that it is guaranteed renewable and convertible. You may want to renew it at expiration, or you may want to switch the policy to ordinary life coverage at some time in the future, when you can better afford the higher premiums. Make certain a medical examination isn't required when you attempt to renew or convert a term policy.

Credit life insurance is just a type of term insurance. Credit life can be quite costly the way it's sold today. While it is presented as a protection for buyers, the creditor himself is the real beneficiary. He gets the proceeds of the policy if you die, in order to liquidate what you owe him. In many cases the creditor is also the salesman, making 50 per cent or more in commissions on the premiums.

Then, too, you must compare rates carefully. Some credit life insurance decreases in coverage as your debt drops. This is almost always true on "home mortgage insurance." Other policies pay the full face amount regardless of what you owe. Naturally the last mentioned kind is the most expensive, by about double. But at least your heirs would get some money after your debt is liquidated.

There may be times in your life when you want special term insurance to protect your family for a few years, perhaps while your own finances are in rather poor condition. Term insurance can be a great help under the right circumstances.

c. *Endowment life.* An endowment policy is just barely a type of life insurance coverage. It is more a savings plan with term insurance or regular life insurance attached. You are guaranteed a lump sum of money after so many years. Endowment plans are written for a fixed number of years, just like the fixed-payment plans. But endowment plans cost a great deal more because they build up greater cash values than the twenty- and thirty-year pay arrangements.

During noninflationary periods, endowment plans can be a fine investment. But they pay relatively small dividends, as compared to interest on savings accounts, and most of them pay off in "dollars" regardless of what the dollars will purchase. In general, endowment plans belong in your savings budget, rather than in your budget for life insurance protection.

Education plans, annuities, and *family income* plans are variations of the three main types I mentioned. An education plan is an endowment-type policy. An annuity can be arranged for under most other policies with cash values. All you do is pay in a certain amount of cash, or convert the cash value you already have, to assure yourself of a certain number of dollars in income —immediately or in later years. Your annuity can be geared today for life, or a fixed number of years. Some annuities are "variable," which we will discuss later.

The family income plan combines term insurance with regular life coverage. The premiums are low for, say, five years, based on the term insurance idea. And while no cash value accrues during that part of the program, if the husband dies his wife receives a small income for a specified number of years. If the husband doesn't die during these first few years, his premiums rise as the policy converts to a regular life plan. The plan has a great deal of merit, since it gives a young husband low-cost insurance while his income is small.

Life insurance companies have been selling another rather new idea which is called the *family plan*. Under this plan, every member of the family is insured, even those not yet born. The trouble is, a family can afford only so much protection, and under the family plans too much may be spent insuring the wife and children and not enough on the main wage earner, the husband. The real economic loss would arise if the husband died.

I could go on listing one variation of life insurance after another, but there would be little point to it. Most persons want to know the following about life insurance: (1) how much they should have, (2) the type of plan they should buy, (3) which life insurance companies to patronize, and (4) what dangers to avoid.

HOW MUCH?

Just because typical families spend about 3 per cent of their incomes for life insurance premiums doesn't mean you should. But it is fairly good guide to follow. Spending that much for premiums may be less important than taking out enough insurance to leave your family the equivalent of at least two years' income.

As you get older and perhaps richer, you may want to increase your coverage. That could come from having more members in your family, a desire (plus the ability) to leave them better protected, or a need to have more cash in your death estate. You wouldn't want the family business or your home to be sold to meet debts.

Don't worry about not being able to afford immediately all the coverage you'd like. While it is true that premiums go up as you get older, that merely makes up for the period you didn't pay *any* premiums. It averages out quite well.

SPECIAL BENEFITS

As I indicated, regular life insurance is hard to beat for the typical family. Just make certain the main breadwinner has the bulk of the coverage on *his* life. The family income policy has many advantages, too, especially for young families. Group insurance, either regular or term, is especially economical because it is less expensive to insure a group than it is to insure each individual separately. Term insurance is for special occasions, and when you want maximum protection at lowest cost, without worrying about the savings features.

Under any policy you may want to pay a little extra to have your premiums forgiven (waived) while you are disabled—temporarily or permanently. It doesn't cost much more. Another feature worth considering is the "double indemnity" clause, which doubles the face amount of your death coverage if you die from an accident rather than from an illness.

As your wealth and income increase, you will want to check with your life insurance agent, as well as with your lawyer and tax man, in order to make the most of our income tax laws. These laws change constantly. There are many ways to protect your estate and minimize the taxes your widow would pay.

WHICH COMPANIES?

Life insurance companies are not all the same. Some are stock companies, some are mutuals, and some are more or less clubs and co-op associations. Some companies pay higher dividends than others. A dividend is the result of a number of factors which result in a life insurance firm earning more money than the premiums justify. Higher profits than expected are the rule these days. In the case of a mutual, member policyholders might get the excess profits almost automatically. But in the case of a stock company, it might depend upon whether or not your policy is of the "participating" kind. In most cases it pays to take out a policy under which you will participate in the dividends. So check dividend records of various insurance firms.

There are still some true "mutuals" operating in the life insurance field. If you buy a policy from such a company you may be asked to make up any losses the firm suffers—pay your share, that is. That can be quite expensive, so make sure of your potential liability. Most mutual life insurance companies issue *nonassessable* policies today.

A few life insurance companies operate out of states which offer little effective regulation. To put it bluntly, quite a few life insurance companies have gone broke, especially in Texas, before that state cleaned house somewhat. Always make certain the life insurance company is licensed to do business in your own state. That's particularly true on mail order insurance.

Another thing to watch out for is the "hard sell." Some life insurance companies have mobile squads in the field, covering each territory to the point of saturation. They stay in one town a week or more and then move on. If you don't want more insurance, and don't need it, learn to say "no," even if the salesman gets out the crying towel thinking about what might happen to your loved ones.

By and large, life insurance is a highly respectable, clean business today. It has a fine record of solvency and integrity. But as I said, no two companies are exactly alike in any respect. Deal with those you know, those with good, long-established reputations. But compare rates on identical coverages, even among the best companies. Above all, select a reputable, well-trained insurance agent, one you trust and respect.

The best bargain around is the G.I. insurance that is issued by the Veterans Administration to those eligible. If you have that type of insurance, hang onto it.

As to whether to convert term coverage to other permanent types, it depends upon your needs. Many persons cash in their regular, ordinary life policies in their later years, or convert to annuities. There is no point in having any kind of life insurance unless you have dependents, or unless there are some tax and business advantages. You aren't necessarily losing anything by keeping your term insurance, G.I., or other types, as long as you are certain you can renew or convert it; you are paying for protection as you go.

THE DANGERS

Avoid weekly and monthly payment plans for buying life insurance. Someone has to pay for all that bookkeeping and collecting expense, so it shows up in substantially higher premiums. You can get lots more coverage for the same amount of money by paying your premiums annually or semiannually. It just takes a little planning (that second checking account I mentioned under Income Management).

Beware of high-cost burial plans. Life insurance itself is a form of funeral plan. There are cases of $500 burial insurance policies costing more than $1000 ordinary life policies. Changing the name on the policy doesn't change the basic nature of the coverage.

A salesman may try to switch your policies to those of another company, or even to other types of policies with the same firm. You may have to take a medical examination to qualify for the new policy. You may have to pay another entrance fee. Ask plenty of questions if you get the switch proposition. There are times when a switch is advantageous, helping to reduce your premiums and adding additional paid-up insurance. Just make sure you understand what the switch will do for you. Generally speaking, the older policies have better features than newer ones.

The important thing is to understand the primary function of life insurance, which is to protect your family from undue hardship arising from your death. If that is what you want, concentrate on that angle.

No one can protect his family from all hazards. It isn't possible. Nor is it realistic for a person of modest means to buy so much insurance that his family will live as well, or better, if he dies. They make horror movies about that sort of thing. Budget for life insurance as you would budget for any other expense of living. Your family probably likes to live fairly well now, too, while you are alive to enjoy life with them, and have enough money to provide them with a decent standard of living. It *is* possible to be "insurance poor."

Medical insurance

Most persons live in fear of a serious bankrupting illness or accident. That can happen to anyone, and I firmly believe that most persons should guard themselves against such a hazard. Too many persons feel, however, that they should get "first dollar" insurance coverage on all the minor ills that beset them.

First we will analyze health insurance from the standpoint of what is really "insurance" and what is really "prepayment." Insurance in its true sense is a "share the risk" idea. You don't buy insurance on the assumption that you most likely will put in a claim, or several claims. In fact, both you and the insurance company assume just the opposite. Under the belief that claims are improbable, premiums are relatively low.

Under most health insurance plans, the insurance idea has taken quite a beating. Now it is assumed that most persons, the assureds, *will* put in a claim—many claims—over the lives of their policies. Consequently health insurance premiums are skyrocketing. This has come about because few people are willing to save enough money in advance to pay *small* medical bills. They want the health insurance company to start paying immediately, almost as soon as the bills arrive. And they want the insurance company to pay the "first dollar" of expense.

Other things being equal, the easiest way to save on health insurance costs is to count on paying the expenses of small illnesses yourself, and to stay willing and able to pay the first few hundred dollars of even the big medical bills. "Gamble" isn't quite the word to use, from the angle of making adequate financial preparations, but it is the word to use when trying to

determine the likelihood of an accident or illness happening to
you. We can't predict trouble in advance, but we can make
preparations in case it occurs.

Employer-paid plans should be considered as the base from
which to plan your overall health insurance program. The coverage given by your employer isn't exactly free, since the con-
tribution he makes to the insurance company is really part of
your total remuneration. So while you may not have to pay income taxes on the so-called free premiums, you should consider
them part of your "total income," just as gifts and free rent
would be. And you should also realize that the cost of those
free premiums is part of your overall "medical expense."

I make this point for an important reason. If you decide you
should allocate 6 per cent of your gross income for total medical
and dental expenses, including health and accident insurance,
first deduct from that 6 per cent a sum approximately equal to
what the "free insurance" would cost you otherwise. Six per
cent is a typical percentage for young families in the middle-
income range, those earning from $6000 to $12,000 per year.

Health insurance has two main purposes: (1) to help you pay
doctor, hospital, and other medical bills; and (2) to replace
income you might lose from being off work due to illness or
accident.

The first purpose is the most important for the majority of
American families, since, for one thing, most employers continue to pay disabled workers for reasonable periods of time.
And second, most illnesses and accidents don't involve long periods off work. A high percentage of "income replacement" health
policies require a waiting period.

Here are the main types of health insurance plans, with my
comments on each of them.

TYPES OF PLANS

a. *Loss of Income Insurance*

As I mentioned, some policies of this type require waiting
periods of thirty days or more before you are eligible to put in a

claim. The longer the waiting period, the lower the premium. If your employer has been following the practice of keeping disabled employees on the payroll for a month or more, you certainly wouldn't need "first day" protection. And remember, you usually must go to a hospital to receive benefits.

b. *Surgical Expense Coverage*

These policies pay all or part of the doctor's bill. The policies list various operations and how much the insurance will pay toward each type. Quite often a doctor's bill will exceed the amount allowed.

c. *Hospital Care*

Under this type of policy, the insurance pays so much "per day" for room and board (often considerably less than you will be charged) and also pays specified amounts for dressings, X rays, laboratory fees, and operating-room costs. You need to check local hospital rates carefully to see how well you would be covered under this kind of a policy.

Sometimes hospital care and surgical expense policies are more or less combined (Blue Cross—Blue Shield), but actually the policies are separate entities.

d. *Regular Medical Expense Insurance*

Under this insurance plan, you may be covered for non-surgical doctor bills, including calls made to the hospital and calls made to your home. It may even cover trips you make to the doctor's office. You must make certain you aren't duplicating your coverage under some other policy, and you need to consider the cost carefully too. You might be wise to underwrite these expenses yourself.

e. *Major Medical*

These plans are quite similar to those called "Comprehensive Plans." You might even call them "calamity insurance." In general they pay for the prolonged, serious disabilities, those which could almost bankrupt you. They have two main features that make them attractive to some wise persons, and unattractive to persons obsessed with "first dollar," "first day" coverage.

1. The insured must pay the first few hundred dollars of the expense entirely on his own. That is called the "deductible" and can vary from $250 to $1000 or more. The higher the deductible, the lower the premium.

2. The insured usually must also share in the cost after the deductible has been applied. A typical percentage to be paid by the insured, after he has paid the deductible, is 20 per cent of the remainder of the bill. Here again, the higher the percentage to be paid by the insured, the lower the premium.

One other thing: All of these policies are limited as to total dollar amount of the insurance company's liability. If the insurance company refuses to pay more than $5000, the policy would be less expensive than one in which the insurance company agrees to go as high as $10,000.

The only difference between a true "major medical" policy and a "comprehensive type" is that the latter also includes some of the features of the more basic insurance plans.

Some persons use the major medical plans to supplement their other coverages, including that furnished by their employers. Other persons buy only major medical or comprehensive coverages. To my way of thinking, the comprehensive coverage is enough, at least for those families that set aside enough cash to meet small medical bills, plus enough to meet the deductible.

There is an important distinction between genuine "insurance" and "prepayment." Let me illustrate in this way. If an insurance company or association selling prepayment-type insurance expected you to incur $700 in doctor and hospital bills over a year, the firm would have to charge you an annual premium of about $770—10 per cent more than you would normally pay in medical bills. It must do this in order to pay its overhead in issuing policies, screening applications, servicing the smaller claims, and guarding against fraud. So it is quite costly to get prepayment insurance. We Americans have forced ourselves into the position of paying more than we need to for medical services because we won't stay solvent enough to underwrite our own small medical bills. Medical prepayment plans are like consumer credit—we pay too much in order not to have to budget in advance.

On the other hand, a comprehensive medical policy protects a family from a bankrupting loss. Such policies cost very little if the deductible amount is reasonably high.

WARNINGS

No matter what type of medical insurance you secure, heed these warnings. Medical insurance is the fuzziest of all consumer spending areas because it is so difficult to shop for and compare.

1. Check on the insurance firm. Ask your friends about their insurance companies. Make sure the company is authorized to do business in your state.

2. Don't be awed by all the diseases covered, although they might make up a long and impressive list. Take more interest in what *isn't* covered—the exclusions. Too many exclusions can make a policy almost worthless. We aren't allowed to pick our diseases, you know.

3. How much will the insurance firm pay during any one calendar year? Per-year limitations may not be the same as total limitations under a policy.

4. Is the policy cancellable? It can be worth a great deal to know the insurance company can't drop your coverage the first time you put in a substantial claim.

5. Will the insurance company deny any claims where you have a duplication of coverage? You may be paying twice for some coverage without the chance to get double benefits. Check your policies carefully.

In summary, medical insurance is absolutely essential to any family today. But I have shown a number of ways to economize on it. While this isn't a medical book, nor one on health, it has been said over and over again by medical authorities that the way to cut medical bills is to stay in good health. That means proper food, a decent amount of exercise, plenty of sleep, and a philosophical attitude toward life. Those, plus a willingness to provide in advance for small medical bills, will help enormously in cutting your total outgo for good health. And they will make it possible to keep your overall asset-management plan intact, without undue worry.

Casualty insurance

As you accumulate physical property from your earnings, you must insure that too. Actually you must insure your belongings from two angles—considering what can happen to your property itself, and considering what your property can do to damage other persons and *their* property. Here is a check list of the casualty insurance programs most families need:

a. Auto Insurance

Auto insurance is a two-part thing. The part that reimburses you for damage to your car is called "physical hazard insurance." That in turn is divided into (1) collision coverage and (2) comprehensive coverage.

The other half of the overall auto insurance package is the "liability" part, which protects other persons and their property against what might happen to them as a result of your driving. But it also protects you, the insured, against lawsuits coming from your own negligence and irresponsibility. Most states more or less require drivers to carry liability coverage in order to protect innocent persons from financial losses not of their own making. A liability policy also has two basic parts, "bodily injury to persons" and "property damage." The "bodily injury" part is the most important coverage, since juries have been awarding high damage settlements to those injured by automobiles. Most persons have a fairly good understanding of the nature of auto insurance, so we'll concentrate on ways to save money—showing how to buy it, what to include, and some often overlooked points.

HOW TO PURCHASE

Rates for auto insurance vary a great deal, according to where you live, your driving record, who drives the car, how much the car is driven, the value of the car, and how the insurance firm sells its policies.

Even if you finance your car with a dealer, you ought to insist on the right to place your own insurance, paying cash for the coverage if you can. A few of the larger finance agencies offer competitive rates on insurance, but many of them load the premiums with coverages you may not need or want. Shopping for insurance by comparing coverages and companies is an obvious way to save money.

You can't easily change where you live, so if you live in a heavy traffic area, expect your rates to be high. But wherever you buy your insurance, make certain you obtain the rates you are entitled to. If there are no young drivers of your car, ask for rate benefits. If you haven't had any accidents, stress that point too. You may get a prime rate if you are a nondrinker. If you own two cars, the second car should get a lower rate.

A person driving 15,000 miles a year should expect to pay a higher premium than a person driving only 10,000 miles a year. You should bargain on all those points.

The value of a car determines how much you pay for collision and comprehensive coverage, which includes fire, theft, vandalism, and other miscellaneous hazards. So one merit in keeping a car longer is the reduction in insurance premiums. Also, compact cars often qualify for a 10 per cent rate reduction.

Some companies are able to charge lower premiums because they eliminate the salesman's commission (usually about 25 per cent) by selling through their own agencies on a wholesale basis. This can be a real cost-saver. On the other hand, some persons are willing to pay a little more because they feel that an independent agent will give them better service. They also feel the agent will intercede with the insurance company for them on disputed claims. This is often the case. It depends on the insurance company, the agent, and other minor considerations. I simply want to point out the choice.

In general, follow the same guides I pointed out on shopping for other types of insurance. Check the company, make certain it is licensed in your state, ask other persons for recommendations, and demand all the rate reductions you are entitled to.

COVERAGES TO INCLUDE

Most persons have little choice about taking out liability coverage. State laws demand it, or almost demand it, by threatening to revoke driving licenses when a person fails to meet his financial responsibilities. Insurance companies will go only so high on the property damage coverage, limiting their liability to $5000 or $10,000. This is usually perfectly adequate.

But many persons fail to take out high enough limits under bodily injury coverage. The premium difference between $10,000 and $20,000 is very slight. Many persons carry $50,000 in bodily injury coverage, just to be safe. Juries sometimes award damages in excess of the insurance company liability.

Some auto policies carry a medical insurance clause protecting both the driver and his riders against medical bills from accidents. From the standpoint of the driver-owner, such insurance can be quite high-priced, especially if he has other accident insurance. After all, it covers only driving accidents. As to whether the insurance is a good buy to protect the guests in his car, it might depend on whether he is liable for them under state law. Comprehensive coverage is almost always desirable. It is relatively low in cost anyway. But some insurance companies offer a "deductible" comprehensive plan, which is a better, more economical buy.

Many persons overbuy on collision coverage. The lower the deductible amount, the higher the cost; if you must pay only the first $50 of repair on a collision, the premium cost will be much higher than if you were required to pay the first $100. The $50 deductible is not only higher in dollar cost than the $100, but you pay a great deal in extra premiums just to avoid a "possible" $50 loss.

Let me put it another way. If an insurance company had to insure the automobile of a marginal driver, the company would rather he bought $50 deductible—even $25 deductible—rather than $100. Insurance companies make more money on the low deductibles than on the high ones.

So, to reverse that thought, it usually pays a careful driver to buy high deductible insurance. It will pay him to gamble a little, relying on his careful habits over the years, to count on being able to come up with an extra $50 or so if he gets in an accident. Twenty-five dollar deductible is rarely a good buy, even for a mediocre driver.

On older cars—quite old ones—collision insurance may not be necessary at all. By the time the deductible is applied to a collision loss, and the salvage on the old car sold for parts or junk, the insurance company may have a net loss so small it barely exceeds the annual premium charged.

A finance company may require collision insurance on an older car, partly because it makes a profit selling the insurance. In such a case, a car-buyer would be money ahead to borrow against something besides the car and let the car go uninsured for collision. The risk would be worth it. But even very old cars should be covered for fire and theft.

On newer cars, most persons would be wise to take the three major auto coverages—comprehensive, collision, and liability. But most car owners would also be wise to consider the higher deductibles, and do some of the risk underwriting themselves.

SPECIAL POINTS TO CONSIDER

1. Some auto policies are "assessable" or "reciprocal." Check that point carefully, since you may be required at some future date to pay extra money. This is especially true if you have had trouble getting auto insurance and have been forced into a "pool" of bad driving risks.

2. Make certain your auto insurance can't be cancelled during its regular term. A company has the moral and legal right to refuse to renew your policy if your driving habits are bad. But

you should demand that your policy be of the type which cannot be cancelled until it expires.

3. You may be offered an auto policy with all sorts of special features you do not want. Don't be too thrown by all those extras, since everything has a price. Buying a "bulk package" can be economical, but it also can be as foolish as buying a sofa and chair combination with ashtrays, footstools, and doilies. Keep your eye on the main items and the price of each.

b. *Homeowner Insurance*

If you own a home you now can include several types of casualty insurance in one package. That package plan is known as the "homeowner policy," or as the "comprehensive dwelling policy." Even if you rent a house or live in an apartment, you can obtain these coverages to insure your furniture and personal belongings.

The comprehensive package is a little more flexible than the homeowner one, so discuss that aspect with your casualty insurance agent. But in general these broad-coverage policies insure you against loss from fire, hail, wind, vandalism, burglary, and miscellaneous hazards. Fire is the basic coverage, however.

You may get protection on a deductible basis against falling trees, just as with auto collision coverage. But you may have to pay extra for earthquake insurance or for brush fire insurance. It depends upon where you live whether or not you need such insurance. And you won't be covered by flood insurance, so bear that in mind. Landslide insurance is very hard to obtain, too.

These package plans usually include personal liability insurance, a must for everybody. Make certain you have it. A regular fire policy wouldn't include insurance to protect you from lawsuits against you by persons damaged in some way while on your property.

You may also want a personal property floater to reimburse you in case you lose or misplace valuable pieces of personal property, although regular comprehensive dwelling policies afford a limited amount of protection against loss of property while traveling. Such coverage can be invaluable during times you are moving from one home to another. Regular moving insurance on your furniture, the kind furnished by moving companies, is computed on a "thirty cents a pound" basis (it may be raised to sixty cents), although you can get better coverage by paying higher premiums. A floater policy would reimburse you for the value of your actual loss, usually on a small deductible basis, however. A floater policy isn't necessary unless your personal belongings have sufficient value to warrant insuring. If you own expensive jewelry or furs, a floater insurance policy is a good buy. Rates are fairly standardized among insurance firms. These policies are called floaters because they follow you all over the world—float around, in other words.

Most homeowner policies are now written on a three-year term, which saves you money, since the third year coverage is written at one-half of the regular premium.

There are definite economies in combining so many basic coverages under one policy, especially on the three-year term. But aside from picking one of the best insurance companies and comparing rates, here are a few things to remember about home insurance.

POINTS TO REMEMBER

1. Part of the value of your homestead is just plain land. You can't insure that against fire and certain other losses. Base the insurable value of your home on the house and improvements alone. The land will remain after a fire or hailstorm.

2. See if your state laws allow coinsurance. Under that kind of insurance, if you underinsure your home, you might receive only a certain percentage of a partial loss from the insurance firm. The insurance company would feel that since you fudged on the premiums by underinsuring your home you should share in any losses as coinsurer of your own property. If an appraiser decided your home was worth $25,000 and you had insured it for only $20,000, you might get only 80 per cent reimbursement on a partial loss. Most states don't allow this on homesteads, but you should check your local situation to make certain you have enough coverage on your home.

3. Even if you finance a new home, reserve the right to buy and select your own home insurance. Some financing agencies try to insist on furnishing your insurance too.

4. Make sure just what type of home insurance you have. If you have the basic fire policy, without personal liability and other important coverages, either change to a more comprehensive plan or give some thought to extending the coverages under the policy you have. In addition, take out personal liability and consider a floater policy.

5. No home insurance policy insures you for everything. If you choose to live in an earthquake area, or one subject to landslides and flooding, just realize you are gambling. It may be time for the federal government to step in and offer to reinsure casualty insurance firms that cannot afford to offer complete coverages to homeowners.

Casualty insurance, medical insurance, and life insurance are the means whereby we try to protect our "master plan" from being destroyed or seriously set back. Long before any of these insurance plans came into popularity, persons lived, worked, saved money, and amassed wealth. Even today, many persons choose to gamble with luck and adversity. It is a choice open to all of us.

c. *Cut Costs of Casualty Insurance*

When you add the premiums you pay to guard against all the hazards, they amount to a pretty penny. It is not unusual for an $8000-a-year man to pay 10 per cent of his income in total insurance premiums of the three types.

One way to reduce your total insurance expense—the premiums you pay for psychological security and to offset the chance factor in life—is to take some of the risk on your own shoulders. Save enough money to be able to underwrite the smaller losses yourself. Be your own insurance company and plan to cover hazards which wouldn't seriously harm your net worth or your peace of mind.

As some insurance men say, your need for insurance should be measured not by the likelihood of the loss occurring, but by your ability to stand the loss if it does occur. A prime example of being overinsured, in my opinion, is a man who pays an extra $20 in auto insurance premiums, just to change his deductible from $100 to $50. Twenty dollars to insure $50 isn't insurance at all—it is a type of "poverty" thinking. It is an admission you would be hard-pressed to raise an extra $50 for an accident that isn't even likely to occur.

Family improvement as security

When the young wife looked out the window in order to view the family car in the driveway, she said to me, "Sometimes I think we're in terrible shape financially, but when I see the fine automobile we own, I know we are getting ahead after all."

Rather typical American thinking, I guess. Over the years we have come to think of security in terms of physical assets. Few families would even consider saving cash money until they had acquired all the comforts of modern-day living—the niceties, the luxuries, the conveniences, and the social necessities. After all these have been purchased, and perhaps paid for, then comes the savings and investment program.

I want to treat this subject of family betterment before I jump into the more financial aspect of security planning, because I suspect many Americans have been sold a questionable bill of goods. If the typical housewife prefers a new hi-fi set to a share of stock in International Business Machines, that is her privilege, even if she hasn't one nickel in the bank and has to buy her hi-fi set on the "never, never" pay plan.

I can only wonder how much conditioning it took over the years to bring about such a change in our value standards, to turn us into such fine consumers. I do know this: Consumer economists have had to revise suggested budgets to include family betterment as one of the main categories. How else could they account for all the consumer products we fill our homes with?

The acquisition of consumer goods—consumer assets—now takes up a substantial part of the "family improvement" section for most families. And family improvement itself, as a budget item, often takes 20 per cent of the budget.

I want to make three main points about all this: (1) those who load up with all the consumer goods before they tackle their genuine security program may never get off the starting blocks; (2) there are ways to acquire most of the modern comforts and conveniences without sacrificing security; and (3) family improvement or betterment has a meaning not related to consumer, durable goods.

WARNINGS

1. *Consumer Goods Won't Give Security*

Keeping your home stocked with the latest in durable goodies is a never-ending procedure. Even if the goods last a long time, you soon fall out of love with them. Manufacturers build "psychological obsolescence" into their products. New and "improved" versions come out every year, even every half-year in the case of some autos.

Most consumer goods lose value (depreciate) so fast that replacing them strains the earning power of the most capable wage earners. Not only that, but buying all these "assets" on credit further increases their cost and seriously reduces your chance of actually saving money. Having a house and garage full of short-lived "things" isn't a form of security; it is just a substitute for genuine security.

2. *How to Own Things You Really Need*

Many smart people have whipped the problem of living in the modern manner. There's nothing particularly ingenious about their solution, either. They first ask themselves what they really need, from the standpoint of function, labor-saving, and economy. They aren't impressed with chrome, blinking lights, brilliant enamel, or false prestige. Some of the goods they pay cash for. Many they buy second-hand. But whatever they buy they treat carefully and invite to stay in the family until age and frailty call for retirement and replacement. In the meantime, these wise people seek status in more lasting ways and ignore the commercial pleas to buy newer and fancier things. They get no more "kicks" thinking about replacing their consumer assets prematurely than they would get from reading the "jobs wanted" ads under the "domestics" column. After all, an appliance is just a servant. So is an automobile.

3. *What Betterment Actually Means*

To lump the acquisition of consumer goods under betterment can be misleading, because the term "betterment" implies that you are adding something of lasting value to your life. Things that don't last, don't last. It is about that simple.

However, some expenses coming under the general definition of betterment are well-justified, even before you manage to acquire much net worth or savings. More education for you or your children is one example. Giving to your church is another, if you are a religious person. Doing a reasonable amount of entertaining might be another. Even vacations can be justified as a form of presaving betterment if they add to your general well-being.

Family betterment is a valid expense of living. We shouldn't try to live by bread or money alone. I simply want to show the true meaning of this particular budget expense before going on to pure cash savings.

The all-important emergency fund

Before embarking on a long-range saving and investing program, a family should set aside a fund for emergencies. Such a fund would be in addition to short-term savings specially earmarked to buy consumer goods, pay for vacations, and the like. The emergency fund should be at least the equivalent of two months' salary—perhaps three months'.

If you earn $500 a month, you should have an emergency

savings account of at least $1000 in a safe place, preferably earning some interest. Think of this fund as part of your savings program that won't be used to live better or to speculate with. The fund could be the cash value in your life insurance policies; it could be in a bank, savings and loan firm, credit union, or government savings bonds. It shouldn't be kept at home.

But from now on, when I talk of savings and investments, I am mainly talking about money over and above that emergency fund, and over and above cash you may be accruing to meet annual expenses, such as replacing things which wear out.

HOW TO MEASURE A SAVINGS PROGRAM

Consider the features you already have

When planning a balanced, long-range investment program, you should gear your plans with (1) Social Security, and (2) any benefits you may receive from programs sponsored by your employer, union, or other associations.

During 1961, the average retired couple in this country had an income of about $2500 a year, or $200 a month. About two-thirds of that income came from retirement plans, government and private. Only one-third came from earnings.

Yet during 1965, it would have cost the average retired couple about $3500 a year minimum to live in a typical city. So approximately one-half of our retired persons are living on incomes well below the respectable level of subsistence, even though many of them are still working part-time.

While most persons in this country can expect to receive Social Security benefits at retirement age, it is unlikely that those benefits will be sufficient to provide more than a minimum standard of living. Social Security wasn't intended to cover more than that.

And while almost 50 per cent of the private labor force is covered by pension plans, those plans pay only about 30 per cent of what each employee earns just before he retires. The point is, Social Security benefits plus private pension plans afford only a modest standard of living to the retired people of this country. If you want to retire with any degree of comfort and security, you must supplement your benefits from Social Security and pension plans with additional investment income.

Also, you must consider the fixed nature of retirement income plans. Inflation and a higher cost of living can make a serious dent in the purchasing power of retirement dollars.

We are living long lives these days, thanks to medicine and research. Most persons who retire continue to enjoy life, and most of them are reasonably healthy. But it does take money to live the good life, and the burden of being sure you have the money falls on you.

Let me give this as an example. Suppose the Social Security payments for a man and wife were raised to $250 a month by the time you retire, over 25 per cent more than today's coverage. And suppose, in addition, that you could expect another $175 a month from your private pension plan. You might think the total sum—$425 a month—would support you in grand style. Perhaps it would, but the chances are the cost of living would have soared, too. It likely would take about $500 or even $600 a month to live graciously by the time you received the $425. That is life, and that is inflation.

But enabling yourself to have a good retirement income is only one of many reasons to build up an estate. You may want to buy into a business. You may want to leave your children enough of an estate to give them a good start in life. You may just want the feeling of having something substantial behind you in case you want to change jobs.

An increasing number of people are saving to live abroad, in warm, pleasant areas where taxes are low, people are friendly, and the pace is less hectic. Some persons save in order to see the world, traveling as the mood strikes.

If a modest subsistence pension isn't enough, start now to add to it. Retirement comes sooner than you might imagine. The first thing you must do is start a regular, systematic savings plan. You must save so automatically that it soon becomes routine and virtually painless. To put it in a different manner, you must consider "savings" as the first of the modern-day essentials. Live on what you have left.

There are at least three main factors to consider as you begin to save money, at least for those first few hundreds or thousands of dollars. We will discuss these next.

The important elements of a savings account

Because many of our financial institutions have become so large, even in comparison to the size of other businesses, some persons think only in terms of interest rates, feeling *all* savings institutions are safe.

This feeling partly stems from the public relations departments of the savings institutions. The financial ads show pictures of Hercules, giant rocks, and magnificent waterfalls in order to associate these things with the strength and stability of a particular firm. But how, for instance, does an innocent saver compare the relative safety of an Atlas-like firm with another whose image is tied to Boulder Dam? Comparing images isn't very businesslike.

First I will enumerate the general factors a saver should consider when entrusting his cash to the safekeeping of any firm. After that I will try to relate these factors to the more important industries offering to hold and invest our cash.

SAFETY

Safety should be the number one consideration of any savings program, and by that I mean getting your dollars back intact. As a general rule—one demonstrated by history—the higher the return promised, the greater the risk. So let's be practical—when you are promised 6, 7, and 8 per cent on your savings, you are assuming a certain degree of risk. There is no magic way to keep your money absolutely safe and still earn top interest rates.

Even when financial institutions are competing vigorously for your money, and therefore offering fantastically high interest rates, the "times" themselves may be dangerous. Savings institutions can get themselves into traps offering the public too much for money and then getting involved in risky investments.

Interest rates tend to creep up when money is scarce, usually during boom times. And it is precisely during such times that savings in general become less safe. After the Big Crash in 1930, interest rates dropped to 1 per cent on savings accounts at banks. By 1966, during a period of enormous boom and expansion, savings rates had jumped to 4 per cent at banks, even higher at savings and loan firms. Supply and demand determine interest rates up to a point. Beyond that point speculation takes over.

Safety is a relative thing at best. In relation to savings institutions it can depend upon (1) how the firm is licensed and regulated, (2) how it is insured, and (3) how liquid it keeps its investments.

AVAILABILTY OF YOUR MONEY

Your cash might be "safe" from the viewpoint of eventually getting your money back, but if it took too long, you could be broke or badly bent. You should always keep the availability of your savings in mind, the ease with which they could be liquidated, in other words. At least some of your savings and investments, particularly the first few thousands of dollars, should be at your disposal at all times.

EARNINGS

The interest you earn on your money is important, but it isn't so important as being certain the principal itself is safe, and also reasonably available. Better to earn low interest, or no interest at all, than to worry about getting nothing back, or getting your savings back so late you are badly hurt in the meantime.

Many persons will sacrifice a point or so of interest in order to know their savings are both safe and liquid. There are times when you should, too. As a rule, any savings plan offering to pay more than United States Savings Bonds (Series E and H) would entail some risk.

CONVENIENCE

The only real merit to having a convenient place to save is that you may save more money if you have less of a struggle doing it. It has been proved that persons will save more if small sums are deducted from their pay checks at regular intervals. This is the time-honored way people acquire savings bonds and shares in credit unions.

Picking a savings institution close to where you work or live may result in more savings. If you can mail in your deposits that may help too. Convenience as a factor in savings relates to human nature, not to the safety, liquidity, or earning power of the institution. These factors are the ones you should consider as you begin to save money. Later we will get into the matters of diversification, capital gain, and overall balance. But first we will discuss the more important fixed-income savings institutions, as they stack up against the guides just outlined. These fixed-income institutions promise you your dollars back plus interest or dividends. They are really plans to invest in the dollar.

Fixed-income dollar plans

COMMERCIAL BANKS

We will start with the commercial banks because they are the backbone of our entire money system. If our banks aren't safe, nothing is.

From the safety angle, most banks belong to the Federal Reserve System, which brings them under some control by the United States Government. But our commercial banks are privately owned, make no mistake about that. Don't let the word

"Federal" confuse you. Some banks are *chartered* by the Federal Government; others are chartered under state laws; but all the banks are privately owned and operated. Furthermore, the banks themselves have a great deal to say about the policies and rules of the Federal Reserve System, even though the "Fed" is a quasi-governmental agency. Member banks buy shares of ownership in the Reserve banks.

Another safety factor is that most all banks have their deposits insured through the Federal Deposit Insurance Corporation, which does some auditing on its own.

Because of the rules laid down by the Federal Reserve Board and the FDIC, most banks operate under a rather rigid set of rules. Your deposits may be insured up to $15,000 by the FDIC, even more if you juggle account names around by various wife-husband combinations.

Nevertheless, the FDIC is not the United States Government; not quite, anyway. The FDIC is an "instrumentality" of the Federal Government. Congress has only a limited responsibility to support the FDIC if things got really rough—not only a limited responsibility, but perhaps a limited ability. After all, Uncle Sam has his money in the banks and when he needs cash in a hurry, he borrows from them, too.

I make these comments to distinguish between "normal" safety of an insured bank, and "ultimate" safety in event of a national economic disaster. The FDIC itself, the insuring agency, in 1964 had about $3 billion in the kitty to bail out insolvent banks. The FDIC has the power to draw on the U. S. Treasury for another $3 billion if necessary. For that matter, some Congressmen believe the Federal Government has the "moral" obligation to back up the FDIC all the way. But a moral debt is not the same as a legal one, and there is always the problem of wherewithal. Nothing is absolutely safe, although an insured bank, one belonging to the Reserve System, is in my opinion as safe as any private investment you can make.

When it comes to availability, or liquidity, banks rate about tops in that department, too. But remember this—when you put your money in a bank savings account, you will have a "time deposit." In other words, you must give the bank "time" to refund your money if the bank asks you to. A savings account is not the same as a checking account, which entitles you to your money on demand.

To my knowledge, the right has never been exercised, but a bank *can* ask you to wait ninety days for your savings account money, if conditions warrant. That is why savings accounts pay interest, whereas checking accounts do not, except as an offset to service charges.

The longer you leave your cash in a bank savings account, the more interest you will earn. How much you will earn depends on the times and the demand for money.

To sum up, banks *are* safe. If you pick a bank where your deposits will be insured by the FDIC, you should have no cause for alarm under normal or near-normal economic conditions. But if you are a worrier, thinking about the worst that might happen, pick the most liquid, well-managed bank you can find. Some banks are safer than others, from the standpoint of ultimate safety. To learn which banks are safest, try to find out where large financial firms keep their idle cash. Because their deposits are not insured over the $15,000 figure, they must pick banks with care. But even large financial institutions sometimes choose the wrong banks, as witness the failure of the San Francisco National Bank during 1965.

MUTUAL SAVINGS BANKS

These banks are mostly in the East. They have shown a remarkable record of safety, and they concentrate on serving families of modest means. All mutual savings banks are state-chartered; all are nonprofit; all are heavily invested in mortgages.

In general they pay somewhat higher rates on savings accounts than do commercial banks. Some of these mutual organizations also offer member-savers a combination plan of cash savings, low-cost life insurance, and a way to accumulate Federal savings bonds.

Being "mutuals," the savers are part owners. They buy shares in the mutual banks; these shares pay "dividends" rather than "interest." When you save at a commercial bank, the bank then owes you (the creditor) money. Creditors earn interest. Owners earn dividends. But when you buy shares in a mutual of any kind, you become a shareholder-owner and receive profits or dividends. This may sound like hair-splitting, but creditors (interest-receivers) come ahead of part owners in legal liquidations. It is only important in event of serious trouble, but worth mentioning.

Consider how your savings (shares) are insured, and also consider the management record of the mutual bank itself. Over the years, money saved in these firms has been safe, liquid, and quite profitable.

SAVINGS AND LOAN ASSOCIATIONS

Most savings and loan firms are mutuals too, although in the West the trend has been toward private ownership. It is always important, from long-range considerations, to know whether you are a creditor of a savings institution or a member-shareholder. There has been a tendency to pooh-pooh that distinction over the years, since savings and loan firms now have "share insurance" under the Federal Savings and Loan Insurance Corporation (FSLIC) just as banks have deposit insurance under the FDIC. As of this writing, most savings and loan firms provide share insurance under the FSLIC up to $15,000 on each account.

As a practical matter, savings and loan firms, those which have share insurance, are just as safe as bank savings accounts. The only degree of difference would arise from the nature of the savings and loan associations in the event of an economic catastrophe. It is always more difficult to insure an owner-shareholder than it is to insure a creditor.

Savings and loan firms have almost all their assets invested in real estate mortgages and loans to improve real property. These loans would not be very easily convertible if the economy and overall price structure had slipped badly. Then, too, the FSLIC, the insuring agency, has as even smaller percentage of money in the pot to meet its commitments than does the FDIC. Again, Congress and the United States Treasury can come to the rescue, up to a point, assuming they are willing and able. But here we run into the philosophical problem of national liquidity in the event of a severe economic collapse. Economists have gone crazy over that problem.

At this point I must pass, since it is probably against the law to cast doubts upon the ability of the FSLIC to meet its legal commitments under any eventuality. Your guess is as good as mine. I can say this, however: The FSLIC always has performed its duty when various savings and loan firms went under. A number of noninsured savings and loan firms have gone broke, so do make certain your shares and deposits are insured by the Federal instrumentality.

Some savings and loan associations are chartered by the Federal Government. Others are chartered by the states. As long as the firm has FSLIC insurance, whether it is state-chartered or not it receives some Federal auditing. But if you are worried about getting your money back in highly portentous times, pick your savings and loan association with care. Some of these firms operate much more safely and efficiently than others.

As to the liquidity and availability of your share-money in a savings and loan firm, your passbook is the key. It may state that you must give so many months' notice before demanding your money. Or the passbook may refer to the bylaws of the association, which specify the waiting period.

These waiting periods are seldom enforced, but they could be. And until a savings and loan firm has gone beyond the waiting period, it cannot be declared insolvent. And until it has been declared insolvent by some court, the FSLIC has no legal duty to reimburse shareholders.

I will admit these warnings are pretty far-fetched, but some persons want to know what would happen *if*, and the answers are so hard to come by that few people care to comment. But I do know that the Federal Home Loan Bank, which regulates Federal savings and loan firms, has been worried enough at various times to tighten certain lending rules. And I also know that a great deal of pressure has been applied by state agencies and the Federal authorities to keep dividend rates within reasonable limits.

One thing about savings and loan companies—they usually pay about the highest rate of return on savings. Some of them were paying 5¼ per cent in 1966. But a true "mutual association" cannot "promise" any specific dividend rate. It depends upon earnings, and can only be "anticipated" to the public.

In general, insured savings and loan firms are safe, liquid under normal circumstances, and they pay a high rate of return on savings and shares. My advice is to pick the safest one you can find, even if you must sacrifice a point or a fraction from the dividend rates. But savings and loan firms are not banks and you must keep the distinction in mind, from the standpoints of the diversity of investments, the liquidity factor, the relationship you have (creditor or part owner), and the nature of the insurance on your shares.

CREDIT UNIONS

Credit unions are more than just "mutuals"; they are more like co-ops, working for their members. They, too, have established a fine safety record. While some credit unions have failed, most savers have been rescued from serious losses. But here again, a saver becomes a "member-owner," not a creditor. And few credit unions have share insurance comparable to the FDIC or the FSLIC. Credit unions do bond their officers and managers, but that is not the same thing as share insurance. Dishonesty that results in a loss is not the same as failure because of unpredicted economic causes.

In time the share insurance idea may be adopted by credit unions in general, but until it is, a shareholder-saver should insist on adequate bonds for officers, efficiency of operation, and a reasonable degree of liquidity.

You should ask if there is any waiting period, which could be enforced if you need your money back in a hurry. Credit unions can be Federally chartered or state-chartered. In general, Federal charters mean closer auditing and tighter lending rules.

So far, credit union savings have been highly liquid and readily available to those members wanting to withdraw funds. But some credit unions have had to close when their industry sponsors failed or moved to new locations. Most credit unions are tied to particular companies, serving the employees of those firms. Remember, there is no share insurance in most cases, which puts a burden on a member-saver to take an active part in the operation of his credit union.

Rates paid to credit union saver-members have been fairly high, somewhat higher than banks and close to the dividend rates paid by savings and loan associations. Some credit unions have too much money, which often means low rates to both borrowers and savers. Others are always short of funds, and must compensate for the situation by paying quite high rates to attract savers. It all depends upon the particular credit union.

There are reasons besides interest rates to save at credit unions. These mutual savings institutions usually offer low-cost life insurance, as well as life insurance on loans and savings accounts. There are a number of other fringe benefits a credit union member can avail himself of, including free financial counseling in some cases.

GOVERNMENT SAVINGS BONDS

It is hard to beat Series E or H savings bonds when it comes to fixed-income savings. The interest rate is quite high—4.15 per cent as of this writing. There is no need to have share insurance or deposit insurance, since the Federal Government is *fully* behind each savings bond it issues. And the money is quite available.

You can acquire Series E bonds by having the money checked off your wages. Or you can buy them from a bank or the United States Treasury. You must hold a Series E bond for seven years to get the full 4.15 per cent interest. Series H bonds, however, pay out interest every six months, on the same sort of schedule; they are for persons needing a regular income.

On Series E bonds you can postpone declaring your interest until you cash them in. For some persons approaching retirement, when their incomes will be lower, that can be a tax advantage. Or you can convert Series E bonds to Series H bonds and postpone paying taxes on the interest that way.

From the standpoint of fixed-income, dollar-type savings, it is very hard, almost impossible, to beat Series E and H bonds. You have genuine safety, a high degree of availability, and a good return on your money. Furthermore, the Federal Government has made it convenient to buy these bonds.

You do have to hold a Series E bond for at least two months, and a Series H bond must be held for six months. Neither Series H nor E bonds are negotiable, and they cannot be pledged for loans. But they are registered and you can get your money back if you lose them; so keep track of your serial numbers.

LIFE INSURANCE SAVINGS

Many persons confine their savings programs to life insurance alone. The money in such cases would be very safe, at least with a well-run life insurance company. Most states require life insurance firms to stay very liquid by placing a high percentage of their funds in reserve. Also, state laws are strict regarding the type of investments allowed such firms.

As I indicated before, you can always borrow against your cash value (or surrender value) when you need money. You can turn in a life insurance policy for cash. So money saved with a life insurance company is usually highly liquid and available.

Earnings on your life insurance savings are a somewhat different matter. Your cash value doesn't actually draw interest. A certain anticipated interest rate on your savings is used to determine the premium charged. That rate is usually 3 to 4 per cent. The life insurance firm hopes to earn much more than that percentage, by investing your money, and it almost always does. If you have a "participating" policy, you will get some of the extra profits from dividends, and if you allow those dividends to build up, you may get paid interest on the dividends, but not on the overall cash value of your policy.

Of course, if you try to borrow on the cash value in a life insurance policy, without cashing the policy in, you will have to pay interest of 5 to 6 per cent. So the liquidity in a life insurance policy has a price upon it.

Thus, savings through the medium of life insurance is usually highly safe, quite liquid, and moderately profitable from the point of interest and dividends. The liquidity comes at a rather high cost, however, and you can beat the profit return at many institutions. But, to be fair, profit from savings is not the main— or even an important—feature of life insurance. The main point is the financial protection you would afford your heirs from the first moment your coverage went into effect. No other savings plan offers that. And because of the tax advantages in having money come to your heirs through life insurance plans, you are compensated for the other minor disadvantages.

MISCELLANEOUS SAVINGS PLANS

You could put your money in postal savings, but the return is so low that savings bonds are a better investment, with just as much safety and almost as much instant liquidity.

There are certain "thrift certificates" issued by private lenders, especially industrial loan firms, which carry a high rate of return. But these certificates carry no share insurance, and they may not be as liquid as represented. A "thrift and loan" firm is not the same as a savings and loan association.

You may buy corporation bonds, but until your wealth is quite substantial, my advice is to stick to Series E and H bonds if you want bonds at all. Remember, corporation bonds fluctuate in price.

You could purchase "municipals," the securities issued by various local and state authorities. These aren't taxed by the Federal Government, but until you get into the really high income brackets, you won't need the tax advantages of municipals, as I will show later.

Then there are real estate mortgages. These carry considerably more risk than the main savings plans already discussed. That is especially true of second mortgages or second "trust deeds," even though the rate of return promised is awfully tempting.

With a bit of luck you might make some big money dabbling around in the unconventional savings plans. Each such plan requires considerable checking into by investors. It is my contention that few persons can afford to do much gambling with their savings.

On the other hand, all savings plans involve some gambling; nothing is absolutely safe. It was not my intention to undermine confidence in either the FDIC or the FSLIC. They are the best techniques we have come up with to protect the life savings of ordinary citizens. Neither of the two agencies can afford to have one dollar on hand to insure each dollar of savings. Nevertheless, we citizens are entitled to a peek behind the scenes now and then, and even do a little auditing. It's our money they are insuring. I began revising this book during the middle of 1966, while witnessing the most fantastic interest-rate war of modern times. If all of our banks and savings and loan firms come through this period unscathed, I shall be terribly surprised.

It all started when the Federal Reserve Board hiked the "discount rate" in order to curb inflation caused by the war in Vietnam. Unfortunately, it came at a time when a number of savings and loan firms were caught with rather high mortgage delinquencies, plus a slow housing market. In a nutshell, the S & L's were feeling a pinch anyway, and despite rising foreclosures they couldn't unload their properties without losses, as well as a strain on their liquidity. Many of the commercial bankers admittedly disliked the saving and loan institutions anyway, and weren't a bit sorry to see them crowded to the wall.

It suddenly became very important for savings and loan associations to retain the savings they already had, and to maintain public confidence in order to prevent a "run." As bankers consistently raised their interest rates paid on savings accounts, the S & L's tried to stop them. The Federal Home Loan Bank threatened a loss of borrowing privileges to those S & L's exceeding the going rate of 4.85 per cent allowed in California.

This rate held for a while—until the banks went to 5 and 5½ per cent on certificates of deposit. Then the dam broke and S & L's first went to 5 per cent, then to 5½ on passbook accounts and to 5¾ on long-term certificates, a relatively new type of investment. A few S & L's promised to pay 6 per cent.

A certificate of deposit is simply a written promise to pay a specified sum of money, plus interest, to a saver provided the money is left on deposit for an agreed time. That time limit might be only ninety days, or six months, even three years. The longer the time, the higher the agreed interest rate. Bank certificates of deposit can be either "negotiable" or "nonnegotiable," depending on the agreement. But the savings and loan firms were not allowed to issue negotiable securities, which works to their disadvantage in an interest-rate war.

When the war over interest finally broke, the claims and counterclaims confused almost every potential investor. First the public was told about special "bonus" plans, because the S & L's were not allowed at that time to advertise their higher rates on certificates. The banks countered with equally puzzling commercial messages. Few savers understood the real meaning of certificates, which is a rather interesting story in itself.

Several years ago, when money was rather cheap and plentiful, corporations were embarrassed by all their idle cash. By law, a bank could not pay interest to a business firm on a "time deposit" or savings account. So the certificate of deposit came into general use as a means of getting around that legal restriction. A businessman finally could earn interest on his surplus funds, which he could "invest" at a bank for a short period of time—typically for six months. And since the banks could count on having that money on hand until their certificate-notes matured with no reserve requirements, it gave them greater freedom in lending. The banks therefore could afford to pay slightly higher interest rates on certificates than on passbook savings accounts, although not all of them did this for quite some time. Almost everyone was happy with the new arrangement.

The tight money situation changed everything. Some banks

dropped the semantic nonsense and issued "bank bonds." Others offered to issue certificates for as little as $50, payable in ninety days, in order to attract small savers. The original certificates of deposits aimed at business firms rarely were issued for less than $5000 and usually for much higher sums. The "C.D.'s" as the certificates were called, became a more familiar borrowing instrument to thousands of Americans by 1966.

As long as an individual held his cash investment at any one bank to not over $10,000, he had the same FDIC protection as any other small depositor. Even if his particular C.D.'s weren't fully negotiable, he could always borrow against them at his bank without much penalty, should he have need of cash before they matured. In mid-1966, when the interest war in California reached its greatest frenzy, a man with $10,000 had a number of baffling choices. He could obtain 4 per cent (the legal maximum) on a regular savings account at his favorite bank, subject only to the usual restrictions governing "time deposits." He could get 5¼ per cent at one of the nation's largest savings and loan institutions, on a regular passbook account, which also involved some little-known but very real withdrawal restrictions. He could get 5½ per cent on a bank certificate of deposit, at a number of small banks, provided he didn't mind having his money tied up for a year to eighteen months. And he could get 5¾ per cent if he invested at least $5000 in a giant savings and loan firm for at least three years.

So which route should he take? Did it matter that one bank was larger than another? Did it matter whether the particular institution was charted by the State on the one hand, or by the Federal Government on the other? How good was the FSLIC? Was one better than the other, and if so why and how? And as I have shown, these questions are not easily answered.

The Senate Banking Committee met in a closed meeting for several days during June of 1966, trying to work out some agreement between the bankers and the savings and loan officials. Just when it seemed a workable solution was in sight, the head of the U. S. Savings and Loan League demanded more concessions from the bankers, asking them to limit interest rates on C.D.'s of under $100,000 to 4½ per cent. The bankers refused and the committee adjourned, willing to let the chips fall where they might. As the July 1 deadline approached in 1966, speculation mounted. Would people juggle their savings accounts around to earn higher interest rates? Or would they prefer more safety and lower earnings? For that matter, where would money be absolutely safe during a period of strained national liquidity? Many investors simply withdrew money from both banks and savings and loan firms to put their cash under the mattress or in safety deposit boxes. A great deal of currency simply disappeared, further tightening the monetary situation.

It soon affected almost every phase of the national economy, all but the war spending. The statistics began to show a mixed trend. Auto sales declined. Housing starts (new construction) fell off sharply and so did new housing permits. Retail sales began to skid noticeably, although credit buying held up fairly well. The credit consumer is always the last to know what's going on. Federal officials alternated between warning of inflation on the one hand and hinting about a possible recession on the other. It was indeed a delicate balance. How it will all come out is left to the future; this book has a deadline.

Ordinarily, most readers would not be bothered with having to choose between passbook savings accounts and the more sophisticated certificates. Indeed, under normal or near-normal circumstances, a saver should expect to earn more interest (usually called dividends) at a savings and loan firm than at a bank. Banks have to hold back higher reserves than do the S & L's, whereas the latter are almost always *fully invested*. And because they are fully invested in *real estate*, which isn't very liquid during a crisis, they should pay higher interest rates to savers than should banks. Only during odd (or serious) times would these paradoxes happen, causing many a widow to sit up nights worrying.

Even under normal times, safety has a relative meaning. You always should measure money by its purchasing power, rather than by the fancy numbers on the bills. Getting back $10,000 after ten years, even at 6 per cent interest, isn't much of a bargain if the money has lost one-third of its purchasing power.

Regardless of how the tight money situation works itself out, inflation is the real demon of the future. This means that as your savings build up, you must place some of your bets on things other than dollar bills, in spite of the high interest rates and deposit insurance. It would be just as great a mistake to place all your money in safe, fixed-income "dollar" accounts as it would to sink your entire fortune in the stock market.

When you "save money" at a financial institution, you become a creditor of the firm; it simply "owes" you money. You have loaned money to the private financial institution. But as you get into "equities," common stocks and share arrangements (even at a mutual-type S & L), you become an "owner," with a some-what greater chance of losing money, because the law protects creditors ahead of owners.

It may sound odd that you must take "risks" in order to play it safe, but that's what it amounts to. It's more a question of courage than of being foolhardy, however, because it requires prudence and foresight to take proper risks.

HOW TO ACHIEVE GROWTH
AND HEDGE AGAINST INFLATION

Why cash money isn't everything

We now have a monetary system based mostly on paper, with the paper money being backed by gold and bankable securities. Only 25 per cent of the backing is gold. Since the rest of the backing is "commercial paper" held by our banks, you can see what a large role paper plays in our currency setup.

In general, paper money is only as good as the faith people have in it. We keep paper money passing around pretty fast these days, since it is downright silly to hoard it. That tends to keep prices moving up, resulting in inflation. The conventional type of inflation comes from too many dollars chasing a shortage of goods.

We certainly don't have exactly that kind of inflation in this country, not with our tremendous supply of products and commodities. We have a sort of engineered inflation. It comes from a number of causes:

a. Easy credit is one of the causes, because it creates purchasing power without actually putting more dollars in circulation. Much of this stems from the money pyramid the Federal Government created by using only twenty-five cents in gold to back each dollar in currency, and by borrowing from our Reserve Banks on IOUs. The banks then use the Federal IOUs as a base for making even more loans.

But private lenders have helped create additional buying power, too, through easy credit policies. Even checking accounts are a means of increasing the purchasing power of a fixed supply of money without resorting to the printing presses. Modern methods of banking have increased the velocity of exchange, too—the speed with which money gets around to buy things.

b. Many of our largest industries are dominated by a few giant corporations. These industries seem able to raise prices from time to time, without the limiting effect of unrestrained competition. And some unions have helped to feed the inflationary fires by raising the cost of labor in excess of the rate of increased productivity.

The Federal Government recognizes the inflationary effects of the wage-price spiral, but has been unwilling, in our type of society, to fix wages or prices. We believe in free competition and pricing.

c. Inflation does seem to help some people—those heavily in debt. It reduces the effect of a debt by making the debt repayable with cheap, easier-to-come-by dollars. In our economy, all debts are expressed in terms of dollars, not purchasing power, although at one time, back in 1933, many debts were repayable in terms of the value of gold. We knocked out the "gold clause" qualification back in 1934, and since then debts have been payable in terms of paper money, legal tender, regardless of what the money would buy.

But many politicians cater to the masses, the debtor class, so to speak. And it is historically popular to cheapen paper money in order to reduce the punishment of being in debt. Sometimes this is justified, in my opinion, to ward off depression and prevent social trouble.

Those are the reasons why *paper money* isn't everything. And it goes to show why a person of any substance must place a certain number of his bets on long-lived "things" rather than just on paper. We likely will have more inflation in the future, even if it's only gradual and virtually painless. This is a credit economy and it isn't likely to change. Nor is it likely that giant corporations and giant labor unions will be considerate enough of the public interest to keep a tight rein on wages or labor costs. And there certainly isn't much chance that politicians will refrain from trying to cure poverty or economic inequities by cheapening the currency. Not that inflation really helps those who stay chronically and heavily in debt. Both prices and interest rates keep going higher and higher to offset a debased currency. But the people in debt *think* they are being helped and that is what makes for votes.

Many persons wish they could get their hands on gold, but that privilege was taken away back in 1934, too, except for coin collectors; and just recently, the Federal Government removed the silver backing from most of our currency. Gold and silver coins are valuable in themselves, because the metals in the coins are useful, portable, scarce, and desired by humans.

All we can do is try to compensate for the inevitable by investing in assets that tend to gain in dollar price as the dollar itself loses purchasing power. Common stocks are one of those things; they tend, as a group, to rise in dollar value during inflation—not always, but usually. Common stocks represent ownership in things of value; that's why they are called "equities." Those things of value may be land, plant equipment, inventories of products, or simply earning power from services rendered to people.

Common stocks

EXPLANATIONS AND DEFINITIONS

When you purchase a share of stock, you get a certificate indicating your share of ownership in the particular corporation. Only corporations issue shares of stock; partnerships and proprietorships don't have stock issues.

There are two main types of stock, too—common and preferred. While there are mixtures of the two types, as a general rule common stock indicates the real ownership, with voting rights along with the chances for big profits or big losses. A preferred stock is a cross between a common stock and a bond, and it usually carries a fixed rate of dividend. But a preferred stockholder does get a better break than a common stockholder if a corporation fails. So does a bondholder, since he is a creditor of the corporation, not an owner. Ownership assumes the most risk, because it makes the most profit. So the holder of common stock carries the most risk, but has a greater chance for profit, has more say in management, and represents the only true securities-type hedge against inflation.

WHERE TO BUY STOCKS

You buy common stocks through broker-dealers—stockbrokers, in other words. These brokers in turn buy their securities through the various exchanges, of which they are members. There are only two big national exchanges, the New York Stock Exchange and the American Exchange, but there are a number of regional exchanges around the country. A beginner in the stock market ought to stick to stocks listed on the two main exchanges. The New York Exchange is the most tightly regulated and offers the most protection to the general public. Regional exchanges, as of this writing, offer more chances of wheeling and dealing by members. But tighter regulations may be coming.

Many stocks are sold "over the counter," which means they aren't listed on the exchanges. For both tax and privacy reasons, some financial institutions, including banks and insurance companies, prefer to sell their shares over the counter. Some of these shares are fine buys, but most persons would be wise to stick with stocks listed on the big exchanges, making certain they are buying under true market conditions, and that the stocks can be quickly liquidated if needed. Listed stocks must provide detailed financial information. There is a bit of razzle-dazzle in trading over the counter and too many opportunities to manipulate prices.

The important thing is to pick a reputable brokerage house which belongs to the big exchanges. Also make sure the individual broker, or customer's man, assigned to you merits your confidence and trust. No two brokerage firms operate exactly alike. They have differing rules on conflict of interest, personal holdings, and selling methods. Ask a friend experienced in stock dealing, or a banker, for a recommendation. Most of the large brokers have branches over the country.

WHAT YOU NEED FROM COMMON STOCKS

As I mentioned, one virtue of common stocks is that they tend to rise in dollar price as inflation goes on. Not all stocks do this, but most of the good ones do, at least over a considerable period of time.

But aside from that, you want your stocks to be marketable. You want to be able to sell them for their current price. Stocks listed on the exchanges can be quickly marketed.

You want a good rate of return on your money, too. Bear in mind that corporations are in business to make money. As a stockholder you would share in any profits. But "earnings" are not the same as "yield." Most corporations keep 30 to 40 per cent of what they earn in net profits in order to expand, retire debts, buy other companies, or just grow. So while the yield you might get from a stock would correspond roughly to interest and dividends from other investments, it is not the only profit you might make. A corporation might earn 9 per cent after taxes and pay out only 6 per cent to its stockholders. In such a case, the corporation would be retaining one-third of its profits for specific reasons. Those reasons could easily result in your share being worth more on the market, sooner or later. Don't confuse the yield with the earnings.

In fact, the true "growth" corporations pay very little in dividends; they retain all or most all of their profits in order to get larger. A company might act like a growth company, even call itself by that name, without actually being one in the true meaning of the word. A growth company is usually one closely related to natural resources, utilities, and technological developments that virtually insure its growth as the population increases. A "glamour" company, on the other hand, may be far more speculative in nature than one tied to products and services with a bright future. Many persons confuse the two types. A so-called glamour stock may be appealing simply because it is new on the market, or because it has a fancy, growth-sounding name.

Which brings up the question of speculation. The main difference between speculating and investing can be put in this way: An investor concentrates on income and the safety of his money. The speculator wants higher profits from taking extra risks. It is impossible to draw a clear-cut distinction; nevertheless, most of us would be wise to buy stocks with investment in mind. Leave the speculation to the professionals.

In general, buying stocks should be a long-range proposition. Getting in and out of the market, or switching stocks frequently, is too costly for small investors. The big boys can do it because they buy in large enough quantities to warrant low commissions. Small orders for stocks, say less than one hundred shares of a particular stock, can cost up to 6 per cent in commissions. Go into stock buying with the long run in mind, until you get big enough to afford otherwise.

WARNINGS

To be really professional about buying stocks, you would need to spend years just learning the business. You would have to have a decent understanding of such sophisticated subjects as the future of certain industries, the status of particular firms in those industries, the capabilities of management teams, profit to sales ratios, current assets to current liabilities ratios, cash flow considerations, and price-earnings ratios. Few of us can become market analysts. For that reason alone, one investment adviser claims a person shouldn't fool around in the stock market unless he can raise at least $75,000 and be willing to lose it.

On the other hand, some staunch defenders of the capitalistic system want all of us to own some stock, to bring about a "people's capitalism." Neither of these viewpoints is quite realistic in my opinion. I contend that most of us can afford to own shares of common stocks and that we ought to try. But I doubt if enough people ever own stocks to warrant changing the name of our economic system.

Here are a few sound rules to follow as you begin to buy stocks:

1. Make certain you have a decent life insurance program, one meeting your immediate and foreseeable needs.

2. Have at least two or three months of income saved in some safe institution, and keep that money aside from any stock investing.

3. Pick the best and most reputable brokerage house you can find.

4. Avoid speculating. Concentrate on income and safety, with good chance for growth—capital appreciation.

5. Dodge the "high flyers," the glamour stocks. Stick to proven, conservative corporations—the so-called "blue chips."

It may be easier to state which stocks *not* to buy than which ones to buy. Don't rely on hot tips and rumors. Even a market letter may be tied in with some firm touting a particular stock issue. Also keep in mind that broker-dealers often "make markets" in certain stocks. In other words, it is their jobs to push these stocks. You should ask about that if you are advised to buy a share in some company. Sometimes the most questionable tips come from the financial pages, which often print what are merely press releases from financial public relations firms.

All in all, your best bet is to take advice from a reliable broker who isn't pushing any one stock because he makes an unusual or personal profit from doing so. The stock market as it operates today is a weird mixture of what might seem "conflict of interest" to some persons and downright lack of ethics to others. On some small, regional exchanges, a broker may be wearing four hats at the same time. He may be buying and selling for his clients, buying and selling for himself, trying to stabilize certain stocks, and making an extra profit off odd-lot sales, those under one hundred shares. Perhaps he can be blamed for forgetting now and then who is paying him. But our Securities and Exchange Commission has been pushing for changes; and in the future, buying shares of stocks ought to be less dangerous for little guys.

As a rule, you'd be safe buying shares in firms you know, those with names that ring a bell, and that stick in your memory. To put it another way, not many large, long-established companies have failed over the past fifteen years. They may be merged, bought up, and go through slack earning periods, but over the long haul they offer a good chance for profits with safety. And in general, huge corporations manage to find ways to increase their prices when dollars cheapen. That means a new price structure and higher per share stock values; in other words, a hedge against inflation.

HOW TO BUY STOCKS ON MONTHLY PLANS

One way to buy stocks is to walk into a broker's office with $1000 or so and select your stock. Another way is through monthly accumulation. Members of the New York Stock Exchange have a plan known as the M.I.P., or Monthly Investment Plan. In that way you can add to your stock portfolio each month by mailing in $100 or more.

One advantage to this monthly accumulation plan has to do with "dollar cost averaging." Each month you would be buying the same stock at different prices. The first month you might pay $22 a share. The next month it might be $24. Several months later, the stock may have slipped, costing you only $21 a share. That would hurt your present portfolio, but it might bring you extra profits over the long run, for this reason: Historically the market tends to go up, just as historically the dollar loses value. If during your accumulation plan you are able to pick up some shares of stock at depressed prices, you should eventually show a greater profit on your overall net investment. It usually works out that way.

But the M.I.P. has some disadvantages, too. Buying in odd lots, small orders, is more costly than buying in large lots. M.I.P.'s carry commissions of about 6 per cent on $100-a-month plans. Another problem is the lack of diversification. All your shares would be in the same firm on a single M.I.P. If you want to spread your investments around, you would have to set up more than one monthly investment plan, unless you acquire shares in a closed-end fund, which I will discuss in more detail later.

A third way to acquire stocks is through investment clubs. You can get together with a dozen or so friends and purchase stocks as a group, either as an association or as a corporation. You may not get rich this way, but you should learn a great deal about stocks and have some social enjoyment at the same time. Under the club plan, each member puts in $10 or more each month, to be invested in jointly held stocks and other securities. A good book on this subject is *The Investment Club Way to Stock Market Success* by Helen McLane and Patricia Hutar (Dolphin Books, Garden City, New York). Or you can write for information to the National Association of Investment Clubs, 1300 Washington Boulevard Building, Detroit 31, Michigan.

But an increasingly popular way to purchase stocks is through specialized investment companies, commonly known as mutual funds. They are important enough today to warrant detailed consideration.

Mutual funds

WHAT A MUTUAL FUND IS

A so-called mutual fund is an investment company. In other words, instead of offering specific products or services to the public, an investment company buys and sells securities of other corporations. You might think of a mutual fund as a sort of an investment club that hires professional management. However, a mutual fund has thousands of members, instead of about a dozen. Moreover, the "mutual ownership" idea has been stretched to the very limit. Most shareholders in mutual funds take little interest in management or the investments. But this is the case with most mutuals. Investment companies of this kind hire professional investment advisers to buy and sell the securities needed to make up a portfolio. There usually is a sponsoring organization behind the mutual fund, which may or may not have some other interest in the fund. A bank is appointed to be custodian of the money and securities on hand.

Some funds sell their shares to the public through their own sales organizations, which may be tied in some way with the sponsor, or the investment advisory team, or both. At one time, mutual funds were rather similar in their operating procedures. Now there are so many funds on the market (well over three hundred) that it is getting almost as hard to pick a fund as it is to pick a single share of stock.

TYPES OF FUNDS

The most important distinction you should make between the various investment companies is this: Some are "open-end," meaning they will accept all the cash offered by share buyers, invest the money, and stand ready to redeem the shares for cash at market value. The market value of a single share at any one time would depend upon the combined market value of all the cash and securities held by the fund, divided by the number of shares outstanding.

The opposite of the "open-end" fund is the "closed-end" fund. Closed-end funds have only so many shares outstanding, just as other corporations have limited shares of stock issued. The way to buy a share in this type of fund is to offer the going market price to a person already owning a share. You do that by contacting a stockbroker, just as you would do to buy shares in a regular corporation. In general, the closed-end funds are for sophisticated buyers, who take a fairly active interest in management and investment policies. Most persons come in contact with the open-end funds, so we will discuss that type primarily.

There are a number of ways to classify open-end mutual funds. One is by defining their general objectives. Some aim primarily at *income*, others strive for *balance*, and still others stress *growth* or capital gain.

Another way to classify the funds is by industry specialization. Some funds put all their money in electronics firms, others concentrate on insurance companies, and still others put their money in land.

Then there is the matter of aggressiveness. Some funds take substantial risks. Others play it quite cool. Some funds churn their securities holdings over almost constantly, while other funds sit on the same stocks and bonds for years at a time. Some funds are highly promotional, using what amounts to "hard sell" tactics to attract shareholders and plenty of cash. The reason is, the sales organization earns more in commissions that way, and the management advisory team earns more, too, since it is paid according to the value of the assets managed.

On the other hand, some of the older funds sell only through regular broker-dealers, aiming most of their promotional material at the brokers themselves. That makes this comment necessary: The size of a fund is no valid indication of its worth to you. Many a fund owes its success to how well it "merchandises" shares, not to how much profit it makes for its shareholders. Some fund salesmen are real "pushers." If they weren't selling fund shares, they might be peddling overpriced siding or used cars. And some fund shares are quite expensive to buy.

THE COST

Some funds cost nothing to buy, although there may be a small charge when you sell. These are called no-load funds. Others cost up to 10 per cent of the value of the money invested without a selling fee. Eight per cent is a rather typical commission (load) that you might pay for a small amount of shares in a mutual fund. To give an example, if you invested $2000 in a fund, you likely would pay $160 in commissions, leaving only $1840 working for you. On larger purchases the commissions often are lower.

It is the "load charge" that results in much criticism of the fund theory. Broker commissions on regular stock purchases run from about 6 per cent to only a fraction of 1 per cent, much lower than the typical 8 per cent charged by funds. And even if you buy a no-load fund, you must face the realization that the fund may be connected with a brokerage firm which makes a profit selling securities to the fund.

Original cost itself is no adequate guide for buying shares in funds, as I will show later. Overall result is what really counts. But it is safe to say that you should be skeptical of any fund with a very high load charge. The fund's main emphasis may be in selling its shares rather than in making a good profit for you.

Some of the costs of owning fund shares are hidden from general view. While management may ask only one-half of 1 per cent of the assets as its annual fee, other costs of operation come on top of that. The advisers may be engaged in too much buying and selling, thereby paying high brokerage fees to a broker affiliate. The fund may be running up unnecessary bookkeeping expenses. The more churning there is, the more the other expenses tend to mount. Some funds have kept the same securities for years and have managed to show fine results. Don't be too overwhelmed by "constant management." To be sure, a fund should keep on top of the market situation, but activity alone isn't necessarily progress.

You should be cost-conscious about any fund, and not just from the angle of original acquisition. But there is one cost factor you particularly need to watch. That has to do with the "front-end" load under the so-called "contractual" plans.

Under contractual plans you agree, in a general, not really binding sort of way, to invest so much money in shares over a period of, say, ten years. What you really agree to is to allow the sales organization to collect about one-half of the full ten years' commissions during the first year. To give an example, you might agree to invest $10,000 over a ten-year period, usually in monthly payments. If the commission schedule of that particular fund were 8 per cent, you would pay about $400 in sales commissions in the first year, out of the first $1000 you invested.

Some states, including California, have outlawed the front-end load. In such states the commissions can be collected only as a percentage of the money invested, as it comes in. But many states still allow these contractual arrangements.

Funds defend the contractual plans in this way: They say they are necessary to attract good salesmen, and that if investors will just stick to their plans, the original load will be eventually offset by high profits. This may be true, except that human nature being what it is, many persons drop their plans at great expense to themselves. Just be certain what you are getting into.

THE ADVANTAGES OF FUNDS

The main advantage of buying fund shares is diversification of investment. Since most funds invest in from fifty to one hundred different stocks or bonds, the risk of losing money is kept to a minimum. Few small investors can afford to buy enough stocks to diversify in any other way.

Fund shares do go up and down. Taken as an average, fund shares tend to follow the various market indexes quite closely. But fund shares are far more stable than the shares in almost any one corporation. The big factor in mutual funds is that of protecting small investors from losing their shirts on one or two stocks.

Then there is the advantage of professional management. Funds hire supposedly skilled investment teams to follow the market trends and to do the actual investing. How much this is worth to any one fund-buyer depends on the skill of those advisers hired by his fund.

There is one big tax advantage, too. Capital gains from investment companies get the best capital gains treatment. It isn't necessary for a fund to hang onto a security for a long period in order to give its shareholders the 25 per cent tax break.

Most funds offer a multitude of privileges to shareholders. Some funds allow shareholders to switch to other affiliated funds without extra charge. Life insurance plans may be offered along with fund purchases. Paid-up fund plans in some cases can be converted to monthly income arrangements, or switched to annuities. Dividends can be reinvested without cost. A purchaser should always check the total charge for such extra features and not take them for granted.

There are even some "exchange funds" which allow persons with large profits in one or two stocks to trade their securities for fund shares, without immediately paying high taxes on the profits. But under current tax laws, this must be done when the exchange fund is first formed.

The theory behind mutual funds is excellent. It reduces the risk of loss through diversification. It provides professional advice and management. It provides a means of stock accumulation for persons on modest incomes. But there are some possible disadvantages inherent in the mutual fund idea, as it has developed in the country.

DISADVANTAGES

Mutual funds, like most life insurance, are usually "sold," not "bought." Most persons who buy mutual funds are persuaded into the move; they rarely go seeking shares. Nothing wrong with that, except that too much of the selling is of the "suede shoe" variety. The salesmen come armed with elaborate charts showing theoretical performances of their funds. Too many prospects don't listen when a salesman softly warns them that the future performance of his fund won't be exactly the same as in the past. The chart looks very much like a promise.

Sometimes prospects fail to understand the costs, the operating expenses, and the potential dangers of buying funds. Mutual funds are not the be-all and end-all of investing; they are only one tool. Some mutual funds have been mismanaged. A few have suffered fraud from officers. And some have established very mediocre records in view of the commissions and fees charged. A novice investor would be wise to accept a few tips on funds buying.

GENERAL TIPS

The word "growth" has been overworked in investment circles. A number of so-called growth-type funds fared less well than their affiliated balance-type (conservative) funds over the past few years. The truth is, growth is too often confused with speculation and outright gambling. Most newcomers to mutual fund-buying would be wise, in my opinion, to pick balanced, well-managed funds, because in that way they are likely to get more stability. They not only get shares that tend to go up during boom and inflationary times; they also get some protection that the bottom won't fall out of a fund when the general market takes a tumble. This is called "downside protection."

There are a number of publications which show the performance records of the various funds over the years. *Fundscope* is one of those publications. You can ask any stockbroker for the names of other publications that compare funds.

As I mentioned earlier, the size of a fund is no sure indication of its future performance. For various reasons some stockbrokers refuse to push mutual fund shares, but a good broker can tell you which funds are the safest and most likely to earn a profit.

Avoid the "front-load" commission on the "contractual" plans unless you thoroughly understand the arrangements and feel you need that kind of a potential punishment to keep you paying regularly. You can buy a number of good funds on monthly payments without paying commissions in advance on shares you haven't purchased.

Whatever fund you choose, if you choose any, take a long-range point of view; think in terms of ten years or more. It usually is too expensive and too difficult to switch funds every so often. Don't panic if your shares drop in value. That may be the time to buy even more.

Above all, deal only with reputable fund organizations. Talk to your friends and to knowledgeable persons about the various funds.

How laws protect securities buyers

You have three basic types of protection when buying "equities" in stocks, funds, and other securities. The Federal Government provides some protection through the regulation of the Securities and Exchange Commission. But the laws promoted by that agency just barely seep down to the consumer level. Corporations must file certain reports and samples of their advertising before selling stock. The SEC also promotes certain rules regulating the exchanges. But, by and large, the stock market has been a Big Man's game up until fairly recently. Businessmen don't want much government interference in commerce. But now that pension funds, labor unions, universities, and about eighteen million individuals are getting into the market, Federal laws may become tighter.

The states also attempt to control stock selling to some extent, through state securities commissions and under so-called Blue

Sky laws. For the most part, state laws try to stop absolute fraud and deceit. These laws aren't aimed at weasel words, the hard sell, poor management, or conflict of interest.

Most of the protection afforded the stock-buying public today comes from the securities industry itself. Each exchange has its own set of rules. The brokers themselves try to keep a close watch on their salesmen and representatives. And most dealers also belong to a watchdog organization called the National Association of Securities Dealers, or NASD.

Most of our protection comes from what the industry itself sets up to ward off what it considers fraud, lack of ethics, and double-dealing. As a shareholder, you will likely have to use the courts if you feel unjustly treated by management of the company you have invested in, whether that be an ordinary corporation or a mutual fund investment company.

You must face the fact that when you get into the securities market, you will be playing with the Big Boys. To do this successfully, you need a Big Boy or two on your side, working for you. By that I mean a broker who is sophisticated about the market, understands the risks, has access to inside information, and is willing to service your account honestly and frequently.

Variable annuities

A variable annuity is one in which some of the cash has been invested in common stocks. Regular annuities are "dollar" plans, guaranteeing to pay the annuity owner a fixed number of dollars for specific periods of time, regardless of what the dollars will buy.

A few life insurance companies are now offering variable annuities that tend to guard against inflation and cheap dollars. The problem has been that by the time a retired person started receiving his monthly annuity check, the cost of living had gone so high that the monthly income seemed quite small. Annuity purchasers usually buy their annuities with hard-earned dollars, when the dollars bring a great deal. But by the time they receive the benefits, the money won't buy as much. Variable annuities would pay the number of dollars needed to adjust for changes in the cost of living.

As I said, some life insurance firms are offering variable annuities which should help correct the injustices. But because of legal quibbling over how many agencies should police the variable annuity business—insurance commissions or securities commissions—the offering of this kind of annuity is more or less at a standstill. Until the legal wrangling is worked out, most of us will have to wait to get the greatest benefits of the variable annuities, even though the variable annuities principle has long been accepted in European investment circles. And, after all, a number of mutual funds are now combining life insurance with "equity-type" shares to achieve somewhat the same effect as the variable annuities. I'll discuss the variable annuity in more detail in the section on planning for retirement.

HOW MUCH IN EACH TYPE OF INVESTMENT?

Remember what comes first

I have tried to show what security really means, from a philosophical and practical standpoint. And I have tried to show how much we pay in taxes in order to feel secure, sometimes without attaining the most important goals.

Then I have attempted to impress you with the need for a balanced insurance program. You should take out enough life insurance, medical insurance, and casualty insurance to protect you and your family from financial setbacks.

I gave a nod to the intangibles that make for security, including genuine self-improvement, religious or philosophical faith, and recreation. There was a warning against concentrating on short-lived consumer goods to achieve security and prestige.

Next I stressed the need for safe, liquid cash savings—the emergency fund, in other words. And finally, I warned against putting all your eggs in the same basket. The section on stocks and land showed how to hedge against inflation and how to balance an investment program.

So let's suppose you've reached the point where you want to begin a savings and investment program. You may be wondering how much money to place in the fixed-dollar-type programs and how much to invest in the "equities," the stocks and mutual funds. We will discuss that problem from the vantage of whether or not you own a home, how much money you owe in debts—including a home mortgage, your total net worth, and your age.

How to figure a home into an investment program

A house and lot is a type of "equity" investment, just as common stocks are. But more than that, a home is a form of shelter, substituting for having to rent another home or an apartment. So you must measure your home investment in two ways.

I discussed the costs of home ownership earlier in the book, showing that owning a home is a measurable expense, depending upon the "rental value" of the house. That is the proper way to think of the expense of your home. But the land itself, usually about 20 per cent of the total valuation today, is a type of investment too. If your home is sitting on $10,000 worth of land, you have a $10,000 equity-type investment, one likely to rise in value as the dollar loses purchasing power. In fact, owning a little land is the means whereby most middle-income families manage to stay even with the effect of cheaper dollars.

So if you own a house and lot, you could safely concentrate on fixed-dollar-type savings plans until the total amount of your cash equals the approximate value of your lot (excluding the home valuation). That means that if your lot were worth $10,-000, you would be wise to build up savings in such places as banks, savings and loan firms, credit unions, etc., until they total $10,000, too. After that, you could consider buying some stocks and mutual funds.

If the economy fell into bad times, rather serious times, your land probably would drop in value, as would the market price of your home itself. But if you picked safe, insured places in which to save your money, the increased buying power of your cash might offset any loss from the value drop in your homestead.

At least you would have made a conscientious effort to protect yourself from both inflation (cheap dollars) and deflation (dear dollars). And in the meantime you would be in a highly liquid position, earning interest on your savings.

What about your debts?

It is foolish to even contemplate a big savings plan if you owe much money on short-term, consumer debts. Why try to earn 4 per cent on a savings account, other than on a small emergency fund, when you are paying from 12 per cent up to 24 per cent to private lenders?

If you are using only convenience credit, charge accounts, and month-to-month credit card arrangements, that is a different matter. But if you are financing a car, buying durable goods on time payments, or struggling to pay off a consolidation loan, get rid of any such debts before you undertake any big savings and investment program. The money you channel toward *debt retirement* will earn you more money than almost any investment you could find. Look at it this way: You can't get ahead borrowing money at high rates from consumer credit agencies in order to invest in savings plans and stocks. No sensible person would even try.

The mortgage on a home presents a somewhat different problem. Some investment advisers feel you should overlook a home mortgage in an investment program. They point out that the interest is tax-deductible and that if you weren't buying a home on mortgage, you'd be renting a place to live. Furthermore, a mortgage is a hedge against inflation, since you would repay the money with cheap dollars.

On the other hand, the interest rate on your mortgage may be the determining factor. If you were paying only 5 per cent interest, it might be profitable to leave the mortgage as is, making only the regular monthly payments, while entering into an investment program. As long as you can earn better than the 5 per cent from other investments, you would be money ahead. All you would be doing is borrowing from the mortgage company to invest the money at a profit.

But if you were paying 6 or 7 per cent on your home mortgage, you might be hard put to top that rate on any kind of a safe investment. My advice is: If you are paying over 5½ per cent on your home mortgage, aim your investment program at paying off the lien. To be sure, the interest is deductible from your gross income, but the profit you earn from other investments is taxable, too, and at the identical rate, except for minor exceptions and exclusions.

If you *save* 15 per cent of your possible income taxes by paying interest on your home mortgage, you would also *pay* an extra 15 per cent in taxes on your investment income. It balances out.

And while a mortgage is a hedge against cheap dollars, so is your homestead, even after it's paid for. A high-priced mortgage is a costly hedge against inflation. Consider your home mortgage carefully before saving and investing any extra income, aside from your small emergency fund.

In general, you would be wise to get rid of *all* high-cost debts before trying to spread your savings around.

Your total net worth is a factor

As you accumulate assets, the problem is how to spread the risk. The smaller the amount of money to be invested, the greater the need to keep it safe and liquid. So a person with only a few thousand dollars wouldn't go far wrong in concentrating almost entirely in safe, fixed-dollar plans.

Were you to add up all your assets with marketable value and then subtract all your debts, you would arrive at your "net worth." If that net worth were over $10,000, you should begin to diversify, spread your risk more, and hedge against the changing value of our currency.

If half the net worth were in land and half in cash savings, you would be in fairly good shape, as I showed before. You could continue with fixed-dollar plans until they totaled about $10,000, and then begin to buy stocks or mutual funds. But if the money were all in savings plans now, without any land involved, you should immediately begin to diversify.

You might aim at eventually arriving at a balance such as the following, by the time you are forty years old or more. This is only an example:

> $20,000 in fixed-dollar plans
> $35,000 in equities
> $10,000 in land (your housing land)
> ――――――――――
> $65,000 total

The point is, as your worth increases, you need to concentrate more on equities, less on safe, cash savings, or fixed-dollar plans. In the example above, the $20,000 in fixed dollars could be a combination of bank savings, life insurance cash value, and savings bonds—in fact, a combination of any or all of the ones I discussed under fixed-income dollar plans. The equities could be a mixture of common stocks, common stock investment companies, and bonds or preferred stocks with a certain risk element.

The $10,000 in land could be the equity in your home instead, if you felt your mortgage was sufficiently low-cost to leave alone.

In booming times, it is usually wise to have about 60 per cent or more of your total investment package in equities, and only 40 per cent or less in fixed dollars. But the 60 per cent in equities needs to be diversified, too. One or two common stocks would not fill the bill in the $35,000 example. If you can't buy at least ten good stocks in different industries, place your money in the good stocks of a mutual fund instead.

If we seem headed for a slow period, you might be wise to switch your investment package the other way around, placing 50 or 60 per cent of your cash in safe, insured savings plans. The rest you could leave in equities.

Some economic specialists advise against leaving much cash in so-called safe, fixed-dollar plans. These economists are quite inflation-minded. Instead of $20,000 as I suggested in the example, they might recommend only $15,000 or even $10,000. Furthermore, they might urge you to include some short-term corporate bonds under that category. You won't get the same advice from any two persons.

But with banks paying 4 per cent on savings as of this writing, and savings and loan firms paying even more, some of the damaging effects of inflation are offset. And as of this writing, common stocks are extremely high priced in relation to their earnings. As conditions change, investment arrangements should be changed, too.

From the standpoint of the middle-income person, the trouble with getting advice from financial experts is that most of them serve particular industries. A stockbroker would lean heavily to stock purchases. A banker naturally wants you to keep your money at his bank.

But there are new developments that may help. Some banks are now offering "pooled investment plans," in which some of the money goes into securities. A few banks offer services under the Keogh bill, which allows self-employed persons to set up tax-free retirement plans.

Some mutual funds offer balanced investment programs. And I already mentioned the variable annuity policies which are bound to come into greater popularity sooner or later.

It costs less to invest money on your own, without professional advice and management. That is why I offered some general thoughts on the subject. But managing a substantial sum of money is a tough job at best. Even the most competent persons worry a great deal when they undertake managing and supervising their wealth. In my opinion, it pays to hire honest professionals, even if you do have to pay them.

SPECIAL SITUATION: THE SINGLE, WORKING WOMAN

It used to puzzle me that so many single women considered their financial situations as unique, simply because they were women. After all, women have the same basic economic needs as men have, with somewhat less responsibilities in most cases. Unless, of course, there are the added complications of caring for a dependent relative or a child. Under the heading "single," I am attempting to include the widowed, the divorced, and those women who are acting as "head of households," as the tax people say.

As a reaction to my newspaper column, I often receive letters such as the following:

"Dear Mr. Neal. I've been reading your articles for some time and feel sure that many families must have profited from them. But why don't you aim more of your advice to the single, working woman? There are many of us who could use some practical advice, both in managing what we earn, and in investing what we've managed to save."

It is somewhat presumptuous for a married man to dish up sage advice to single members of the opposite sex, even though an unattached, employed female is lumped in with all the "economic unit" figures compiled by the sexless U. S. Bureau of Labor Statistics. Women do have different psychological and emotional needs than men do, and in spite of all the talk about equality and economic individualism, most women resent being completely on their own. Perhaps subconsciously many career women are afraid of complete financial independence, thinking that it might shatter their receptiveness to a happy marriage, or that it might frighten away the most desirable men.

Could be, but I doubt it. Or to state it in another way, money in the bank need not make a woman unfeminine nor would it scare away any man with a reasonable degree of self-confidence. Perhaps too, their feeling of "being put upon" and of being handicapped makes single women so susceptible to mass advertising of a questionable nature. Each and every ad seems to be aimed especially at her, since it understands her loneliness, her longings, and her possibly drab existence.

What I have written on income management, credit, and spending applies almost equally to single persons as to married couples. Nevertheless, I shall cover briefly what often proves to be the stumbling blocks for the working girl. I shall simply say this or that choice is best—or better, leave it up to the reader to refer back to previous chapters for alternatives or more precise definitions. I don't want to be accused of advising women what to do with money, without having offered a few thoughts on how to acquire it in the first place.

The first step, of course, is to make the paycheck stretch as far as possible, whether the ultimate goal is wedlock or blissful singlehood. For the young, gregarious secretary, or whatever her job, this sort of discipline can be all but stifling. To her it may be far more important to be well dressed, finely transported, stylishly coiffured, etc., than to have cash in the bank. She naturally feels she is investing in her future by grooming her image. Maybe so, and I'm certainly not advocating drabness and utter austerity as a way of life. I'm simply saying that even grooming ought to come from what's left of the paycheck after a few dollars have been deducted for savings. That is why a spending plan is *essential*, even for an underpaid, overworked wage slave, as some women are, of course. I also wish to reiterate that a person can live *almost* as well on 90 to 95 per cent of his or her income, as on the full 100 per cent—far better in the long run.

Shelter

A single woman usually has many choices open to her under the category of shelter. A few younger women can live at home with parents. Apartments can be shared with other working girls. Or, it is often possible to pay for low-cost room and board at a private home, or at a YWCA. The main ingredient lacking in all of those arrangements is privacy, a very important consideration. Nevertheless, whether the net income is $300 per month or $700 per month, if over one-fourth of the net income goes for shelter (including utilities), some other item in the budget will take a real beating. It's the same old story of what a person wants the most out of life, privacy at home, or perhaps better clothing, even a new automobile. The working woman who steadfastly refuses to share her living quarters, or to suffer the indignities of group living, makes sense, as long as she realizes what she may have to give up in other categories of spending. Furthermore, a sacrifice in the "shelter" part of living can be only temporary, to save up those first precious dollars, not a permanent way of life.

What about the groceries?

This is not a book on health or cooking, but it's no secret that many young women become skilled office workers and technicians long before they learn how to boil an egg or recognize a vitamin. Some girls will spend hours preening their exteriors without complaint, but when it comes to scrambling an egg or planning a menu, a gooey pastry washed down with a cola drink will do nicely, thank you. So except for the practicing home economists, who know far more about nutrients than I do, not many young working girls are receptive to advice on the food budget. The point is, a working woman can save money on food by sharing a table with others, by packing a lunch now and then, and by learning as much as she can about nutrition, calories, and shopping techniques. That will pay off while she's single, and it will more than pay off if a husband ever enters the scene. Granted that it is somewhat of a shock to graduate from the Pepsi Generation without being adequately weaned from ground beef, buns, and colored water, there *are* other foods in this world. And many of them can be prepared right at home in the Food Grooming Center, which used to be called the Sink.

The more sophisticated woman, regardless of her income level, usually knows the importance of both proper eating and the cost factors involved. Her problem often is that of loneliness, not wanting to cook for just herself. Without someone to please or impress with her culinary talents, she frequently alternates between two extremes, snack-grabbing and expensive dining out. A group of women who live in a suburb of Los Angeles, but each with her own apartment, partly solved their problems. According to a letter I received, they once a week all eat at the home of one member of the group. Each member selects the menu on her turn, and one of the rules is: The meals must be reasonable in cost. This system has several merits. It provides sociability, economy, and leftovers for the serving hostess. It is, of course, only a personal solution to a universal problem.

I am tempted at this point to overstress the merits of the convenience foods. They do cost more than foods cooked from scratch, of course, but if time and energy are at a premium, these built-in-maid-service meals make sense. But unless a working woman is a social butterfly, a part-time welfare worker, or on call for her employer day and night, she usually has time to do a little peeling and paring. The convenience foods would seem to make more sense for a working wife and mother than for a career woman with time and boredom on her hands. It is highly possible to control food costs without being a drudge or a penny-pincher, and unlike men, attractive girls usually manage a few dinners each month without going Dutch on a date.

Transportation

Few working women really can afford an automobile. As I showed under my section on autos, it is almost impossible to support any late model, full size, American car for much less than $1500 per year. It is, however, quite possible to drive and own (or buy on time) the best known tiny imported car for considerably less than that. It depends on the area, the age of the driver, how much the car is driven, how it is driven, and on how long the car is retained before trading it in. I must emphasize, however, that any working girl with a yen for her own private transportation should figure all the costs very carefully before signing an order. A private auto can cost more to support than a lazy, indigent husband. Most working women would be wiser to live within walking distance of work, use whatever public transportation is available, and/or rent a car on weekends now and then if need or the urge strikes. I cannot emphasize too much my warnings on this point.

To the attractive young thing with flying tresses and a sports car, I can only say "good luck" with your creditors. The truth is, most women have not yet learned, as many men have, that the automobile can too easily become the master rather than the servant.

Insurance

Most large employers furnish some type of medical insurance to their employees. In such a case, a woman should check up on what her protection really amounts to. A talk with the person in charge of the group plan is usually advisable. If the medical coverage has obvious limitations, such as a low limit of total liability, or if it pays only a fraction of the bill, it might be wise to supplement it with a Comprehensive-deductible-participating policy. But since most employees receive paychecks for a reasonable time if they are off sick, the "loss-of-income" policies would seem to be rather costly for the average working woman. You should determine how long you would be paid in case of a serious illness or accident. If that period is limited to only one or two weeks, you might be wise to take out an insurance policy which would begin to reimburse you for wages lost *after* your employer stopped paying. The decision should be weighed by a number of factors: (1) the number of fixed obligations you have incurred, (2) the extent of your savings, (3) the possibility of help from close relatives, and (4) your general health. Many loss-of-income medical policies are not good investments per se; they are essential only if your ability to absorb a loss of income is very limited, provided your actual medical bills would be paid.

As to life insurance, the average, single working woman usually needs only enough coverage to pay for her funeral. Unless she finds it impossible to save money in any other way, it seems foolish for her to take out life insurance with fast cash buildups. She should be able to earn better interest and dividends through other savings plan. And even though her life insurance premiums would be higher later on, in case she needed to increase her coverage, she would be saving a great deal of money in the meantime by paying *no premiums whatsoever*. Life insurance coverage should be determined by your present and reasonably foreseeable needs, not by the inexpensiveness of the premiums simply because you are young. And the greatest need for life insurance is from having other persons dependent on your future earning power. Ask yourself if you have any such dependents. Ordinary, regular life insurance would be a wiser choice, in my opinion, than an endowment type of policy.

Pitfalls to avoid

Prior to the time a young woman sets out on her own, her main use of the word "no" probably arose from cooling the attentions of overenthusiastic boy friends. But a working girl of today will find the "negative" quite essential in the commercial arena too. No sooner has she found a job and settled into her quarters than the doorbell will ring. A handsome young man (usually) will ask if she has purchased her "pots and pans" yet.

Of course she hasn't. Pots and pans were about the furthest thing from her mind. But now she is informed by the attractive salesman that all the smart girls are stocking up on kitchen hardware as soon as possible, that it's the thing to do. Furthermore, the credit terms are so easy that payments are virtually painless. Just sign here and away we go.

If it isn't a pot and pan peddler, it's a guy selling silverware, or linens, or special knives, or magazines, or sets of this and that. First thing you know, our young lady from Middletown is a credit-consumer deluxe, sending in checks to firms all over the United States. And the next thing you know, the young lady is at the bank or the credit union trying to refinance.

I should point up that these easy-pay contracts are almost impossible to cancel, once you've signed up. And few of the firms involved are willing to take back their merchandise to offset the deal. In fact, these at-the-door credit contracts usually are the working girl's first exposure to the great American system of buying on time.

Advice on using credit

I have already covered the credit system in rather immense detail, which it certainly warrants. But when it comes to the single working girl, the entire subject needs further treatment. Up until a few years ago, women were considered top credit risks. There was just something about the way girls were brought up—taught to be honest, courteous, fair, and all that sort of thing—that made them excellent credit risks. But my, how things have changed. A single young lady with an office job is given a thorough checking by most credit managers today. For one thing, even though she is only eighteen or nineteen, she may have a dresser drawer full of unpaid bills. After all, we have our teen-age credit plans, you know.

Furthermore, since women became emancipated, many of them have adopted the same "catch me if you can" attitude toward their creditors that only hard-bitten males used to assume. Once a girl believes that working at *any* job regardless of salary, entitles her to a new car, a fine apartment, and two weeks every year at a ski lodge, one thing easily follows another. First it's too much credit, then it's a matter of refinancing rather frequently, and finally comes the bill-dodging. By the time she meets that Mr. Right, she's virtually panic-stricken over her obvious insolvency. Of course, many girls are too well brought up for this sort of thing, but the example above is not far-fetched. From a realistic point of view, every girl should avoid such a mess. It is simply a matter of staying out of debt unless the need is all but overwhelming.

The working girl who really cares will go over the section on MANAGING YOUR CREDIT with concentration. As they say, it's easy to "fall" into debt, but you have to "crawl" out. And bear in mind that it is next to impossible to launch a savings and investment program once your creditors are making fair, but harsh demands on your paycheck.

Where to save those first few dollars

As I stressed before, a budget or spending plan should be based on from 90 to 95 per cent of your income after income taxes, social security, and other deducted expenses. If you base your spending on the entire sum you receive each payday, there may never be any savings. So think in terms of your net income after savings. Just pretend you earn less than you do.

The surest way to save money is to have your employer or credit union deduct so much from your wages. You can buy savings bonds through a deduction program, or credit union shares through your credit union. Unless your cash needs are really pressing, you should make some such arrangement as soon as you have a steady job. Credit unions, as I mentioned, pay from 4 to 6 per cent on share accounts. As of this writing, U. S. Savings Bonds (E bonds) pay 4.15 per cent if held to the full seven-year maturity.

Another easy way to save is to open a savings account at the bank where you cash your paycheck, or the one where you use a checking account. Or you can start a thrift account at a savings and loan association. When you cash your check or make a deposit, put some money regularly in your savings account, at least a few dollars each time. Until you have several hundreds of dollars in cash savings, or even a thousand or two, you needn't worry about any other kind of investments. That sum isn't likely to be eroded by inflation to any extent, and if you pick your savings institution with care, the safety of your money needn't worry you. Your main problem will be the temptation to withdraw the money, or cash in your bonds, for some real or imagined need.

In the meantime, however, you may be contacted by life insurance salesmen, mutual fund salesmen, or stockbrokers, offering other plans for your money. While most every thrift plan has some merit—for some persons—an unwed, unattached working woman would be wise to keep her first few dollars intact, in a simple, safe savings plan. There is no substitute for money in the bank (or other safe institution), where you can reach it when you need it.

What to do when you have saved them

But after you have built your thrift account to respectable proportions—say, to a sum equal to two months' gross income— then you can start thinking of earning more profit on your nest egg and spreading the risk somewhat. For the working woman I can think of nothing better than mutual funds. As I stated under the section covering mutual funds, they are really specialized investment companies which invest in the stocks of other companies, and in other types of securities. One problem in contacting a mutual fund salesman, or stockbroker, is that he may try to put *all your savings* into a fund. That is not the plan I have in mind. Keep the cash you have saved where it is, with the exception of a few hundred dollars to start the fund plan, and then make your fund share purchases out of future income.

There are two types of monthly fund plans, which I mentioned previously. One is called the "contractual plan," which usually is to be avoided. Under this plan you immediately would be charged commissions on fund shares you haven't even purchased as yet. And these commissions range from 4 to 10 per cent of the share cost. The other plan is called a "voluntary accumulation plan," and under this system you pay commissions only as you buy and receive each new share. Make certain which agreement you sign. If you aren't certain, have a knowledgeable friend read the contract or agreement before you sign it. The point is, under the contractual plan, out of the first $500 you paid into the fund, as much as $250 might go toward commissions or fees. But under the voluntary accumulation arrangement, not over $50 would go for sales charges. The charge more likely would be slightly over $40. Under the contractual plan, you would eventually pay very little in annual sales charges, because you would have paid most of them in advance. But in the meantime, not as much of your investment would be working and earning for you as under the voluntary accumulation plan. Furthermore, should you drop the contractual arrangement during the early months or years, you might get back only a fraction of your investment.

For that matter, you can invest in some good performing funds for no sales charge whatsoever. One example is the T. Rowe Price Growth Stock Fund. You have to write to the fund itself in order to get a prospectus and order form. The address of the fund is One Charles Center, Baltimore, Maryland, 21201. Another "no-load" fund I have recommended to many working women is the Energy Fund. You can write to this fund for information and an application at 2 Broadway, New York 4, New York. There is no guarantee that either of these mutual funds will perform better over a long haul than a number of funds with a 4 to 10 per cent sales charge. But both of them have done well in recent years, and for a beginner in the investment field, they offer an edge. Without a sales fee, you can withdraw or stop your program without a penalty. Until you know you have stick-to-it-iveness, that's an important consideration.

But I should again emphasize the point that a good dollar-type savings program should normally come first. After that come the funds. You may have trouble convincing a fund salesman of this, but it's your money. Unless you simply can't accumulate your first few dollars of savings in any other way, it would be unwise to put equities (stocks or funds) ahead of cash-type thrift accounts.

Both of these funds mentioned above are basically "stock funds"; that is, they invest most all their assets in common stocks, rather than in cash, bonds, preferred stocks, and so on. With your first few dollars of savings you surely don't need a fund manager to invest your money in bonds or bank accounts. You will have done that yourself, assuming you've taken my advice by concentrating first on savings bonds, thrift accounts, or credit union shares. Your point now is to own some common stocks, through participation in a stock-type fund. So at this stage of the game, pass up the so-called balanced, or bond, funds.

As a matter of fact, your investment program never need be more complicated than this, not until and unless you acquire substantial assets. Then you would be more interested in my section for THE MORE SOPHISTICATED INVESTOR.

Stick to a regular savings plan until you have close to $2000 in cash-type, safe savings, or bonds. Then start to acquire shares in a good, stock-type mutual fund, on a voluntary accumulation plan. Just keep tabs on your fund now and then to see how it stacks up with other similar funds. I related how this can be done under the section on mutual funds. If possible you should let your interest earnings be compounded, rather than withdraw and spend them. And you should also have your fund dividends reinvested, both the earnings dividends and the "capital gains" profits.

The divorced mother

The divorced woman with one or more children to raise has a specially difficult situation, particularly if she earns a typical wage and if any one of her brood is quite young. Although the Federal Government now allows her to deduct the cost of baby care, what she saves on taxes is peanuts as compared to her "extra" expenses. Aside from practicing frugality in all areas of the budget, and I do mean *frugality*, she almost has to eliminate some taken-for-granted expenses entirely. One of those would be private transportation. If she can't use public transportation, her only alternative, as a rule, is living within walking distance of work. She can't indulge in those common recreations of working girls, such as evenings on the town or even movies, without counting pennies.

Unless she has a generous allowance coming from her ex-husband in the form of alimony and/or child support, she can plan on years of living from hand to mouth and making apologies to her young for abnormal sacrifices. All this, even though her former husband may be down to frayed cuffs and sponging drinks. From the standpoint of most American families, divorce is financially impossible, there is no other word to describe it. But as those on the verge of splitting up usually say, so is living together under the circumstances. So let's accept reality as it exists, since over 50,000 marriages are rent asunder in Los Angeles County alone every year.

Two commissioners of the Superior Court of Los Angeles have publicly stated that the greatest single reason for divorce stems from financial mismanagement. While poor finances may be complicated by other problems, as is usually the case, money is still the main cause of it all. A rather typical case of divorce involves overwhelming debt, incurred by two childish, unreasonable marriage partners. Yet after the divorce, the ex-wife expects the creditors to drop dead while the husband gives her and the children preference in the payments. The creditors are under no moral or legal obligation to do so, and they know this. There is no way a judge can restrain them, short of action in the bankruptcy courts, and not always then, depending on the nature of the debts. The moral is, you can't divorce your creditors by divorcing your husband.

Occasionally, or frequently, as the case may be, an ex-husband fails to make his support payments, and the wife is tempted to throw him in jail. Indeed, such a willingness is the only way she can hope to get help from court authorities. And if she actually files charges and has him put behind bars, he can't work in order to make the payments. The futility of all this should have been apparent to begin with in most cases.

The divorced woman with a child, or children, has no alternative; she must face reality. She best decide as soon as possible how much it will cost to live and raise her children decently. Her next step is to decide where that money will come from. Perhaps for the first time in her life she will have to draw up an accurate budget and then live on it. A common expression under such circumstances is "I had no idea what it costs to live."

Assuming a reconciliation is possible, it should be seriously considered. If that is definitely ruled out, the sooner she chooses among the possible alternatives the better. She can plan to remarry, with all the tricks and trappings that entails, including incurring some expenses she can hope to repay only with a complete victory. She can plan to become a career girl in earnest, which means scheming to get some position which really pays. Or, she can make the virtually impossible choice of supplementing her income by working extra jobs every free hour she has.

Unlike the working girl with no responsibilities, the divorced mother hasn't all the time in the world to make up her mind; the bills come due and children must be fed and clothed. Most divorcées remarry. A few go on to good careers. But many such women choose to whine, procrastinate, and drift for years. I only wish I could offer some magical formula which would make $400 a month do the work of $550, but I can't. But I do know for a fact that divorce needn't be the end of the line. Many a divorcée has pulled up her socks, wiped away the sniffles, and moved ahead in the world. It should be the rule, rather than the exception. If she manages to amass a decent net worth, which is far from impossible, the rest of what I have to say would apply to her as much as it would to any other woman, widowed, overlooked, or alone by choice.

Owning real estate

Once a working woman acquires a nest egg of a few thousand dollars, she has another option open to her, one she may never have thought of. She can begin to invest in a home or in multiple dwelling units. It depends primarily on two things, her taxable income and her ability to manage property. Even a small homestead can be an advantage to a single woman whose taxable income (after deductions and personal exemptions) reaches the $4000 figure (that is a before-tax income of around $6000, or $500 per month). Every extra dollar such a person might earn would be taxed at a rate of 25 per cent. In other words, Uncle Sam would get 25 cents out of each extra dollar earned and reported, as of this writing. If taxes go up, the penalty would be even worse.

By investing in a home, a working woman could reduce her taxable income by the amount of interest and property taxes she pays. Since a married couple with children would be taxed at a lower percentage, even on the same gross income as above, a homestead makes more financial sense to "loners" than to family types. Under my section on SHELTER, I went to great pains to dispel the myth that home ownership is a great savings compared to renting. Read it again in case you've forgotten. But when it comes to a single person with a steady job and a rather heavily taxed income, a home offers some great advantages.

It even makes sense in such a case to purchase a home to rent out to someone else. That way you can deduct depreciation, upkeep, insurance, and repairs from your taxable income as well. And although such a purchase is generally a so-so investment from the standpoint of pure rental income, it does make sense from the standpoint of reducing income taxes. In other words, if you would feel too lonely in a home all by yourself, and haven't the time or energy to keep it up, you could rent an apartment for your own living quarters, even while acting as another person's landlord. And you've the same, often better, tax break.

I did not bring up the subject of homes and income property until getting into the other areas of saving and investing open to the single working woman for several reasons. First, it's never wise to buy real estate without some liquid assets. There's the down payment to consider, along with the taxes and upkeep. A shoestring investment in a house is a risky business. And second, working girls just starting their careers usually don't earn enough to worry about taxes. Once both income and net worth increase substantially, it becomes time to start thinking about savings on taxes.

As a practical matter, income property and/or home ownership is about the only reasonably simple route available to the ordinary person when it comes to saving on income taxes. The higher the taxable income, the greater the need to invest in improved real estate. It is not at all unrealistic for a career woman earning $15,000 per year or more to be purchasing on mortgage $100,000 or more of combined homestead and income property. The real point to watch is how much of your real estate investment you are using up, by living in it. For a $15,000 per year single woman to live in a $40,000 home would be rather ridiculous, even if she did save on income taxes. What she saved in taxes might be inconsequential compared to the "rental income" she would be wasting. But for her to own (or be purchasing) a $50,000 home to rent out to someone else makes a lot of sense.

The point that confuses most people over the virtues of home ownership as related to saving on taxes is this: For every dollar they save on taxes, and for every dollar they save from not paying a landlord, they fritter away more dollars by consuming the potential rental income from their expensive investment. The financial virtues of owning houses and other income properties are not to be confused with the virtues of living in them. Except for the tax break given to owners of homesteads, there is no real similarity.

The same general theory applies to owning any kind of property, including consumer assets such as autos, furniture, and appliances. The more of your savings you have tied up in items you use, the more of your potential earnings you will be consuming. There has to be a reasonable balance between wealth for personal use and consumption, and wealth which brings you income. And this applies to single women just as it applies to any other individual. Only *you* can set that relationship or percentage arrangement, because a sensible ratio demands some sacrifice. But in time a temporary sacrifice more than pays off because the earnings from your genuine investments will allow you a higher standard of living. Just what is essential in the way of everyday living paraphernalia is a matter of personal choice.

My overall advice to the single working woman is to be realistic in how much she spends to live decently. Then it becomes a matter of "keeping it simple" in life insurance, savings plans, and investments, while holding to a steady program of thrift and accumulation. After that there is a need to recognize that single women have the opportunities to reduce their income taxes, just as men do. And that without a realistic tax plan, the chance of such women becoming financially secure is more remote.

Financial advice

Single women, including the never-been-marrieds, the divorced, and the widows, often express the need for some man to talk to about financial problems. This is quite understandable, since even well-informed, mature men seek skilled guidance at times. But few experts have the time to offer advice free, and not many women would wish to so impose. On a limited income, there is only so much money available for advice on investments and the like. That is one reason I have stressed simplicity for such a woman. There is no need to obtain frequent advice on ordinary life insurance, a good stock-type mutual fund, or even a simple homestead. Complexity has its price, in automobiles, appliances, *and* investment programs. Even under the most basic program, however, there is an occasional need for change and adjustment. That is why selecting an agent or broker can be more important than the decision over what he has to sell. You must trust and respect a man, or woman, before you deal with him. So take your time before cementing a commercial relationship. It should last a long time.

If you select your agents and brokers wisely, you will have someone to talk to when you need to ask questions, desire reassurance, or feel the need to change your security program. Above all, don't be ashamed at your lack of knowledge when you are considering a purchase of insurance or making an investment. No matter how obvious or foolish the question may seem, ask it. And keep asking until you feel you understand. I know for a fact that most women don't know what type of life insurance policies they own, let alone the special features and options.

And while a great many women own fund shares and common stocks, most of them would be hard-pressed to defend their choice. It always pays to know approximately how much cash (or surrender value) a life policy has. The back of each policy carries such a schedule, usually per each $1000 of face value. You can borrow against the cash value in an emergency.

When it comes to mutual fund shares or common stocks, it doesn't take much time each day to search through your newspaper for the latest market figures. Not that you should consider selling your securities simply because they lose a fraction of their values occasionally. A stockbroker once said to me that he shied away from women clients. "They usually demand a good, safe stock with a guaranteed annual return of at least 10 per cent," he said. Unfortunately, there is much truth in his observation. A woman has to be realistic about getting involved in the stock market, even if she limits her participation to the professional investment companies (mutual funds). She should expect no special consideration simply because she is female. She must be prepared to take losses just as men do. And there isn't any such animal as a good, safe security guaranteed to yield 10 per cent. If a woman—young, old, or medium-aged—wants to play around with the bulls and the bears of Wall Street, she should grow up emotionally first, which can be a pretty big order.

Now, there are women and there are women. Some of the supposedly weaker sex are on a par with any man when it comes to wheeling and dealing in securities. I've met women with computer minds and steely nerves, who can laugh it up at a cocktail party immediately after dropping several thousands of dollars in the market. But these are rare types, and from my observations most women investors are far more emotional than most men, and far more demanding to boot. The truth is, most women recognize their inadequacies in the field of finance, and to offset this, they substitute emotion and unreasonable demands. I am suggesting instead that a woman first select her securities representatives with care and then that she trust their judgments until there is adequate reason to do otherwise.

What about the woman with very substantial holdings, perhaps inherited from her parents or from a deceased husband? Should she allow a banker, broker, or investment counselor to take complete charge? In general, I would say yes, assuming that whichever specialist she chose would render fairly frequent and detailed reports. And I would further recommend that she avoid giving a "discretionary account" to anyone, not even to her lawyer. She should insist on being at least consulted or told before any switch in investments is made. And if she consents, she should expect a written memorandum outlining just what has been done. The usual fee for managing a "living estate" is ½ of 1 per cent of the asset value of the estate. But since few banks or investment counselors can afford to actively manage any investment program for less than $500 per year, that means an estate of at least $100,000. Some advisers and banks refuse estates of less than $250,000. Now, however, there are some "pooled investment plans" offered by both banks and registered investment counselors which accept much smaller estates for management. You would have to check the banks and advisers in your area. But if you pay over ½ of 1 per cent of your estate value for management, you would, in my opinion, be much better off in one or more high-quality mutual funds, even if you had to pay a substantial sales charge at the time you purchased your shares. The funds often hire investment advisers with more skill and experience than a modest-sized local bank can afford.

As for allowing a stockbroker to manage your estate, this would present the greatest risk, in my view. A broker may charge you nothing for management, but he is in the business of selling stocks, and there is always the temptation to boost his commissions through too active management. That is called "churning," and it is very difficult to identify or prove, especially if you have given your broker total discretion over buying and selling. I have met several formerly rich widows who had been charmed by a brokerage house "customer's man" into allowing him full leeway in the market. As I said, these widows were formerly rich.

What about your men friends? Should you seek advice from them in order to keep your estate growing and earning? My answer is "no." Advice which costs nothing is usually worth about the same. Furthermore, just because a man is successful in his own business definitely does not make him an expert in the stock market. A man may be flattered into trying to help you, and impress you, but unless you have adequate proof of his investment credentials, forget it. And let's face it, a single woman often finds it hard to separate a man's magnetism from his skill. The typical well-to-do widow is soon parted from most of her wealth. Statistics are hard to come by in this field, partly from embarrassment on the part of the fleeced, and partly because no one is keeping tab. But I personally have met many women who went through sizable fortunes because they failed to distinguish between personal rapport and financial advice. To be blunt, the world is full of male opportunists who live almost exclusively off lonely but wealthy women. If you have money and need help and advice, pay an honest professional for it, even if he has the homeliest face in the city. It is terribly hard for a woman to admit that a man is after her money, although most men take it for granted that legions of women would gladly pick their pockets. Men even joke about it. But most women assume it would never happen to them. Or even when they realistically keep up their guards, it's only temporary. On the other hand, you've got to trust someone, so it may boil down to how well you judge character.

For the woman with some wealth who prefers to go it alone, I have some thoughts on that too. She can weigh some of my ideas as they appear under the heading of THE MORE SOPHISTI-CATED INVESTOR, which includes INCOME PROPERTY.

SPECIAL SITUATION: THE MORE SOPHISTICATED INVESTOR

The following section was written particularly for those persons who have, in one way or another, acquired rather substantial assets, but who feel somewhat at a loss when it comes to managing their wealth. For the purpose of easy, quick definition, "substantial assets" might mean in the area of $50,000 on up. That sum, of course, is tied to the present value of a dollar. Furthermore, persons with considerably less than $50,000 surely will find this material of some value, even though I firmly believe that smaller estates can be invested safely and profitably through a combination of insured "dollar savings plans" and mutual funds. I have already discussed those arrangements to some extent.

I am sure there are many individuals who suspect they may be missing something by sticking to the tried-and-true "simple" systems. And there's something to that. My purpose is to survey the other investment plans available to the man or woman who chooses to sample the menu and get out of a rut; and in doing so, my problem is in getting down to the bare essentials, rather than in trying to compete with the voluminous books on investing.

Nothing is *absolutely* safe, from the standpoint of getting back all of what you've invested, at whatever time you want it. Safety and liquidity carry a price tag. Also, we've reached a point in our economy when income tax advantages often carry more weight than sound investment procedures. At the very least, our tax laws often tip the scales in favor of speculation, as opposed to genuine investment. The man who ought to have more of his money in bonds, savings plans, and/or mortgages, in order to balance off his equities (common stocks), may think he can't afford the earnings (interest) from such fixed-income investments. So, he goes "all out" in the stock market. The profits from his stock dealings are treated as long-term "capital gain," provided he holds his shares a sufficient time before cashing them in (six months at the time of this writing). Such long-term profits are never taxed at over 25 per cent, and sometimes at a lower rate if the investor were to add one half the profits to his ordinary income. That would depend on his tax bracket. For these reasons alone, many investment programs make little sense from the standpoint of balance, hedging against shifts in dollar value, or even earnings. Many investment portfolios are geared mainly to our income tax laws, rather than to sound investment rules. And because of the complexity of our commercial laws, along with our tax laws, investment possibilities are overwhelming in their sheer numbers. Before getting into pure "equities," let's first take up the matter of bonds, most of which promise to pay a certain interest rate over a given period of time, and the principal at a specified date. Like stocks, they usually fluctuate in dollar value.

A. *Bonds*

CORPORATE BONDS

Bonds, which represent a form of "debt," rather than a share-the-risk investment, are broken down into three broad categories: corporate, municipal, and government. Within those broad definitions are a number of subdivisions. The common reasons for buying corporate bonds are (1) relative safety, (2) income, and (3) balance. Since bonds are a form of debt, usually a bondholder would be paid ahead of a stockholder in the event a corporation failed or was dissolved. Bonds pay a stated interest rate, which in normal times is below the yield of common stocks, mainly because there is more "risk" in stocks. The interest rate paid on a bond is almost always less than the actual "earnings" of a share of stock in a good firm, on a percentage basis, although not all earnings are declared in dividends. During times when stocks are priced very high, in relation to their earnings, bond yields may exceed dividend yields on stocks. This was true during the bull market which began to taper off in early 1966, and it was true in 1929. Stocks were yielding less than 3 per cent on the average, whereas bond yields were up to around 5. Therefore, from the standpoint of income alone, some bonds made more sense than most stocks.

As to balance, it's an old investment rule to have so much

of one's estate in the form of dollars (bonds, etc.) and so much in equities (stocks). It's a matter of having some assets fixed in terms of dollars and some in "variables." Our colleges and universities make a fine example of that rule, and here is the manner in which they invested their endowment funds early in 1966. Taken as a whole, 58 per cent of their money was in common stocks, 31 per cent in bonds and cash, and 10 per cent in mortgages. The remaining 1 per cent was in preferred stocks. So you can see how important bonds are in the make-up of conservative investment programs. Corporate bonds usually come in $1000 denominations, although some are issued for considerably less than that, even as low as $100. But there are many kinds of bonds—collateral trust bonds, general mortgage bonds, income bonds, and convertibles—not even considering the different businesses involved, such as industrial bonds and railroad bonds. A debenture is a type of bond backed only by the *general credit* of a corporation, and many convertibles are also debentures.

So much for the basic definitions. Corporations usually issue bonds for specific purposes, such as to expand or buy some other firm, and by issuing bonds they avoid increasing their capital stock. Increasing the number of shares of stock would mean "cutting" more investors in on expected profits, and it would reduce existing stockholder equities. The interest cost of a bond, however, is fixed as far as the corporation is concerned. This does not mean that bond buying is a cut-and-dried proposition. There are bonds and there are bonds. Bonds are rated according to quality by organizations such as Moody's and Standard & Poor's. Moody's has nine ratings for bonds, with Aaa as the best rating, down to C, the lowest. It can depend on the quality and earnings of the corporation, the security behind the bond, the sinking fund (amount regularly set aside to redeem the bonds), and the actual interest rate.

With all these factors to consider, it becomes quite clear that the ordinary investor needs a lot of information and a great deal of professional guidance before getting his feet wet in the corporate bond market. Yet the bond market is no longer the exclusive province of large institutions. Individuals have been heavily in bonds for about ten years now. Some are happy; others are sick.

Bonds today require about the same degree of active management that common stocks do. In the first place, one rarely buys a bond at par value; there is either a premium (stated value plus a bonus) or a discount (buying at less than face value). As far as the issuing corporation is concerned, it has assumed the exact obligation stated on the face of its bonds, along with the interest. Investors, or buyers, on the other hand, may feel the bonds are worth more or less than the face amounts. Therefore, bonds fluctuate in value a great deal. A corporation also may elect to redeem its bonds before maturity, or "call" them, at a predetermined price.

Some bonds are "registered," that is, listed in the name of the owner, which requires a legal transfer at the time of sale. These bonds pay interest automatically. Other bonds are payable to the "bearer," and have coupons attached, which an owner must detach and mail to the company or its paying agent before receiving his interest.

Probably the most sophisticated bond is the Convertible. Some investors feel that Convertibles allow you to be both in and out of the equity (common stock) market at one and the same time. A Convertible bond is usually unsecured (a debenture) and it can be exchanged (converted) into so many shares of common stock. The common stock involved may be that of the bond-issuing corporation or of an affiliate in some cases. The "spread" is often the key to such an arrangement, since the market value of the common stock at the time the Convertible bonds are issued is always below the price at which it would pay a bond-holder to convert. That difference is the spread. Thus, if the common stock tied to the bond rises in market value—gets closer to the option price or actually surpasses it—the Convertible bond itself becomes more valuable. Other investors will pay more for it. Since these bonds are quoted in percentages of stated value, such as 100 per cent, 120 per cent, or (if at a discount) some-

thing like 90 per cent, it is not unusual for a Convertible bond
to shoot up to 150 per cent. In such a case, a $1000 bond would
be worth $1500, regardless of what the investor paid for it. In
the meantime, the investor is earning semi-annual interest at the
rate of 4, 4½, or even a higher percentage—but on the basis of
the face value of the bond, not the market value. Rather than
actually converting to the stock when the option feature makes
it profitable, holders of these bonds usually take their profits
in the bonds themselves. Another attractive feature of Convertibles is that, theoretically at least, there is a limit to how far
down they will go, even in a bearish stock market. Since the
bonds carry interest, they have a built-in "investment quality."
If a $1000 bond pays 5 per cent, that 5 per cent alone should
keep the bond selling at near to its stated value. For instance,
should the market value of the bond decline to 90 per cent,
or $900, that 5 per cent interest would become over 5½ per cent
to any new owner of the bond.

Most of the above is theory, however, and no one really
knows how far down Convertibles might go in a seriously declining market, or even in a runaway inflationary situation. But
it sounds great on paper, and a few speculators such as Seth
Glickenhaus have made fortunes in Convertibles.

A third important feature of Convertibles is "leverage." While
stockbrokers themselves cannot lend more than the usual margin
amount on bonds, (30 per cent in mid-1966 or 70 per cent
margin), banks can lend more. Brokers are governed by Federal
regulation "T," whereas bankers come under Federal regulation
"U" regarding loans made against securities. The term "leverage"
means using borrowed money to pry loose more profits, being
able to invest a greater sum than with one's own limited capital.
Even some mutual funds use leverage. At any rate, a number
of banks, especially in the East and Midwest, have been loaning
up to 80 per cent of the market value of a Convertible bond,
which means a 20 per cent "margin," as opposed to 70 per cent
margin at a broker. Not all banks will do this, however. But
since the bonds pay interest themselves, the cost of any 80

per cent loans against them are more or less offset by the 100 per cent earnings of the bonds. Some investors have stretched the loan advantages of Convertibles into tax-savings features as well, by borrowing against the bonds shortly before the end of a tax year, and by paying interest to a highly co-operative bank in advance (prepaid interest).

Because I believe Convertibles offer substantial advantages to the investor with sufficient cash, imagination, and courage, here is just one example of a Convertible issue with which I happen to be personally familiar. A brief history of the particular bond shows what *can* happen.

Back in late 1965 Foremost Dairies decided to raise some extra capital via the Convertible route. At that time, Foremost common stock was selling for around $12 per share. In order to make its new bond issue attractive, Foremost offered an interest rate on the bonds of 5½ per cent and added a convertible feature which was also appealing. The $1000 bonds could be converted to 55.5 shares of common stock. Thus the "spread" was only $5 or so (the difference between the current market price of $12 and the effective profitable option price of $17). The bonds would mature in 1980, fifteen years later, assuming they weren't called in earlier.

Well, investors gobbled up the bonds immediately, paying a premium price of 110 per cent ($1100 for each $1000 bond), which of course made the "yield" closer to 5 per cent than to 5½.

But it wasn't more than a few months later than Foremost common stock took off, rising to 27¾ on the New York Stock Exchange in February of 1966. The Convertible also soared as a result. In February the bond was selling for 153½ per cent ($1535 for each $1000 bond). In the meantime, holders of the bonds were receiving their 5½ per cent interest on a semi-annual basis. But—when the bear market set in later in 1966, Foremost common dropped to $17 per share. This, of course, also depressed the bond. The Convertible, for a while, retreated to 100 per cent, primarily because even 5½ per cent was below the going rate of interest. Abnormally high interest rates can temporarily distort the investment picture.

Since Foremost did not fall close to its old price of $12 (when the bonds were originally issued), it is impossible to say what might have happened to the Convertible. But since it paid 5½ per cent on face value, it is hard to believe it would have dropped much below 100 per cent.

To sum up on bonds in general, they help balance any sizable investment program, say of $100,000 or over. But there is no particular reason why even a small investor should not buy them, especially the Convertibles. Brokerage commissions on bonds are much lower than on stocks. However, the investor with only a few thousand dollars should consider the following: In mid-1966 E and H bonds were paying an effective rate of 4.15 per cent if held to maturity. There is no sales charge involved. There is little or no risk to consider. So is it really worth it to try for an extra 1 per cent or so, considering the extra costs, the active watching, and potential risk? I think not. On the other hand, one can buy only $20,000 of E and H bonds, so the man with a large sum to invest may need to give serious consideration to other types of bonds. Government bonds, however, are more popular with individuals than are the corporates.

GOVERNMENT ISSUES

Securities issued by our Federal Government fall roughly into three classes—"bills" (less than one year maturity), "notes" (one to five years maturity), and "bonds" (over five years). But it is common to refer to Treasury obligations as either bills or bonds. The longer the maturity, the higher the interest yield in most cases. Uncle Sam has more trouble finding buyers for his bonds than for his bills and notes, partly because of inflation and partly because interest rates vary so from year to year. In addition to the usually higher interest rates on long maturities, our Federal Government allows some estate tax advantages on certain issues. These bonds can be applied toward an estate tax at "par value." Since long-term bonds frequently sell at discount (below par), this last feature can be important to older persons. It would be important to check with a tax man, lawyer, or estate planner.

When the stock market looks shaky, many large investors sell part of their stock holdings and buy short-term "treasuries," thereby staying highly liquid while earning interest. The U. S. Treasury auctions off its bills every Monday through the Federal Reserve Banks on a "bid" basis. In other words, the "discount" is the interest. If your banker or broker buys you a $1000 treasury bill, maturing in three months, for $990 or 99 (the percentage of par), you would earn 1 per cent for just three months, which is an annual rate of 4 per cent. Over the years, and depending on the money market, these bills have yielded from less than 1 per cent per annum up to almost 6. The longer-term securities of our Treasury Department carry stated (and limited by law) percentages of interest, but these issues, too, sell above or below par. As an example, on May 26, 1966, 4¼'s were selling for 93.20 per $100 to yield 4.74 per cent. Here again, it is hardly worth the time or the effort for small investors to get involved, considering the advantages of ordinary savings bonds. But from time to time, treasuries offer great advantages for the investor who wants out of the stock market for a while—the "bull" who has suddenly turned "chicken." Bear in mind that obligations of the Federal Government have no income tax exemption, except for certain "housing authority" bonds, which really aren't true Federal issues. But there is nothing safer than an IOU of Uncle Sam, which is a factor to consider. The real "tax exempts" (Municipals) are not quite as risk-free as most people think. The Municipals are issued not just by cities as the name implies, but by states and their various subdivisions as well.

MUNICIPALS

Bonds and other similar types of securities issued by our states, counties, cities, and other political subdivisions are not taxed by the Federal Government because of the division of power established under our constitution and because "the power to tax is the power to destroy," or so the saying goes. Because of this feature, Municipals carry rather low rates of interest as compared to the general money market. Persons with very high incomes can profitably invest in Municipals even at low interest rates and come out ahead. A man in the 50 per cent tax bracket, for instance, would have the equivalent of a 6 per cent corporate bond when he bought a 3 per cent tax-exempt. On the 6 per cent corporate he would pay Uncle Sam one half his interest, thus netting 3. So if the best he can do in corporates is 5½ per cent, he'd be better off in a 3 per cent Municipal.

Before large investment houses get involved with Municipal bonds, they call in their lawyers and their accountants. Among the questions to be answered are the following: Did the political division have the authority to issue the bonds? Is the political unit financially sound? Are the bonds properly drawn? Is the financing scheme itself sound? Will there be a ready market? To be sure, you could accept the word of your broker or bond man that all this has been thoroughly checked out, and maybe it has. But during the Big Bust, a few cities and other political units failed to pay off as promised. Now and then the bond rating firms downgrade the bonds of a political authority. It happened to New York City recently, and it happened to the State of Oregon when it got carried away with some costly welfare plans. Unless the rating authorities were simply being capricious, we can logically assume there *are* risks in Municipals, even though our "governments" and taxpayers are behind them.

My personal opinion is, and many others agree, it is rather foolish to get involved with Municipals unless your taxable income reaches into the 40 per cent bracket. A number of brokerage firms have been publishing charts showing how advantageous Municipals are to even the man with a modest income, from a tax standpoint. But as I hope I have shown in a rather limited treatment, taxes are only one point to consider. And there are times when even the wisest and richest investors fall foolishly in love with tax exempts. As one friend of mine said, "I won't put my money in anything but Municipals, even though I know

I can net more after taxes in other investments. I just hate to pay taxes." As in the case of corporate Convertibles, it is possible to borrow heavily against obligations of the various governments. In the case of U. S. Treasury obligations, it is possible to have only 5 per cent invested, or a loan of 95 per cent; interest paid to buy Municipals is not tax-deductible, however. Only an investor interested in "leverage," or temporary tax-saving, would want to borrow a great deal against his bonds, unless, of course, he were an out-and-out speculator. Many persons do speculate in public bonds, despite the supposedly antisocial aspects of the act. The main thing to watch is the trend of interest rates. When interest rates are rising, bond prices fall. The reason is quite obvious. Investors discount the bonds in order to obtain higher yields, over and above the promised rate of interest.

Bear in mind that ours is not a "free" money market. It is controlled from top to bottom, starting with our Congress, which, among other things, determines the amount of gold backing to our currency, followed by our administration which can incur a deficit or run a surplus, and continuing with our Federal Reserve Board, which controls the amount of debt in circulation. *Debt,* of course, is *money* in our society, because most money finds its way into circulation through credit. The greater the amount of debt, the more money we have floating around in the form of Federal Reserve Notes. The "Fed" also sets reserve requirements for commercial banks, determines margin rules for stock buying, and enforces lending rates. By setting the bank "discount" rate (what it costs member banks to borrow from Reserve Banks), the Fed influences interest rates all the way down to the man who finances a home or car. But it also influences what Uncle Sam or New York State has to pay for money. Perhaps the greatest impact of the Federal Reserve Board comes from buying, or not buying, the IOU's of our Federal Government. That is decided by the Fed's *Open Market Committee,* a group of twelve men who meet in absolute secrecy.

When the Fed is buying Treasury obligations, money becomes fairly free and easy, for the simple reason that new money is

created like magic. The Federal Reserve Banks simply use Uncle
Sam's notes as a further base for expanding credit, treating them
as money, meanwhile setting up a line of credit for our Federal
Government, all of which is more or less a paper transaction.
When the Fed refuses to buy Treasury obligations, acting through
its Open Market Committee, or actually sells some of what it
already has in the open market, credit becomes tight and money
becomes relatively scarce. That's because member banks and individuals have to dig down in their pockets and vaults to buy
what the Fed doesn't want any more. So, the money supply is
reduced, and interest rates start to rise.

A logical question is: Does the Fed cooperate with Congress,
the Administration, and the U. S. Treasury in manipulating the
supply of money? The answer is "sometimes yes, sometimes no."
The Federal Reserve Board is theoretically independent, and up
until recently it was dominated by "banker thinking." As of
this writing, the Fed is more evenly divided as to money philosophy and it is more difficult to anticipate future moves. We had
been in a relatively tight, high-cost money period during early
1966, which particularly benefits insurance companies, since their
cost of money is rather fixed. But tight money periods rarely last
very long. They sometimes bring on recession for one thing,
and second, they are extremely unpopular with governments,
many business firms, and ordinary citizens. The future would
seem to hold easier credit and less expensive interest over the
long run, which to an investor would mean higher bond prices.
As interest rates drop, bond *prices* go up—the reverse of what
happens when money becomes more costly.

But an important point for the bond buyer to recognize is the
political and pressure-group implications of our money market.
There is also the chance that Congress will in time remove
some of the freedom of action now enjoyed by the Federal
Reserve Board. While this would certainly present perils, the
Fed hasn't always hit 100 per cent in its attempts to curb inflation. Tight money can stop a small boom in its tracks. It can

send an older boom into a recession. It has been compared to using a tourniquet to stop a nosebleed. And, of course, the stock market tends to move in opposite directions from the bond, or money, market. If for no other reason, that's why bonds, both corporate and government, balance a sizable investment portfolio.

B. *Stocks*

PREFERRED STOCKS

A preferred stock is a cross between a stock and a bond. It is partly in "obligation," since the dividend rate usually is fixed and because a preferred stockholder would be paid ahead of a common stockholder if trouble developed. But preferreds are also a type of "equity," or share-the-risk venture too, since regular dividends may depend upon the year-to-year earnings of the corporation. As I pointed out earlier, college endowment funds averaged only 1 per cent in preferreds, so preferreds can be ignored almost entirely in an ordinary investment package without much danger or loss. A preferred stock can carry an almost unlimited range of added benefits, too numerous to go into here. But in general, preferred issues carry a rather high rate of promised dividends (higher than bonds of the same corporation in many cases), and dividends may be accumulated from year to year. In other words, should a corporation fail to pay dividends to its accumulated preferred stockholders during any one year, it would have to catch these up before paying any dividends to its common shareholders. Preferreds sometimes can be converted into common shares at a fixed price (just as Convertible bonds) and have numerous protections built in. In general, preferreds are limited as to profit potential, although some types involve "participation" in extra profit, with a fair degree of security involved. Some preferred shares carry voting rights, others do not.

To give an idea of the comparative yields of the types of

securities discussed so far, and to show how they vary from year to year, here are some pertinent tables. I've included common stocks which I will discuss in more detail later.

(1950)

TYPE OF SECURITY	TYPICAL YIELD IN PER CENT
U. S. Government long-term bonds	2.32
Corporate long-term	2.50
Preferred Stocks	4.14
Common Stocks	5.30

(1963)

U. S. Government long-term bonds	4.00
Corporate long-term	4.09
Preferred Stocks	4.30
Common Stocks	3.20

By February of 1966, at the peak of the bull market, bond prices were falling sharply, as interest rates were rising. Both corporate and government bonds were nearing or exceeding 5 per cent in yield to maturity. Stock prices on the other hand were at their peak, which meant that dividends were down in relation to share prices. Dividend yields on many quality issues had dropped below 3 per cent. In fact, considering that investors were often paying up to 40 times for a share of stock what that share would probably earn, sometimes total earnings of stocks, not just dividends, were below what bonds would yield. The answer was, of course, that many investors didn't care about dividends; they were primarily interested in capital gain—price appreciation of their shares, which to many conventional analysts meant that a bear market was just around the corner. In the long run, earnings always count. Yet when the stock market is climbing dizzily, few investors care to analyze what is happening. Conventional wisdom at such a time is "old hat," obsolete, and downright subversive.

In fact, reading the above might remind older readers of

exactly what was happening back in late 1929, just before reality set in. I might add that back then, just as in 1966, interest rates were suddenly tightened, stock margins were increased, and storm warnings were flying. Only time will tell how different those two eras were and how much we have learned about heading off recessions. But regardless of what the future holds, boom, bust, or muddle through, the stock market undoubtedly will continue to operate, and most large investors will continue to put the bulk of their assets in common stocks. During slow times they may be willing to pay only ten times what a share will earn in a year. During boom times they may pay at a 20 to 1 ratio. When the ratios get beyond that figure, trouble usually lies ahead.

COMMON STOCKS

When one speaks of getting into "the market," most people think in terms of common stocks, although by now any reader should be aware that the market abounds with many other alternatives. At any rate, buying a share of pure "common stock" is the most publicized way of matching wits with the bulls and bears. Owning common stock is genuine "risk taking," being willing to win or lose in the search for profits; although you can't lose more than you invest, under the limited liability of a corporation. It means being part of a joint corporate venture with a percentage of voting rights and legal participation in the firm's profits—if any.

Of course, under our complex system of corporate organization, a small shareholder has little to say about management or control. He usually allows someone else to vote his shares, under proxy arrangements. For the most part, owners of common stock simply acquiesce in what is going on, showing approval by keeping their shares, or showing disapproval by selling them. Except for a few professional dissenters who attend meetings of stockholders, that is. Buying common stock today is more a matter of vicarious profit-seeking, not of influencing decisions of management. Democracy is for politics, not business.

While some investors manage to ride out the ups and downs

of the economy while holding on to the shares of only one corporation, such as AT&T, for instance, it is generally wiser to diversify one's holdings. At various times certain industries do much better than others. And we must consider the political tides as well as the economic ones. The mere threat to investigate the rate structure of giant American Telephone was enough to depress its shares substantially. Words from Washington have been known to send entire industries into headlong retreat. Then there's the matter of price-fixing to consider. Take that nice little old lady in Scranton, Pennsylvania, who alternates between attacking "creeping socialism" and complaining about the high cost of living. Her favorite blue chip pharmaceutical stock may be responsible for her higher medical bills, because of entering into price agreements with other drug companies. So, she has to balance the cost of drugs against the lower value of her stock when the anti-trust lawyers step in.

During the past few years, scarcely any American industry of any importance has been able to boast of no skeletons in its pricing closets. The courts have been overactive in hearing such cases. The typical American businessman really can't make up his mind which fellow is the greatest bum, the guy who "cuts" prices or the guy who "fixes" them. One thing is certain, getting caught manipulating prices can be costly to a corporation. So much so that integrity and respect for law could in time become a prized commercial virtue. If so, the Junior Chamber of Commerce may have to use other criteria than "unrestrained ambition" in picking its young men most likely to succeed. In the meantime, American investors probably will continue to select their shares on the basis of profit, not from which church the president of a corporation contributes to.

CHOOSING A SHARE OF STOCK

There are many ways to measure the potential of a corporation. You can obtain a copy of Standard & Poor's Stock Guide, for instance, which ranks stocks according to earnings and dividend records. This book also shows the principal business of each corporation, along with price fluctuations in its shares and current price-earnings ratios. At least that would be a good start, even though it is based on past history. But *my*, how performances can change over the years. Take, as an example, the thirty "blue chip" corporations making up the popular Dow Jones thirty Industrials in terms of potential capital gain.

In 1956, International Nickel showed a higher percentage of price gain than any of the other twenty-nine issues. In 1957, just one year later, International Nickel skidded to twenty-eighth in performance. It has never headed the list since, although in 1961 it rose to number three. In 1956, Sears, Roebuck & Co. showed the poorest price appreciation performance. But from 1958 through 1964, it was in the top six half a dozen times. By 1965, however, the giant retailer had dropped back to twenty-one. Investors were beginning to worry about the huge volume of Sears credit accounts.

But even though International Nickel, as just one example, skidded around a great deal on the "hot performance" list, an investor certainly would have felt no pain hanging onto it. The company has paid dividends without interruption since 1934, has a good earnings record, and beyond much doubt, a bright future. On the other hand, had an investor dumped International Nickel back in 1962, when it failed to move up, he might well have picked Chrysler Corporation as a substitute. After all, Chrysler was the fastest-moving issue in the thirty Industrials during 1962 and 1963. Many brokers were logically touting the third-largest automaker. But by 1965 Chrysler had dropped to next to last on the list in share appreciation. And so it goes. Brokers, of course, like action—that's what makes for all the buying and selling. It all boils down to the cost and worry of active management of a portfolio, compared to sticking with one or more high-quality issues.

Active management can cost the investor with a modest-sized portfolio a good deal of money in brokerage commissions, even if the advice he gets is above average. There's the added problem of paying taxes on capital gains. Unrealized gains, of course,

aren't taxed at all. While an investor ought to keep tab on his
investments as frequently as possible—accepting the advice of a
competent broker when such advice makes sense—there is a
great deal to be said for letting good things alone. Particularly if
wise selections are made to begin with. As just one example,
Founders Mutual Fund of Denver, Colorado, has made *no*
changes in its portfolio whatsoever from its original selection for
many years, through ups and downs in the market. Yet Founders
has an excellent dividend record, shows consistent share appreciation, and holds up very well in a generally declining market.
That is because it originally selected a diversified blue chip
portfolio. This would seem to make some of the more "actively
managed" funds look bad, yet wise management often involves
a hands-off policy. As a matter of interest, about one-half of the
stocks making up the Founders Mutual Fund portfolio—nineteen
of the forty to be exact—are also included in the Dow Jones
Average of thirty Industrials. They are all blue chips, of course,
and well balanced as to industries. So, by following the Dow
average, you can obtain a fairly accurate picture of how Founders
is doing. This is not to mean that Founders is the best fund you
can buy, because several funds recently performed somewhat
better overall. It is simply to show that an investor needn't rush
to sell his shares during troubled times, and to show what can
be done by careful original selection, plus sustained confidence.
Incidentally, the forty stocks making up the Founders portfolio
own no less than 600 subsidiaries, which gives you diversification
within diversification.

An investor with $100,000 or so could do far worse, in my
opinion, than selecting one or more stocks in several of the
following industries and then allowing the profits to hatch: oils,
steels, autos, chemicals, electronics, office equipment, metals, food
processing, retailing, aircrafts, and farming equipment. He might
pick only five or six widely diversified stocks, or he might add
airlines, utilities, and a few other industries if he chose. It could
mean, of course, relatively high brokerage commissions at the
outset, because he might be buying in odd lots (less than 100

shares of any one issue) and there is an extra charge on odd lot sales. But this original cost would be offset by the lack of frequent shifting of stocks. And in this example, I am assuming the investor would have about 40 per cent of his total wealth in cash, bonds, or the equivalent.

This does not mean "never" changing the make-up of a portfolio, it simply means ignoring the minor fluctuations of individual shares. If a broker phoned you to suggest eliminating one holding in order to buy another, he ought to give you an excellent reason before you act. An example of an excellent reason would be as follows. Let's suppose you had held some shares in one or more savings and loan firms during early 1963 (not as a saver-depositor, but as a stockholder in a nonmutual type of S & L). So, let's pretend the broker had called you to say this: "We have come to the conclusion that the housing market is being saturated with overbuilding, and that land in the western part of the nation is way overpriced. In addition, it looks like a period of tighter money is on the way. This could hurt the savings and loan industry seriously and we think you should liquidate your shares." This proved to be the case, of course, and the broker in the hypothetical example was able to give some concrete reasons why you should have sold such shares. S & L stocks dropped considerably by 1964 and remained depressed.

On the other hand, suppose a year or so later he had this to say: "I don't like the way AT&T is acting, considering the coming rate investigation. Why don't you sell out now and perhaps buy back in later? I think some of the airline stocks will be really 'hot' in a few months."

Well, AT&T did rather poorly in 1965 and early 1966, eventually hitting a new low. And certain airlines did very well indeed, spurred on by the war in Vietnam for one thing. But when the market break came in 1966, some of the better airline shares dropped sharply, while "Ma Bell" held rather steady, in the meantime paying her usual dividends. To accept and act on the advice offered in the second example might mean a complete shift in your investment outlook. You would be subjecting yourself to whimsical, more or less "constant" management, playing the volatile issues against the more conservative "investment quality" shares.

Had the broker in this second example offered reasonable proof that the telephone industry was in for a period of prolonged trouble, that would have been a different story. You would have had every right to weigh his words, check up on them, and, if logical, accept his advice.

Now and then, every investor should give his package a thorough going-over, perhaps by consulting an objective investment adviser. What might have been considered a blue chip back in 1928 could well be bankrupt by now. There are many such examples. But considering the size and diversification of our huge corporations of today, it is only reasonable to assume most all of them will continue to grow and prosper, even though many of their names and separate entities may disappear in the trend toward merger and giantism.

It goes almost without saying that humans differ in their psychological approach to investing. What might seem only wise and prudent to one man or woman would seem outrageously dull and conservative to others. There are many variations to playing the market, just as there are many variations to playing poker.

Some investors feel that investing in a "mutual fund" is too dull. Such investors, right or wrong, feel capable of setting up their own portfolios, and of making their own adjustments periodically. Nevertheless, from time to time, a huge corporation may pour one million dollars into just one mutual fund. Furthermore, it is getting exceedingly difficult to diversify by industry classification. More and more large companies are becoming "funds" themselves to a great extent, by branching out into many lines of business. Take International Telephone and Telegraph (ITT) as just one of many examples. While ITT might seem to come under either the electronics or utility classification, this giant firm owns Avis Rent-a-Car, Aetna Finance (a small loan company), and the American Broadcasting Company. So in a way, ITT has become a diversified holding company, or even an "investment company." Litton Industries has reached out into so many manu-facturing fields that classification becomes very difficult. As time passes, and barring more vigilant anti-trust action, many more large American corporations will become super-corporations, with tentacles reaching into most every field of endeavor. In many cases, the firms they acquire through merger or outright acquisi-tion have themselves branched out into diverse fields, so the trend is compounded. As a result, most American investors will be putting their money into "investment funds," in one way or an-other, whether they planned it that way or not. It may become just a matter of semantics, degree, or SEC registration. At any rate, it's worth discussing the "old pros" of the investment com-pany field.

CLOSED-END FUNDS

Several times in this book I have dealt with mutual funds, the open-end type which accepts and then invests all cash offered, meanwhile standing ready to redeem shares at market value. There is another, and older, type of investment company which is called a "closed-end fund." The closed-end investment com-panies offer a chance to diversify modest-to-sizable estates at relatively little cost and no active management. Whereas the true "mutual funds" charge sales commissions of around 8½ per cent, except for those with no sales charge at all (the no-load funds), the closed-end funds are generally traded on the major exchanges at regular brokerage rates, typically at about 2 per cent. It has been assumed by many observers of the market that the more sophisticated investors prefer the closed-end funds to the mutual funds, but this has never been proved.

The closed-end funds began their history as holding compa-nies, in most cases, gradually shifting their operations to that of true investment companies. This required a change of registra-tion with the Securities & Exchange Commission. Now any in-vestor has many of these investment companies to choose from. Two examples are the Madison Fund and The Tri-Continental

Corporation. Because shares in these specialized firms are traded on the market in the same manner as shares of IBM, the shares reflect what investors are willing to pay for them, and not necessarily what the shares are worth in terms of holdings in other securities. And unlike shares in a mutual, open-end fund, the number of shares in closed-end funds is strictly limited. If you want such a share you must buy it from some other investor, at his price, almost always through a broker.

It would be wrong to assume that because many of the sixty-odd closed-end funds now operating gave up their holding company status they've stopped trying to influence the managements of other corporations. The closed-end funds do vote their shares, they do influence policy, and they do have an inside track on what may happen to the shares of certain corporations. For that matter, some of the managers of open-end funds hold somewhat the same power. The Puritan Fund, for example, threw its weight into an MGM proxy fight. So far this power has not been noticeably abused, although the potentials for a concentration of influence are obvious.

Since the closed-end funds do not make daily tabulations on their asset holdings, it is difficult to know what such shares are really worth in terms of book value. An investor may be paying a premium or buying at a discount without knowing it. But *The Wall Street Journal* does publish an unaudited report each week on the closed-end funds, showing both "value" and price. Earnings of a closed-end fund may be more important than whether or not its shares are selling below asset value. The shares in Madison Fund were commanding a 20 per cent premium in August of 1962, whereas two years earlier the shares were selling at a 30 per cent discount. Tri-Continental shares have been consistently below asset value. Some closed-end funds command a 50 per cent premium. When one of my clients wrote to Tri-Continental for an explanation of the discount in May of 1966, he received this answer from the President, Fred E. Brown:

1. A number of people still remember how many closed-end funds failed during the depression.

2. There is only limited sponsorship (sales efforts) for closed-end funds.

3. Too many investors were currently interested in individual shares rather than in broad diversification.

4. The belief that closed-end shares should sell at a discount because of tax liability on unrealized profits.

5. Tri-Continental had issued a number of stock warrants, which if exercised could dilute the profits per share.

6. Tri-Continental retains its profits, rather than distributing them, which makes the fund suffer in comparison to certain mutual funds.

Who knows, in a few months or years, shares in Tri-Continental may be commanding a premium, which would require an entirely different answer from the president, whoever he then may be. At any rate, shares in the better closed-end funds do offer investors the chance for diversification, professional management, decent dividends, and growth. And at a somewhat lower acquisition fee than from buying into a typical mutual fund. Any broker would be happy to sell you shares in a closed-end fund.

Whether you invest on your own, with or without professional advice, or choose one of the various open-end or closed-end investment companies, you'll still want to stay abreast of the market. That means interpreting the market reports, analyzing the market comments, and, in general, keeping your perspective.

THE MARKET INDICATORS

By far the most popular and widely heeded indicator is the Dow Jones Average of thirty Industrials. While these thirty Industrials represent only about 2 per cent or so of the shares listed on the New York Exchange, they amount to about 30 per cent of its market value. So the index is more representative than its critics contend. More importantly, the Dow Industrial index is very representative of overall American industry, and it portrays the actions of the leading corporations in most of those industries. What many critics object to about the Dow thirty is not selectivity, but the size of the figures involved. When the Dow was trying to break through the 1000 mark in February of 1966, a 1 per cent drop in the average came out as 10 points, a rather frightening figure. Points aren't dollars, of course, they are simply "points" in a highly complex system of measuring change.

The price change in an individual stock is often expressed in points too, such as 3½ points, but in such cases points *do* mean dollars. Not in the indexes, however.

The Dow system also has a way to measure the action of a select group of railroad stocks, and one for the utilities as well. And to appease certain critics, Dow Jones also has a sixty-five-stock average, which includes industrials, rails, and utilities. This would seem to give a more representative view of total market action, but that index has never been widely accepted.

Now almost everyone is in on the market tabulating act. The Associated Press has an average of sixty stocks. The UPI recently came out with an all-inclusive indicator which records the average change in all listed stocks from the previous day's trading. Standard & Poor has a number of indexes, including its rather popular "500 stock index." And now the New York and American Stock Exchanges have bowed to pressure and are publishing daily composite indexes of all trading. Perhaps in its own way, each index adds a little something to one's market perspective. But I doubt you can go too far wrong following the Dow Jones averages, especially if you balance them a bit with any of the more inclusive indicators. While a rise, or a slide, in the popular averages may not affect your personal holdings on any one day, major securities movements affect all stocks in time. That's why so many analysts make a living just writing and talking about the "market."

Especially when the market is declining many stockbrokers rely heavily on semantics to bolster the courage of their clients. The brokers often say there is no such thing as a "stock market," that there is only a "market in stocks." The inference is that certain stocks of good quality, or those influenced by special situations, may be rising while most other shares are falling. This is all well and true. But a general "bear" market, if it goes deep enough, usually drags most all issues down with it. That is why the financial reporters stress the number of shares which decline each day as compared to the number which advance. Although the New York Exchange lists over 1600 issues for trading, with most of them being common stocks, only about 1400 are traded on any given day.

Another figure to consider is the number of issues reaching new low prices for the year, compared to the number which reach new highs. It isn't so much that these computations have any immediate, direct effect on the stocks you own; it is mainly because so many other investors think there is a pertinent relationship. The stock market as a whole, and over the years, acts from logic—based on how individual corporations, industries, and the general economy are doing. At least that statement would be true if logic means "just cause." But from day to day, or even month to month, the market often acts in an entirely irrational manner. Investors react to news, rumors, planted information, and hysteria. And they especially react to a breed of men known as the "technical analysts."

THE CRYSTAL BALL CROWD

Predicting how the stock market or individual issues will perform could not, under the wildest stretch of the imagination, be called a science. Even the study of economics is not a true science, since it involves that great unpredictable—human nature. Nevertheless, there is a great deal to be said for the conventional stock analysts and the business economists who spend their lives trying to rationalize the market. The economists in particular have a wealth of statistics within easy reach these days, and when they add up all the information available, a certain logic emerges from it all. These "fundamentalists" make notes on how certain industries are doing, how inventories are controlled, and how the cost-of-doing business affects those industries. Certain companies always do better than others in the same field. Management shifts are important to watch, as are cash, and cash-flow considerations.

Cash-flow is merely net profit plus the amount set aside for depreciation, an important factor considering the changes in our depreciation allowances and investment tax credits. At any rate, the so-called economic and conventional analysts at least have statistical support for whatever they predict. Any investor with a substantial sum to worry about needs to keep reasonable tab on the health of the economy and on the health of the firms and industries he has invested in. He can do this by subscribing to any number of business publications and from reading the business and financial section of his daily newspaper.

And since I have used the air waves as a part of my communications career, please allow me to say that radio and television offer the busy person a chance to keep up with the major events on Wall Street. Incidentally, the number of radio "business and financial" reports has tripled over just the past three or four years. By and large, news media financial reporting deals with facts, documented trends, authentic analysis, and statistics, which, however, many investors place little faith in. These persons much prefer to know, for instance, whether or not "Oils Unlimited" broke out of its "head and shoulders" formation.

From the standpoint of the "chartist" or "technical analyst," such talk is not gobbledy-gook. It is all part of a nebulous system for predicting market behavior, based part on arithmetic, part on conventional wisdom, and part on psychology, with a good sprinkling of pragmatic history tossed in. Chartists often talk in terms of "line formations," "gap formations," "triangles," "rounding bottoms," "triple tops," and "widening tops." They are referring to the patterns made by the up-and-down movements of individual issues, or of the market indicators as a whole. Such analysis is primarily human interpretation of stock movements and trends, particularly the rails and industrials, using those tools which have become respectable within that particular theory group. The Dow Theory is the most widely followed technical analysis, although I have yet to find a man who can actually define the theory itself.

How good are these ill-defined predictions? Opinions differ, and so do the results as they appear in print, depending upon who is making the case. A chartist may warn his clients that if the market falls below a certain point, look out. A number of Dow Theorists advised their clients to sell all stocks and real estate holdings during May of 1966, because all the bear market signals were flying. It is questionable how many clients went to that extreme. But since many investors did get out of the market to an unusual extent, based on the warnings, it becomes clear that analysts not only interpret market actions, they affect them as well.

There is only one moral I can draw from all this, since it is very doubtful that any chartist owns a crystal ball. The moral is to pay attention to what these seers are saying and forecasting, for the simple reason that many investors do place great store in this type of analysis. In other words, if a group of men are capable of creating a near-panic, they deserve more than normal attention. And while the chartists and other technical analysts use methods which would not qualify as scientific, the data they feed into their "guess machines" often have a sound economic value, however suspect the systems and the conclusions may be.

SUMMARY ON THE STOCK AND BOND MARKET

To sum up on bonds, stocks, and funds, I still hold to the view that most persons with $50,000 or less to invest would be wiser in the long run to stick with the safe fixed-income savings plans, balanced by careful selection of one or more mutual funds. As wisdom and net worth increase, an investor can try his hand at corporate and government bonds, in order to increase his potential on dollar earnings. There are enormous possibilities in the Convertibles, provided an investor doesn't grab at the first offering he is exposed to. When something becomes too popular, look out.

On the equity side, while a person has the opportunity to pick his individual shares in order to diversify, the closed-end funds, or some of the super-corporations, give him better odds at lower costs. Regardless of which route he chooses, it only makes sense to keep up on what's going on in the economy. And even if an investor is a hardheaded realist who sneers at ouija boards and squiggly lines, it would be sheer folly to ignore the chartists and other technical analysts. The truth is, a genuine "fundamentalist" with an advanced degree from Harvard Business School may be hard put to earn $15,000 a year while he studies true "stock values." But the chartist, who may have spent most of his life as a song-and-dance man, could well be drawing down $100,000 per annum or more, which gives you a rough idea of what you are up against trying to make sense out of the stock market.

At the very least you should ask your "customer's man" (the broker's representative) whether he's a chartist or a fundamentalist at heart. Then you'll know if you're getting the facts or the "feel" of the market. While all brokerage firms belonging to the New York Stock Exchange have to meet the same requirements as to financial condition, rules of operation and disclosure, some account representatives are more honest and competent than others. And this *does* matter.

The New York Exchange not long ago admirably chose to bail out some of its bankrupt members' customers over a salad oil scandal in the East. Other Exchange members, as a result, were voluntarily assessed millions of dollars in total. In Japan, just a few years back, the government had to salvage the largest brokerage house in that nation. The failure of a large finance company in Canada almost toppled the government and started a panic on the Toronto Exchange. If one or more very large brokerage firms in this nation were to go under because of dishonesty or stupidity, it might sorely tax the ability of the New York Stock Exchange members to come to the rescue again. It used to be that the established life insurance companies would always buy up their bankrupt competitors, in order to protect the "image" of the industry. But that practice came to a virtual halt when life insurance firms in our Southwest began to fail in fairly large numbers. Now the insurance industry is more inclined to let the chips fall where they may, meanwhile stressing "Pick your company with care." So it may be with the securities business. If you leave large sums on deposit with your broker-dealer, recognize that it is *possible* to lose that money. There is no Federal share insurance covering broker deposits. To sum up, pick your brokerage firm—and your personal customer's man—as you would select a surgeon.

In wrapping up this section on stocks, bonds, and funds, I have not attempted to include trading on the commodity markets or advice relating to the more esoteric forms of stock speculating, such as "puts" and "calls." These are a form of speculating, not investing. The average investor would be better off, in my opinion, shooting craps at Las Vegas.

The same applies to "going short," which amounts to betting that a particular issue will drop in price. There are valid reasons for large investors to hedge their bets in this manner, under certain circumstances, but these reasons hardly apply to the "peoples' capitalism" type of fellow. Going short, or "taking a short position," means (on paper) borrowing and then selling another investor's share of stock, hoping you can replace it later at a price lower than the current one. There have been tons of money made and lost on shorts, involving such reputable firms as RCA and Piggly Wiggly. Many analysts consider a large "short position" as a support for the market, since at some time the shorts have to buy in to replace their borrowed stock, which is about all most of us need to know about this technique.

When you own common stocks or shares of a mutual fund, you're really in the "real estate" business, because there are "real" items of wealth backing up your investments. But most investors think of real estate in terms of land and buildings, which brings us to the next general subject for discussion.

C. *Mortgages, land, and income property*

MORTGAGES

A lien instrument against a piece of land or improved property is called a mortgage and it is essentially income-producing. Mortgages are stated as repayable in so many dollars, thus there is no chance for capital gain, at least not unless interest rates dropped drastically enough to make an old high-rate mortgage worth more than its face value. So it becomes rather obvious that persons with high incomes are not very interested in mortgages these days, considering that they would lose a substantial part of their interest income to the Federal Government. By and large, the mortgage loan business has become a specialized field for large financial institutions, such as investment bankers, savings and loan firms, banks, and insurance companies. Many older persons on limited incomes still show an interest in mortgages, however, for several reasons. The tax bite doesn't affect them as much, for one thing, and second, mortgages are usually well secured, which brings peace of mind. A third reason is that mortgages normally carry higher interest rates than bonds, savings accounts, and the various "mutual-share" arrangements. Thus a person who (1) needs income, (2) isn't taxed too heavily, and (3) wants security, could logically invest money in mortgages. There is one important thing to watch, however; the higher the interest rate, the greater the risk in most cases. The mortgagor who is willing to pay an unusually high rate of interest is either dumb or a poor credit risk. And even though mortgages are secured, they aren't very liquid. Lack of liquidity, the ability to cash in, is a serious drawback to mortgages as an investment tool. Then too, if a mortgagor defaults, costs of foreclosure can be high. There's also the problem of delay, since in most states foreclosure on a regular mortgage can take up to a year. The California deed of trust, however, was designed for relatively fast, easy repossession.

One must also consider the cost of servicing a mortgage. Payments must be collected and posted. Receipts must usually be mailed out, showing the portions of the payment going to interest and principal. A mortgagee must be sure he is protected by fire insurance if there are improvements on the real estate, and he must check to see if property taxes are being paid. Some individuals who invest in mortgages pay special "service companies" to handle all these details, with 5 or 6 per cent of the payment being a typical charge. But that cost reduces the net earnings on the investment.

Only if an investor is in a tax position to afford pure interest income do mortgages make a sound investment medium these days, and only then if he can expect to gross at least 2 per cent more per year than he could earn on safe, insured savings plans. The further qualification is that he invest only in sound mortgages backed by a good equity in the property. The trouble is, many investors get carried away with the thought of earning 6 or 7 per cent, compared to only 5 per cent or so in bonds or certificates of deposit. This is especially true of second mortgages, or second "deeds of trust," as they are called in California.

Back eight or nine years ago, savers in California and in certain other states were offered 10 per cent on second trust deeds. But many of these investors lost everything when the trust deed companies failed or absconded with the funds. The invested cash had been placed in "pooled" trust accounts, with no one investor having a claim against any specific property. That situation has been more or less corrected, but investors by the thousands still put their money in "seconds," hoping for higher than usual rewards. It's the old story of "the higher the rate promised, the greater the risk."

Only in areas where land prices are booming or inflating rapidly do seconds make any sense at all, except in the case of a seller of property who is willing to gamble because he has received such a good price for his property. Even then, he's probably willing to sell his "second mortgage" at a discount ranging from 5 to 20 per cent. At the very least you should try to discount a second mortgage by 3 to 5 per cent per year.

A mortgage is one thing, a second mortgage is another. Any serious dip in land or housing prices may result—and has resulted —in thousands of families abandoning their mortgaged homesteads. When equities disappear, people do too. While holders of the first mortgages may eventually bail out or suffer moderate losses, most second mortgage holders are left holding the bag.

Even the first mortgage investors may have their cash tied up for
months or years before liquidating. Over the years, second mortgages have proved to be a poor investment for most individuals,
even though the rates of interest involved were very high. What
about your Aunt Minnie who made a fortune in "seconds"?
Well, she may have hit a period when everything was moving
up, getting out at just the right time. Maybe she was just lucky.
On the other hand, maybe she was doing a little "loan sharking"
on the side, charging higher rates than the law allowed. As a matter of fact, that's where most of the profit in second mortgages
comes from. You have to have the stomach for that sort of thing,
which is why I never felt too sorry for many of those persons
who got clipped by the "10 per centers."

LAND

Our population explosion and our income tax laws (they figure
into everything) have resulted in an enormous interest in raw
land. People more or less rightly assume that since there will be
so many more of us, land will automatically rise in price. But
not just any old land. Unless the land involved is in or near an
expanding metropolitan area where 80 per cent of us will soon
be living, it can take years for it to show an appreciable price
increase, which points up the questionable wisdom of paying
several hundreds of dollars for a so-so plot on a desert. For that
matter, there are thousands of unimproved, uninhabited lots in
lush Florida, patiently waiting for their unhappy owners to start
things moving.

The recent land boom, or craze, has two distinct aspects. First,
there are the numerous small investors who bought lots in highly
promoted sections of the country. The other phase has to do
with "big money" and "big incomes" looking for ways to dodge
taxes. Taking the little guy first, he never wants to miss out on a
good thing. And in the case of land promotion, he gives the
promoters quite an edge. Unlike the fellow who dabbles in
the stock market or in commodities, and who expects a quick

buck or nothing, the innocent land buyer accepts the fact that he may have to wait years to turn a profit. And during those years of patient waiting, the promoter has plenty of time to fleece more sheep. His office isn't crowded with unhappy victims for a long time, and by the time things get a little tight he can move on or file bankruptcy. I've visited several oversold land developments in Arizona and California, only to see flat, sagebrush country, without water in many cases, and often without marking stakes. One spot which sold for $3000 an acre in 1958 won't bring one-half that figure at this writing. The promoter is finally having trouble with the state and is being sued by his customers. All this despite the promise of a new freeway and hints of rapid industrial development. Several years from now, perhaps, the land will bring its sale price of $3000 an acre, but you certainly can't count on it.

Most land buyers pay a small sum down, financing the balance. So they have an interest cost to consider; but even when they pay cash, their investment isn't paying a nickel in interest or dividends. Over a period of time, even the small land taxes mount up. I'm not saying you *can't* strike it rich investing in small chunks of raw land; I'm simply stating it as plainly as possible that the odds are weighted against you. To be sure, plenty of land in our major cities sold for only $100 an acre twenty, thirty, or fifty years ago, whereas it now would bring $50,000 a lot. But in most cases that type of land has changed owners scores of times, with each owner making only a normal speculative profit. To select a spot with true potential and then hang onto it for a decade or so is unreal to contemplate. Only the huge landowners can afford to make such killings.

At the very least, the individual who is toying with the idea of putting money in land ought to visit the site in person. He should be aware of the cost, the waiting period, and the lack of income from his equity such an investment involves. And then, assuming he is sufficiently liquid and solvent after his purchase, he can rest assured that he now has a claim to the source of most wealth, land. He may even hit the jackpot, but not likely. Here is one way to tip the odds in your favor, however. Select a spot where you'd like to build a cabin or a second home and then try to buy some land in that area.

This has become much easier to do now that millions of Americans are interested in the second home idea, where they can escape hordes of people over the weekends and commune with nature. Farmers and other landowners have been understandably reluctant to sell off small pieces of their land to strangers, because once an acreage is subdivided it becomes harder to unload the remaining larger parcels to commercial developers.

But now there is money to be made in developing large parcels of attractive and far-out land for recreational purposes. When Shelter Cove, which is north of San Francisco, was subdivided into small units for second homes near the sea, the 4500-unit development was virtually sold out in six months. Now the same developer is experimenting with an even larger parcel in the heart of the California redwoods area. The individual lots will sell from $3000 up to perhaps $10,000 a lot, and each lot will run about one-fourth to one-half of an acre.

This mass-development of second homes and retirement areas is a relatively new concept, but my guess is that it will have a great future. Some of these lots can be purchased for as little down as 2 per cent, and the terms are only 1 per cent of the original balance per month. Thus a family could invest say $6000 or less by paying down only $120, and payments of $60 per month. By accelerating the payments whenever possible, the land could be paid off and become the necessary equity for the financing of a 1000-square-foot home costing about $12,000.

In a few years the family would have a place to go to on weekends, holidays, and vacations. The adults may even choose to live there after retirement. This is precisely what many people had in mind when they sunk thousands of hard-earned dollars in desert and sagebrush country, only to lose most of what they had invested. The point is, you may have to pay more originally, much more in fact, when you invest wisely in potential recreational land, than when you buy cheap scrub land. But if you buy wisely, it is hard to lose. Even if you decide not to build on the land, you should be able to sell it and turn a decent profit after a few years.

Here are some guides to follow when you buy that double-duty land. By all means, try to visit the selected spot if you can. If it's too far away, at least talk to some people who have been there—people you trust. Make sure the place has natural beauty, along with natural recreational facilities, such as water, campsites, and fishing areas. To be a really good investment, there should be tennis courts and a golf course.

In order for the land to gain in value, it ought to be fairly near a large urban area, close to a highway and with airport facilities. The temperature should not be extreme during any season, otherwise it will be a part-time recreational development. How cold does it get? How often (and when) does it rain? If the development promises all-weather sports, is there enough snow to attract the ski crowd?

While many of us think we'd like to rough it, that feeling wears off rather fast once we're away from civilization for any length of time. The successful developments of the future will have sewers, electricity, water, and telephones available at each lot site. That's one reason you'll pay more for a good piece of recreational land. And you can't rely on promises to obtain these amenities. You should expect a warranty arrangement when you buy an undeveloped lot. Some developments are being handled through bank trusteeships, so you can be certain of clear title if the developer goes broke. And in many cases the developers are required to post bond that they'll carry out their promises.

It always pays to understand your own prejudices too. A piece of land selling for bargain prices may lure many people you don't care to socialize with. They may be interested mainly in very casual living, whereas you have developed somewhat plusher tastes. Buying land near a seaside development could virtually isolate you unless you love to fish, or unless your leisure outlook is water-oriented. Persons who buy recreational land near the sea may be quite different, as a group, than those who buy on the desert or in the mountains.

If you love natural beauty, make certain there are rules regarding the destruction of nature and rules regarding the types of buildings allowed on individual sites. After all, you're not interested in duplicating the mass-produced suburbia you are trying so hard to escape (I hope).

The reputation, experience, and integrity of the developer are very important to check. If he's handled any similar projects in the past, it would be worthwhile to look at them, especially if they've had time to jell. The best-laid plans are sometimes thwarted by humans themselves. We try hard to allow freedom of choice in such things as housing and recreational developments, but one or two bad apples can ruin a thousand acres of carefully implemented plans.

If you check all these things before you buy land for that second home or retirement cottage, you should do well. At the very least, you'll have a place to visit and enjoy long before you retire. You may not make a fat profit should you decide to sell, but if you chose wisely, there ought to be a decent financial reward.

But, as I said before, "big money" is going into land because of the tax angles. This is especially true in California, where prices of certain land has been inflated almost to the bursting point. The tax angles amount to this: (1) the possibility of paying lower taxes on profits because of the capital gains treatment, and (2) the chance to "prepay" interest, all of which is treated as an expense for the year in which it is paid. In fact, the trend is so popular in California that special "land hunting" firms have done exceedingly well themselves without investing a nickel in the land being traded around. Three of these firms are Ramco, Property Research Corporation, and Economic and Land Research Corporation.

These land hunters act mostly as brokers, usually getting 10 per cent of the sales price from the seller. And they concentrate on what is called "predevelopment" land, mostly in California, but they accept money from anywhere. That would mean land which has already shown a certain amount of price appreciation, because of being fairly near some large city or development, but which has not been seriously bid up by housing developments or industrial complexes. The theory is that proper research, including the study of freeway planning, population push, and natural advantages, will almost guarantee a buyer a future profit. The profit, hopefully, should come in from three to five years, not merely because Americans are impatient, but because it is costly to inventory nonproductive real estate.

The real kicker comes from the "prepaid interest," however, and that's how the land hunters really earn their cut. It becomes necessary to find a farmer, ex-farmer, or ordinary landowner who wants to sell out, and who is in a low enough tax bracket to accept several years of interest in advance. Otherwise, Uncle Sam would make up in taxes from the seller what he lost from the buyer. Some hunters hint that they have now devised a way to sell land under which the buyer can prepay tax-deductible interest with the seller getting somewhat the same tax break, probably through a combination of trusts and deferred payment plans. However, each such proposal has to be tested in the tax courts. But, as an example, suppose a piece of land worth about $250,000 is purchased for 20 per cent down, and the balance at 6 per cent over ten years. The 20 per cent would come to $50,000. Since 6 per cent on $250,000 amounts to $15,000 per year, three years would come to $45,000. So the buyer pays the $50,000 down all right, with $45,000 paying three years' interest in advance, and only $5000 going to the principal. Assuming the buyer is in the 50 per cent tax bracket, or higher, about one-half of what he paid down would come from his savings on income taxes alone. And he would have paid three years' interest in advance, with nothing coming due for that period of time, not even payments on the principal according to many such land contracts. As a result of all this, the high-income buyer bought land at the expense of the Internal Revenue Service, with the added chance of a fat capital gain.

If, for instance, the land later brings $300,000—hopefully in three years—the investor can cash in a profit of $50,000, on which he wouldn't pay taxes of over $12,500. Should the land double in price, the tax-subsidized windfall is that much greater. At the very worst, the investor has lost $25,000, but he originally *saved that much* in taxes, and his loss would be deductible too. At any rate, that's what the land boom is all about, with minor deviations.

Here again, years can pass without disenchanted buyers complaining. Should a recession develop, or should land fail to inflate as predicted, the land hunters may be forced into other lines of business. The real weakness of the scheme probably lies in a certain amount of pseudo-research. But since a reasonable number of investors have already made big money, it is only common sense to include it in this discussion.

Unfortunately, a great deal of the money made in land has come from obviously unsavory techniques. Large landowners, waiting for their sale profits, have been known to influence tax authorities in order to get ridiculously low assessments. Otherwise, as I mentioned before, it becomes very costly to inventory sizable estates. And since it takes "big money" to finance "big land deals," some appraisal firms have been getting their share of the bonanza through phoney appraisals. It became so bad in certain parts of the nation that land appraisal associations had to expel some of their members and tighten their rules. One should realize immediately that land speculation has always been a field for wheeling, dealing, and peeling. Sometimes it only takes a hundred-dollar bill, peeled off a bankroll, to raise a land valuation sufficiently to make up for a nonexistent down payment. But as I said earlier, most Americans don't let their Puritan upbringings affect their financial statements. My only advice is to recognize that land speculation can be a pretty fast, and often dirty, game. Maybe you'd prefer the cleaner career of an income-property landlord. Well, let's take a look at that.

INCOME PROPERTY

Long before William Nickerson wrote his book *How I Turned $1,000 into a Million in Real Estate—in My Spare Time,* many Americans were dreaming of retiring as landlords. During the 1920s, thousands of American families bought duplexes, under the mistaken impression they were living rent-free in one-half of their investments. Nickerson undoubtedly did make a million, but he was writing the book back in 1958 when the latest rush to Los Angeles was just beginning. Furthermore, Nickerson really wasn't interested in the landlord business, he was more interested in making money *from* would-be landlords. His idea was to turn over income properties as soon as possible, after minor improvements and hiking the rents, which, of course, increased the "investment value" of each apartment.

Because of this widely read book—the first of its kind really aimed at the mass market—the possibilities of a quick buck in older income properties have been somewhat reduced. Many potential buyers seem fairly well informed on such things as "price to income" ratios. Nickerson, for instance, suggested trying to buy an income property, such as a four- to twenty-unit apartment for not over ten times its adjusted gross income per year. That would be after deducting certain fixed expenses. If such an apartment complex brought in $20,000 per year (net-gross after allowing for free rent to a manager and other fixed expenses) the suggested bargaining price might be $200,000. But in California, where Nickerson made his million, things have changed considerably. Land prices have skyrocketed for one thing. The land beneath our hypothetical $200,000 apartment may now be supposedly worth $150,000 itself, forgetting about the vertical improvements. Whereas back in 1958, the land more likely would have been valued at only $50,000. What's more, the rental income may be about the same as back then. Which means, in a nutshell, that a prospective buyer of such a property would have to inventory a great deal of high-priced, nonproductive land. The building itself would be worth a lesser percentage of the overall price. He ought to try to buy such a property for not over eight times the net rental income, and even then he'd be lucky to make money as a landlord. Before long he'll have to replace the building or drastically improve it to keep the tenants.

Another big change has come in the vacancy rate. Back in 1958, vacancies were running around 2 per cent. During 1965 and 1966 the vacancy rate in parts of the heavily populated San Fernando Valley reached 20 per cent. Foreclosures mounted to the point where home financing agencies were acting more as landlords than as lenders. Other sections of the country suffered less from the overbuilding and speculation than did California, but it shows what can happen. The swing of the economic and speculative pendulum will in time adjust things, but if nothing else, it proves you can't count on inflation and/or the population explosion to bail you out of a bad real estate investment.

While Nickerson and his legion of followers may scoff at the "pure income" aspect of owning rental units, preferring to unload them at the right time on other buyers, you simply can't make a profit selling a near-empty apartment building. Unless there are contented rent-paying tenants, you really have little to sell. It can be compared to bidding up a share of common stock way beyond any sensible relation to what the stock will earn or yield. In the long run, income always counts, and it should determine the cost of any investment. Here is an example of what you might get into buying an apartment complex, and it's partly based on an example which came to my attention. A man and wife paid $250,000 for a twelve-unit apartment with a potential gross rental income of $25,000 per year. Since the price was ten times gross, it seemed like a fairly decent buy. But here are the annual expenses as they proved out over a few years:

Vacancies and losses (4 per cent) $1000
Electricity (halls and exterior)   120
Heat and superintendent   3200
Repairs and upkeep   2500
Insurance   600
Water-sewer   500
Manager   1200
Taxes (property)   5000
Depreciation (25-year life of bldg.)   6000

Total: $20,120

Since the building only grossed $25,000 per year, the net was less than $5000 per year, which is about one-half what the investor could have realized on some 4 per cent bank savings accounts, and with a lot less risk and trouble. You will note there was no allowance for mortgage interest, which would have made this a losing proposition entirely. It may surprise you, but many income properties change hands without any actual expense breakdown. Even when an income property investor consults a tax man, there may be no analysis whatsoever as to genuine profit and loss. Mortgage payments are often made out of the money that should be set aside for repair and depreciation.

The trick these days is to turn your property over before you have to keep a decent set of books, let alone spend money on repairs. In the above example, the building itself was supposedly appraised at $150,000, while the land was worth $100,000. Had the land cost only $50,000, the place would have been a much better buy, from the standpoint of taxes—and eventually from the standpoint of net profit, if any.

In the example given, the disillusioned buyer decided to make some fast adjustments. He began managing his own apartment, thus providing himself with a nonpaying job. He hiked the rents on some units, temporarily upping his vacancy rate, but eventually improving his net return. He cut corners on repairs, deciding to patch and cover rather than genuinely maintain the building. And finally, he decided to completely ignore depreciation (except at tax time). All in all, his books took on the surface look of a reasonably profitable operation, and in time he was able to unload his white elephant on another innocent. In fact, he cleared a $25,000 profit.

I have been exposed to worse examples than the above. I've seen triplexes with monthly rentals of $600 per month (total of the three units) offered for sale at over $100,000. From an income standpoint, $60,000 would be more reasonable. In each case these properties were located on or near very valuable land. Perhaps in time the land under these apartments would bring $100,000 or more. Only time, inflation, the population explosion, and our tax laws will tell. But in the meantime, there will be some unnecessary bankruptcies and foreclosures.

Many income-property brokers have stopped relating net income to total investment; they advertise only in terms of what you can "gross" in terms of your equity alone. You should be interested only in what you can "net" on your equity, relative to what other investments would yield, and relative to the total risk you would assume is order to net anything. Depreciation is the controversial point in all this. You don't actually depreciate the land, only the improvements. Soaring prices for land over the past few years have tended to offset or completely nullify the need to set aside money to replace the improvements (the buildings). Furthermore, our Federal Government allows building owners to deduct depreciation of the improvements from gross income, thereby reducing taxes. That is true even though the land itself may be *increasing* in value. Thus the cost of setting aside money to replace an aging building (which we call depreciation) is usually considered a tax advantage rather than a real expense. But depreciation *is* a very real expense over the long run because as the dollar loses value and as land gains in value, the cost of replacement soars too. If all this be true, you might ask then why has there been such a boom in new apartments, and in income property as a whole? Partly it's from the continuous buying and selling, which in turn keeps boosting property values. As I have mentioned it's from the tax advantages associated with owning something that loses value only on paper (depreciation), even while you aren't being taxed on the *unrealized* price increase of the land itself.

It all boils down to itemizing point by point the real costs of owning an income property. You probably will decide the big money is in the buying and the selling, in finding a buyer who will pay more than you did. That, of course, is not being a landlord, it is being a speculator. And today it's a mighty fast game. There is, beyond a doubt, a great deal of money to be made in being a "slumlord," which means owning shabby properties to be rented to low-income families. The slumlord doesn't keep his units in decent shape; he charges outrageous rents and he ignores safety, health, and public opinion. But even that is changing. In Chicago, for instance, action groups have forced slumlords into reducing rents and improving their properties. The courts have tended to side with the low-income action groups. There's little more to be said about getting rich in that manner; if it's for you, most of this book will bore you to tears.

There is one other explanation to all the building that has been going on in our major cities, and it also has a great deal to do with taxes. A number of new apartment complexes have been financed largely by the Federal Housing Administration. In many cases the FHA guaranteed mortgages up to 90 per cent of the total cost of land and building. Thus a $2,500,000 complex would require only a $250,000 original investment—not even that if the builder managed to obtain a very high appraisal on some recently acquired, inexpensive real estate. The sudden value appreciation (on paper) of his land might pass as his entire down payment.

But the point is, once the complex had been completed, the owner-builder was allowed to "write it off" (depreciate it) on an accelerated basis. In perhaps just five years he could set aside enough for building replacement to match his $250,000 outlay—whether that was real or on paper. What's more, instead of leaving the replacement money in the proper pot, he could pay it back to himself in cash as a nontaxable "return of capital." So in five years the builder would own (except for the mortgage) a $2,500,000 complex without a nickel invested in it. His only problem at this point was to keep enough rent coming in to pay the mortgage, at least until he's able to unload the building on someone else and therefore realize a nice, low-taxed capital gain. Ah yes, it pays to know the angles and the right people. But it helps explain the surplus of half-empty new apartment buildings in our major cities. And it helps to explain why the FHA got stuck with so many multimillion-dollar apartment complexes.

Nevertheless, there are plenty of honest, sound reasons for owning income property, even if it's only a single unit or a duplex. The person who is paying rather high income taxes can save on those by being able to depreciate his rental property. Even a small, older unit worth $20,000 (not counting the land) can be depreciated over twenty years, which comes to $1000 a year. Thus a person with a $25,000 "taxable" income would have that income reduced by $1000 per year, and since he is in the 36 per cent bracket, as of this writing, he would *save* $360 per year from income taxes. Chances are his property wouldn't actually lose $1000 each year, thanks (?) to inflation and rising land costs. Therefore his "paper loss" would save him several hundred real dollars each year.

There is another problem related to investing which should be discussed, and that has to do with changing the dollar value of gold. The United States cannot indefinitely continue to run a balance of payments deficit and still maintain the current gold-to-currency relationship. Even though we out-trade other nations in total, we continue to lose gold, primarily because of our spending on the "hot" and "cold" war.

As of September 1966, the gold we owned was barely enough to back our outstanding currency by 25 per cent, as required by law. The ratio was down to 33 per cent, compared to almost 38 per cent one year prior to that time. In addition, foreign governments and foreign banks had almost $30 billion in possible claims against the U. S. Treasury stock of $13.4 billion. To be sure, we Americans had well over $30 billion invested overseas, but those assets were of little help to our short-term liquidity crisis.

That situation obviously could not continue. Yet were we to cure our chronic overseas deficits, world trade might suffer enormously. We could remove the 25 per cent gold backing to our currency entirely, but that likely would result in a financial panic, and eventually into runaway inflation. Or, we could reprice gold. It is this writer's opinion that gold will sooner or later be priced at around $70 an ounce, compared to the current $35 an ounce. The big question is: What will this do to investments and values in general?

No one can be certain what would happen, but there is the strong possibility the stock market would drop temporarily, but only temporarily. Pricing gold upward is strongly inflationary, meaning that dollar prices of everything would go up. Many investors have been buying shares in gold mining firms, hoping to reap a harvest from higher priced gold. And quite possibly they will.

But we should bear this in mind. Changing the dollar price of gold will not alter very much the value relationship between gold and other valuable commodities. Thus if gold is worth more in dollars, so will other valuable items such as other metals, petroleum, timber, land, and diamonds. That is why many sophisticated investors were hedging against devaluation by putting some of their cash in oil firms and commodities. As of this writing, the British have little chance of keeping the pound at the par rate of $2.80. As the pound goes, so goes the dollar, according to many experts who stay abreast of international finance.

Having all one's assets in dollars, or in securities payable in dollars, could be quite dangerous in times such as these. That is one reason interest rates have been so abnormally high, in order to attract dollar savings. And it is also the reason why France has chosen gold over dollars, even though she loses the potential earnings from dollar-type investments.

The main points I am trying to make are: (1) You can't outguess major monetary moves, so stay balanced in your investments—only so much in dollars and the rest in securities related to natural resources and productivity; and (2) buying shares in gold mines is only one method of hedging against cheaper dollars and devaluation. Other valuable commodities should tend to follow the revised dollar valuation of gold.

As I stated earlier, even a single person making considerably less than the above example might realize tax savings from owning income property. And the larger the investment, other things being equal, the larger the potential tax benefits. But the person who decides to dabble in this type of real estate shouldn't get carried away by the tax savings alone. I hope I have proved that there are many angles to consider before becoming a landlord, even your own. As to that duplex you've been dreaming about, living in one-half the unit certainly won't provide you with free rent. You'd simply be consuming one-half of your potential rental income. You might compare it to buying your own grocery store so you could eat free.

When you come right down to it, investing in real estate has to be measured against the returns offered under other investment plans, including stocks, bonds, and even savings accounts—on a "net income" basis. Real estate is no magic road to riches, even though the ads sometimes make it appear that way. There are a number of tax angles in real estate, and there's also a lot of wheeling and dealing. The important thing is to know exactly what you are getting into, with your eyes wide open. If you do that, there are plenty of interesting, rewarding possibilities from being a landlord.

SPECIAL SITUATION: PLANNING FOR RETIREMENT

Before getting into the practicalities of planning for retirement, let's "talk" about it for a while. Retirement would be simply great if we could disassociate it from the thought of getting old. That's why we're a bit schizoid about the whole idea. Take, for instance, a young man of twenty-six years applying for a position with a corporation. More than likely his first question has to do with the company's retirement plan. This is a bit appalling to the rugged individualist of today.

Yet, what is this young man? Is he really young? From a purely chronological standpoint, he has entered the "middle third" of his life, based on a life expectancy of seventy-five. But to call him "middle-aged" would be violating the semantic code of our youth-worshipping society. It could be that he has every right to begin thinking about his twilight years. Indeed, he would be a fool not to.

On the other hand, the closer we get to actual retirement age, the more sensitive we become. A man of forty, temporarily out of work, wouldn't dream of inquiring about a pension plan when applying for a job. Yet he has only ten of his middle years left. Even though young girls sometimes weep at leaving their teens, and middle-aged men often act like asses proving their youth, the hurdles of age are mostly psychological. The getting old process does involve chemistry, there's no doubt of that, but by and large it's a rather gradual, smooth transition. We create most of our own problems. There is, of course, a vested interest in the "fear of age." Commercial advertising has created a ready market for wrinkle creams, tonics, and "think young" escapes.

This makes us jittery enough, and it is compounded by the scare tactics used by many thrift institutions as they struggle to entice our savings. A good case can be made that older people haven't been thrifty enough, considering the millions of retired persons living on sub-subsistence incomes. But not all older persons can be blamed for their poverty. Most all of us try hard, in our own ways, and failure is hardly unique. I am not trying to make a case for the profligate, and I'd certainly question the man who looks forward to senility. But it's quite possible that if we ignore the bleatings of the marketplace to look young, feel young, and think young, we'll be able to wear our age with more dignity and have lots more security toward the end. Who knows, if more mature people would accept life philosophically they might even earn the respect of their youngers.

So, whether you are on the verge of retiring, already there or threescore years away, stop running scared. If you manage to survive those joyous (?) years of youth and in-between, you'll have accomplished a great deal, with or without hitting the jackpot. Try to put something aside regularly for the day when your earning power will have decreased. How much that should be is a matter of debate and personal choice as well.

How much should you save?

As I have indicated before, long-term savings should not be confused with short-term savings. Saving to buy something in the months or years immediately ahead is entirely different from saving for retirement, emergency, or disability. Perhaps five cents out of each dollar is sufficient for long-range thrift. At least it is fairly realistic.

But now let's return to "this world" again. As of 1966, 8.4 per cent of the first $6600 we earned went for retirement and security. We paid 4.2 per cent and our employers paid the other half—which is really another form of wages. It is very doubtful if the average young husband could save much more than 8.4 per cent and still provide decently for his family. And since that 8.4 per cent is considerably more than five cents out of each dollar, that problem is fairly well solved. What's more, a young man now can afford to concentrate on more immediate money problems. With Medicare included in our Social Security taxes, the deductions will increase year after year, making it even more difficult for wage earners to save additional money. It has become almost useless to debate the wisdom or implications of this government-enforced security program, it is here and most people support it. It is more logical to *plan around it*.

Therefore, under the present scheme of things, it makes more sense for families and individuals to save in order to live better *now* and in the *fairly near future*, rather than to scrimp in order to provide for old age. To a reasonable extent that last burden has been lifted from us. Following this line of thinking, for instance, a young man with a family needn't buy an endowment-type life insurance policy (with a fast cash buildup) at the *expense* of pure insurance protection. In other words, he needn't let his fear of the "poorhouse" reduce the sum of money his family would receive from life insurance should he die prematurely. Social security does enable us to concentrate on other important forms of family protection. In my considered opinion, it isn't necessary to seriously worry about retirement until about age forty-five, or even age fifty-five. One should, of course, strive for solvency, avoid foolish debt, and build an estate if possible. But to run scared all one's life, always thinking about the calendar, is worse than not being born at all. The young man who selects a job *primarily* because of the firm's retirement program already has one foot in the grave. There has to be a sensible, middle-of-the-road approach to the financial problems of old age.

Thrift does involve sacrifice. And because it does, a thrifty person is reluctant to change his habits once the rewards have been won. A really frugal person pales at the very thought of "dipping into capital." Once he has acquired a substantial nest egg, the idea of spending it to live better seems positively foolish. Live off the *earnings* of thrift, yes, but reduce the source of those earnings, no! . . . so reasons the older person who finally retires from his job and wants to take it easy. But let's assume a retired couple wants (or needs) an extra $200 per month income, to supplement social security and perhaps a pension plan. Invested to "earn" about 5 per cent per year, this would require a retirement estate of $50,000 to provide such an extra income ($2400 per year).

There are close to 20 million persons now over sixty-five in this country, and assuming they represent about 15 million "family economic units," these older people in total would have to own assets worth about $750 *billion*. There is barely that much wealth in the entire country, especially when you consider that it's balanced off by almost as much debt. Therefore, even such a modest goal as a supplemental income of $200 per month (from earnings of assets) is an unreasonable goal to hold out to enormous numbers of people. A few of us may achieve such a dream, but most of us will fall far short.

This is in no way meant to discourage those with bigger ideas, or to criticize those who have already managed to acquire substantial assets. It is simply an attempt to make sense out of dollars, and to offer most every family an attainable goal. Even having as little as $5000 in savings at the time of retirement would be well worthwhile. It would give a feeling of having "something in the bank." It would provide perhaps $200 per year in earnings for special occasion spending, and it could even be dipped into now and then without a guilt complex.

A retired couple with considerably more than $5000 in assets might find it even harder to consume bits of capital each year. The more money one has, the more one is inclined to hoard it and make it pay its own way. While this has considerable logic during one's working career, when the estate is being created, it makes less sense as the actuarial tables begin to press in. A man at age sixty-five has about fifteen more years to live, assuming good luck and good health. Thus if he supplemented his regular income by $1000 per year from a $15,000 estate, he would still have money left over at eighty. That would represent the earnings over fifteen years from his "average" estate value of about $7500. At 5 per cent per year, over fifteen years, the earnings would come to $5625—even more when compounded fairly frequently. So after spending his entire original savings over a fifteen-year period, our hypothetical wastrel would still have close to $6000 left.

That's why some of the "monthly withdrawal" plans offered by mutual funds are attracting more older investors, even though, in almost every case, the monthly sums paid to shareholders involve some dipping into capital (the principal sum) for several years. It is usually considered "safe" to withdraw $50 per month, or $600 per year, from a $10,000 fund investment. That would represent a 6 per cent "draw," partly from capital for a while, partly from earnings, and partly from share appreciation (capital gains profits).

Let's pretend, just as a teasing example, that you had retired at the end of 1957 with only $10,000 in savings. But along about the middle of 1958 a mutual fund salesman contacted you and persuaded you to put the entire amount in Fidelity Trend Fund, Inc. Well, $800 would have disappeared right off the bat, going toward the 8 per cent sales charge. So now you have only $9200 working for you. What's more, you elected to draw $50 each month to supplement your social security. By the end of 1958, you would have consumed $300 more from your principal investment, less any earnings of the fund. At any rate, for the next seven years you continue to draw $50 per month, or $600 per year, in order to live decently. And all the time you are wondering if there would be anything left. As a matter of fact, there would have been *quite a bit* left by the end of 1965, some $86,000 to be exact. And that's despite the $600 per year you drew out and the $800 sales commission. Over that period of time, this particular fund earned $3214 in investment income dividends, and many times that much in capital gains and share appreciation. This happened to be a "hot fund," the very hottest in fact, over the particular period covered. But what if you had simply selected a mutual fund at random and made a poor guess?

In the June 1966 issue of *Fundscope Magazine,* well over 100 different funds were analyzed as to the results an investor could have expected under the above arrangement, covering the ten-year period from 1956 through 1965. In each case it was assumed the investor would invest $10,000 and then begin regular $50 a month withdrawals. The worst result depicted was that of a "bond" fund, which would have had a residual cash value of slightly under $6000 at the end of the ten years. So even after taking out $6000 from the $10,000 investment there would still have been almost $6000 remaining, under the worst of the examples.

A retired investor can even hedge a little if he chooses to, by reducing his monthly draw during bad market periods. He can even suspend it for a while if he chooses to, in order to avoid depletion. To be sure, during those particular years covered, an investor might have had to sell some of his profitable shares to pay taxes. But those on retirement plans would have felt little pain because of their small incomes, double exemptions, and tax-free social security. Not every ten-year period will be as good either. Some may even be "bad" from the standpoint of dividends and capital gains. But throughout the history of the stock market, very few ten-year periods have been bad overall.

The whole point of this is to show that a retired person *can* dip into capital occasionally, and rather regularly, without shattering his security. And it also shows how even a modest nest egg can supplement one's retirement income. If you distrust the stock market completely, you could set up a somewhat similar plan under a bank savings account—without, of course, the chance for capital gain.

What you already have

It also is worthwhile to consider what social security itself is worth in terms of an estate. The Research Institute of America figures your social security rights could have been worth $186,000 during 1965. Since the benefits are exempt from estate and income taxes, they could be worth over $300,000 to a family in the top tax bracket. RIA gave the example of a thirty-five-year-old man, who is married, has two children, and earns enough to pay the full social security tax. The value assigned to this man's potential social security benefits was broken down as follows:

Life Insurance Protection	$76,000
Disability Insurance	72,000
Retirement Annuities	38,000
Total Potential Value	$186,000

Very few individuals would amass such a fortune if left to their own devices, and of course, once a man has actually retired, his main social security estate would be that of the annuity value— the $38,000 in the example above. Nevertheless, a man or woman can acquire a sizable retirement estate through systematic savings. Were a young man to save $100 per month until age sixty-five —based on 4 per cent interest per year compounded quarterly— he would have $118,000 at retirement. If, over that forty-year span, he had invested one-half his savings in good quality stocks or stock funds, his estate would more likely be worth $250,000. There is nothing "magic" about social security; it is simply an *enforced* program, and we can either settle for it, or supplement it. Well over 90 per cent of us will mostly settle for it.

The modern problem, as I have repeatedly stated, is inflation, the gradual cheapening of the dollar. As an example, a couple who retired in 1950 received $120 per month in social security, the top figure at that time. Because of adjustments in payouts, this same couple received $168.60 in 1965. Yet because of inflation, the $168.60 was worth only $126.67 in buying power. That is what is known as treadmilling. But it primarily points up the need to hedge somewhat against inflation, even if you think you would be happy on the maximum retirement benefits paid today. At the moment, a fully covered man and wife, both age sixty-five, would receive a monthly sum of $203.85. There is no doubt but that this figure will be adjusted upward as the dollar buys less, but there are time lags to consider, for one thing, and personal spending habits to keep in mind.

A person can retire at age sixty-two, on a smaller benefit, and there is a case to be made for that. You would have to live three extra years to make up for what you would lose by waiting until age sixty-five. But if you continue to work and earn until age sixty-five, you would lose *nothing* by waiting. And then you would receive the top payout during the remainder of your life-time. The decision might depend on your health, your need to continue working, and the extent of your earnings. Retiring at age sixty-two would normally be an expensive decision for a

couple with only modest savings, but a decent earning power. It
would not, however, be very expensive for a man who has accumulated enough assets to bolster his income. While a social
security pensioner has to sacrifice some of his monthly retirement
benefits if he continues to work for wages rather regularly, he
can have an unlimited income from rents, interest, dividends,
and capital gain without losing a dime from his government income. Many a retired person draws full social security benefits
on top of an investment income exceeding $50,000 per year. At
first thought, this would seem unfair, until you realize that most
wealthy persons are only drawing on their own paid-for Federal
annuities. But if we were to follow that same train of thought,
why should a still-working pensioner be denied what he also had
bought and paid for? Social security seems cleverly designed to
thin out the labor force. Perhaps in time, some of the inequities
will be removed, but you can't count on it. All you can do in
the meanwhile is to build your estate as best you can, adjust it
as you approach retirement, and be a bit philosophical about it
all.

Adjusting your assets

It has become almost a cliché to say that older people should stick
to ultraconservative investments. The thought behind this advice
is that a man of sixty-five or so hasn't the time left to recoup any
losses incurred by speculating. Generally speaking, this idea
makes sense, but you can carry it too far. A man of sixty-eight has
over twelve years left in which to live, according to the Vital
Statistics of America. And since virtually every ten-year investment period in the fairly recent history of this country has shown
(1) a gain in the dollar value of a carefully chosen stock portfolio, and (2) a serious decline in the purchasing value of a dollar
bill, putting all one's money into bonds, savings accounts, or annuities doesn't make sense. If you have reason to believe you'll
be around for even five years, you have almost as much latitude

in your investment program as does a man of thirty. So don't avoid the growth stocks or funds simply because you are drawing social security. Even if you are in a low tax bracket because of your age and income, there is no reason why you should choose interest and rents over dividends and capital gain. Income is income, and you can spend capital gain just as readily as interest from a bond or savings account. And even though you feel elderly and are afraid to gamble, you could be speculating just as much by keeping *all* your assets in "dollars" as by having them *all* in common stocks or mutual funds. Except for the estate tax benefits of giving some of your wealth (even your insurance policies) to your wife and/or children, which I'll discuss later, there is no real need to seriously alter an already well-balanced estate just because you reach age sixty-five. If you have had 60 per cent in stocks and 40 per cent in dollars, it might be wise to reverse these percentages. In that way you would make a temporary market decline less punishing.

Certainly you will want to check up on your life insurance policies as you near retirement age. It may well be that you've accumulated cash value close to the face amounts of your policies. You may want to cash in the policies and invest the surrender value—put that money to work, in other words. It doesn't seem logical to pay the full premium on a $20,000 life policy, when $10,000 of that money is your own (to all practical purposes), especially as your actual need for life insurance protection decreases. It decreases when your children are self-supporting. It decreases when your spouse has only so long to live, has a certain guaranteed income, and has modest living requirements. You simply have to ask yourself "Why am I continuing to carry so much life insurance protection, and what is it costing me in terms of better living, higher earnings on my cash investment, and potential growth of my dollars?"

You may want to consider switching your policies to annuities or income arrangements, however. From the standpoint of "investing," an annuity may act as a balance and a hedge against other investments. But it would be rather foolish to put all, or

346 Managing Your Assets

most all, of your assets in an annuity. Many wealthy persons do buy annuities, say at age sixty-five, to make certain they receive a guaranteed income in case their other investments collapse or seriously decline in value. An annuity can be arranged to pay for only a limited period of time—say ten years—or it can be arranged to pay forever.

According to the tables of one very large insurance company, it would cost a sixty-five-year-old man about $27,000 to purchase a guaranteed lifetime income of $2400 a year, or $200 per month. Under this arrangement, he would receive $36,000 over the fifteen years he was expected to live. Should he live longer, he would be beating the odds, getting back more than the insurance company estimated. Should he die before his life expectancy of eighty, his estate (or survivors) would feel the loss.

But the point is, even if he should live *exactly* the length of time predicted—fifteen years—he would have received in total about what he would have received had he put his money in a savings account at 4 per cent compounded quarterly, and consistently withdrew $200 per month. The only way you can be sure of beating the lifetime annuity (with no survivorship rights) is to outlive the actuarial tables. Some annuity buyers believe that life insurance companies are much safer than other financial institutions. Life insurance firms are, of course, more liquid than almost any other type of thrift institution, because they are required to maintain very high cash reserves, so there is that to consider.

Now let's suppose this same sixty-five-year-old man has a wife exactly the same age. Were they to purchase a "last survivors" annuity, under which the $200 per month would continue as long as *either* person were alive, the cost would jump from around $27,000 up to about $35,000. Under present life expectancy tables, the man is likely to live for fifteen more years, while his wife should live for eighteen additional years. Their combined expectancy is twenty-two years. There is no way to outguess the annuity firms on this one. The $8000 in additional cost has to be weighed against the $7200 the wife might receive should she live to the age expected and against all the other possibilities.

The years from 1961 to 1964 brought a period of generally rising prices and cheaper dollars, inflation in other words. And inflation is supposed to hurt the annuity business. No retired person likes to pay "dear" dollars in exchange for "cheap" ones later. Yet one large insurance firm reports that its agents, in total, earned only $57,000 in commissions from annuity sales in 1960. By 1964, commissions from such sales had jumped to over $600,000, which is more than a 1000 per cent increase. We can logically ask why this occurred. Beyond a doubt, many wealthy persons panicked when the stock market fell apart in May of 1962. They then apparently decided to play it safe and put a substantial part of their estates in annuities. The market plunged again—only temporarily—when President Kennedy was killed in November of 1963, which probably caused even more older persons to buy annuities. Then too, there are certain tax advantages in annuities for some people. Going back to our sixty-five-year-old man, he would have to declare as "income" only $571.20 each year for tax purposes. Were he instead to invest the $27,000 at 4 per cent interest, he would have to declare $1080 each year as taxable income. Annuity incomes get a tax break because some of the annual receipts are treated as a "return of capital."

It would seem then, in this author's opinion, that only a portion of one's assets should be placed in annuities, regardless of the type. The annuity portion of one's wealth at retirement should correspond to what a person would otherwise invest in safe "dollar plans," such as bonds and savings accounts. Furthermore, the tax benefits of an annuity would mean more to a person in the high income brackets than to a person living mainly on social security and/or a private pension plan.

One should never consider an annuity arrangement all by itself; it is wise to balance it against other investments and against what the tax break really means. Costs of annuities vary from state to state because of local "load" taxes, and prices also vary from company to company. It pays to shop around, as long as you consider the relative strength and reputation of the insurance companies.

There is always a temptation to gamble on the odds, thinking you may outlive the actuarial tables. And well you may. There is a good case to be made for the statement that our "natural life expectancy" hasn't changed within the recorded history of man. Just as elephants and rabbits, we are built to live so long. The life expectancy tables, however, have to consider infant mortality, disease, war, and such deadly, unnatural things as automobiles. And as you reach age sixty-five, your life pattern is rather well established. You will already have survived many of the "civilized perils." You have every right to weigh your own likelihood of beating the tables in relation to the cost and "investment quality" of a lifetime annuity. An insurance company is working on the law of averages. But you know more about yourself than the insurance company will ever know. As long as a man has other wealth which would support his surviving wife in decent style, he can't be blamed for gambling on a lifetime annuity with no *survivorship rights*. But he'd be a fool to buy such a plan if his survivor would be left destitute in the event he were too optimistic about his general health and longevity.

The younger you are, the more a lifetime annuity costs. And the younger your wife is, the more it will cost to include her in the "last survivor" plan. Some insurance firms refuse to issue a lifetime annuity to a person under fifty. But they are very happy to issue such plans to persons over sixty-five. There is no doubt but that annuities would be more popular were it not for inflation. During the post-depression years, movie stars used to sink their entire fortunes in annuities. Mostly they were running scared, remembering their friends who were wiped out during the market crash of 1929. But since those dreary years, creeping inflation has more than offset fears of another bust. Because of this dread of getting back cheap dollars when a retired person needs money the most, a number of insurance companies are offering "variable annuities," but mostly under group retirement plans. Variable annuities have a substantial percentage of their dollar assets invested in common stocks, in order to provide the necessary growth and anti-inflation hedge. Under this plan, a monthly annuity check would be adjusted more to the cost of living, rather than paid out in a fixed number of dollars. The First Investment Annuity Company of America is one of the variable annuity firms, and according to its own statement, intends to offer individual plans within a reasonable length of time. In its brochure the firm compares what the results would have been under its "Investment Annuity" compared to fixed-dollar annuities. As an example, a $100 per month annuity starting in 1945 would have shrunk to only about $55 in purchasing power by early in 1966. In other words, to keep up with wage increases alone, the annuity owner needed over $200 per month rather than $100.

But had he invested his 1945 annuity money in General Motors stock, as just one example, under the Investment Annuity principle his monthly income by 1964 would have been $1038. In AT&T, the monthly sum would have been $340. If the annuity sum could have been invested in the Dow Jones Averages, which was impossible of course, the monthly income would have been $541 by 1964. However, an investment in a good common stock mutual fund would have accomplished about the same thing.

No one can guarantee that any variable annuity will perform as well as the hypothetical examples given above, for the simple reason that no one knows what the stock market will do. But in a society seemingly based on inflation, the odds are with the man who puts a good share of his assets in carefully selected common stocks, whether in the form of an annuity, a trust fund, or a personal portfolio.

The retirement budget

The first big decision facing a retired couple is over shelter. Shall we sell our large home now? Should we buy a small place or move into a cooperative or condominium? How much can we afford to pay? These are the questions older people must wrestle with at the very time they are able to drop other worries and responsibilities. And in each case the decision is a very personal one, involving human preferences, income limitations, and tax advantages.

While a man and wife are usually reluctant to give up comfortable housing and a familiar environment, financial considerations usually predominate. As I have repeatedly stated, a private homestead is a so-so investment at best, mainly involving a tax savings and a hedge against inflation. But most retired persons quickly drop into a lower tax bracket, because of reduced income and greater exemptions. And even though the land under a home does offset inflation to some extent—by rising in dollar value— the cost of keeping up the home itself, including property taxes, makes the inflationary hedge an expensive one. That is particularly true if an older couple retains an unusually large homestead out of sentimental considerations, or out of fear of making a change. Therefore, it is usually wiser to rent, purchase a much smaller home, or buy into some kind of housing development with special provisions for older persons.

If a couple's income is quite substantial, then it becomes a matter of personal choice. Many retired persons with wealth are buying into condominiums, where they at least own clear title to their own individual apartments. This usually gives them maintenance-free living, along with a tax break on interest and property taxes. The same thing is true under full "co-operatives," where ownership is represented by a share in the entire development.

One bit of warning on both co-operatives and condominiums— our income tax laws are quite complex in these matters, and you should check the legal aspects of the tax benefits before buying a unit or a share. There is the added problem of potential liability should a co-op or condominium become largely unoccupied. Under the co-op arrangement, your share of both taxes and maintenance would increase. And even under the condominium plan, empty units would raise your maintenance costs and probably drop the value of your investment.

If money is an important consideration, as it will be for most older persons, the large developments aimed at so-called "senior citizens" have a great deal to offer. For a small down payment and extended mortgage terms, a retired couple can live better and less expensively than strictly on their own. In parts of Arizona and California these specialized developments have proved quite successful. Not all of them, however. Generally speaking it is wiser to make sure a senior citizens' development is rather fully subscribed to before investing money in one of the homes, condominiums, or townhouse. You should check out the recreational facilities, the type of people, and the costs involved. If you don't like physical exercise or planned recreation, you could save money by moving into a development without all the frills. Always spend plenty of time visiting any community you intend to "join" before signing papers or parting with money.

A number of new community developments are less "ghettos for the aged" than are the strictly old folks' developments. A number of planned residential communities are really communities within communities. They allow children, pets, and younger families in certain specified areas, while restricting other parts to older persons without children. This makes for a better sociological mix, but it raises property taxes somewhat. Children are educated at the expense of the entire community, whereas in the regular senior citizens' developments there are no children to educate. It depends on your personal philosophy.

As an example, the Casitas Capistrano community development along the coast of Southern California started with a number of circular townhouse areas, with the common wall, open-space concept. One area banned children, but only a few hundred feet away families with children lived and had access to a pool and clubhouse. This gave a certain degree of privacy to older people without making them feel isolated from other age groups. These attractive Spanish-style townhouses with enclosed private patios featured up to four bedrooms and three baths and were either one or two stories. The cost of a unit varied from $22,000 to about $25,000, depending on the number of rooms and so on. Since even a retired couple could finance such a unit with only about 10 per cent down and thirty years to pay, those with modest incomes were eligible. In other parts of the West, such townhouses have been available on FHA terms for as little as $17,000. Many older persons prefer them to retirement developments because of the varied age groups. Large numbers of retired people like to travel a great deal, and the townhouse concept enables them to pack and leave in a hurry, knowing their homes and property will be watched and tended to. Such provisions are often included in a monthly maintenance fee.

The retired person of today has a wealth of alternatives available in the field of shelter. While owning (or buying on mortgage) becomes less of a tax advantage at retirement, because of smaller income in most cases, it offers the secure feeling that the rent can't be raised. Property taxes *can* be raised, however, and so can maintenance costs, which makes it imperative to keep the original price of a home within sensible limitations. The higher the price, the higher the taxes and upkeep expenses. Many retired couples have had to sell their homes because of terribly high property taxes. So give yourself some leeway if you buy.

Food becomes less of a problem and less of an expense when you grow older. According to Howard Whitman in his book *A Brighter Later Life* (Prentice-Hall, Inc.), weight control and nutrition are the main problems. Quoting from a guide to diet published by the Council on Foods and Nutrition of the American Medical Association, Whitman said to try to maintain your weight by eating plenty of proteins and cereals, giving proper balance to the requirements of minerals and vitamins. The wisest idea is to ask for a diet from your doctor and then stick to it. But by age sixty-five, a person may need only three-fourths as many calories as back when he was younger and more active. Your eating may not be inexpensive, but what you lose from having to concentrate more on costlier foods can be offset by the lower volume.

Since most retired persons head for warm climates as soon as possible, clothing costs may drop considerably, unless they deliberately choose otherwise. Older persons are not too affected by the whims of fashion designers either. So the clothing budget is easily handled.

Health care for older persons used to be an enormous problem, but now that Medicare is part of our law, the typical retired couple will probably spend from $200 to $400 less per year than in 1965. Transportation costs could be insignificant if you choose to live in a community development. For one thing, there's usually some form of public transportation available, plus a number of auto owners willing to share their trips to town and the recreation areas.

All in all, based on today's dollar value, an older couple can live rather comfortably and without worry on less than $400 per month. Since the fully insured couple on social security and Medicare can count on over one-half that sum, tax-free, much of the worry over getting old should eventually disappear. In fact, it's already beginning to, if the attitudes I've encountered at several retirement developments are any clue. I think it is fair to say that the happiest, carefree Americans are those over sixty-five who have retired with full social security, Medicare, and a little in savings.

The legalities

Even so, there's still the nagging problem of how to pass on one's hard-earned wealth, without losing most of it to the tax collector. Blessed indeed is the man who has a good family lawyer. It's hard enough to save any money these days, considering our various tax laws, without ending up in a confusing maze of estate taxes, inheritance taxes, and probate costs.

The older person actually faces two huge problems when it comes to leaving his wealth to survivors. First he must try to minimize the Federal estate tax and the state inheritance taxes;

then he must arrange his wealth so that the lawyers, appraisers, and probate courts don't get all of what's left, which is no mean trick, since there's a vested interest in the probate courts, which have been called a scandal and an insult to the dead. There is no substitute for a properly drawn will, when it comes to making sure your "intentions" are carried out at your death. And I strongly urge the hiring of a lawyer, rather than a do-it-yourself job. A simple will may cost only $25 in some parts of the country.

As to the taxes, each estate is allowed a $60,000 exemption, plus a marital deduction of 50 per cent of the adjusted gross estate. Because of these allowances, there is little to worry about if a married man leaves an estate of under $100,000 after debts. The net estate, incidentally, should be the base for the lawyer's fee as well, but lawyers have been known to base their fees on the gross estates with no objection from the probate courts.

Most persons are terribly confused about such legal technicalities as "tenancy in common," "joint tenancy," and "right of survivorship," as well they should be. The legal jungle is not for most of us. I do heartily recommend a book entitled *How to Avoid Probate* by Norman F. Dacey (Crown Publishers, Inc.). Even if your attorney disagrees with what Mr. Dacey suggests, such as the use of the "Inter Vivos" trust, you will at least know the *right questions* to pose to your lawyer. What you must try to do is avoid having your wealth fall into the hands of your "estate," where it then becomes a matter of appraising, dividing, squabbling, and taxing.

There are certain legal differences involved in putting real property in joint ownership arrangements compared to doing so with securities. There also are legal problems involved in giving securities to a minor under custodian arrangements, or under the "gift to minors" acts. You should definitely consult your lawyer on these matters.

When it comes to giving money away, you are entitled to one lump tax-free $30,000 gift, plus an additional $3000 per year. But as long as you are married, estate taxes are a problem only if your estate would exceed $120,000 after deducting liabilities.

You do, however, have to worry about probate costs, because even on a $10,000 estate, total expenses of probate could come to $2000. On larger estates, the percentage drops, but the dollar amount is greater.

The wisest thing you can do, even well before you have retired or reached age sixty-five, is to itemize all your assets very carefully, even personal items, to see where you stand. Then see how much, if anything, you would owe the Federal and State government. It may be time for gifts, trusts, joint tenancy with right of survivorship, and revising your will. It might also be the time to think about helping your young children, or grandchildren, with future college expenses.

Either under the "gift to minors" act—a custodial arrangement —or under a trust setup, you may be able to avoid taxes on assets you are holding to give the youngsters later. You can even make a trust "reversionary," which means the principal sum would eventually come back to you, and you'd still save on taxes as long as the trust was for at least ten years and not subject to your revoking it. A youngster could earn up to $1000 per year in tax-free dividends on such a trust setup, assuming he had no other income.

These are just some ideas to explore; the field of trusts, estate taxes, and probate is too complex to discuss here. While it is true that estate taxes hurt the very rich the most, unnecessary probate fees can hurt even a modest saver. And anyone who pays income taxes at all should be thinking about trusts and gifts.

As one fellow put it, "I realize there are plenty of tax-saving adjustments I could make in my personal holdings, but from personal experience it would be mainly a matter of giving the lawyer what he saved from the tax collector." That needn't be, of course. Talking turkey with an attorney about costs is a respectable, rational act. And for that matter, many banks, life insurance companies, and mutual funds have specially prepared forms you can use for trusts. These financial institutions always tactfully suggest you have your own attorney check over their forms, but it isn't absolutely necessary when small sums are involved.

To summarize this treatment on Planning For Retirement, it certainly helps to have a healthy attitude toward both age and retirement. How you hope to live will determine how much you will eventually need. Even a small amount of savings will prove enormously helpful, and quite often sufficient. Take stock of what you already have, including your social security estate, and then plan around it. Adjust your holdings as you reach or approach retirement, but don't be too conservative. Set up a workable living budget, and if you need to, dip into capital occasionally. And finally, remember the tax collectors and the probate judges. You can effectively protect your heirs with a little planning.

But even with all this, you'll have to keep your eye on money, what it is worth in terms of buying power. Gradual inflation is not a communist plot; it never was. The idea of slyly and somewhat painlessly trimming the value of a dollar bill is strictly capitalist in origin. It goes back to the British economist John Maynard Keynes, who greatly influenced the thinking of our President, Franklin Delano Roosevelt. Keynes felt that prosperity could be retained, revived, or stimulated through government borrowing and spending. Our present set of politicians, Democrats and Republicans alike, still more or less subscribe to this thinking, even though they occasionally attack it for political reasons. Most Western European nations continue to base their economic policies on the ideas of Lord Keynes.

No one yet has proved Keynes completely wrong, although he has plenty of critics waiting in the bushes to say "I told you so." As a result, you can expect our Federal Government to go on spending and spending, especially when the private sector of the economy slows down. Most of us are willing to go along with this thinking, under the logical assumption that a little inflation is better than a heaping helping of deflation and depression. And when you get right down to it, many of Keynes' severest critics are a bit hypocritical about it all. Take the conservative bankers who have a vested interest in the juicy national debt, especially when Uncle Sam has to pay 5 per cent for his money.

But what happens when the economy gets a bit shaky? The bankers are the first to pull in their loans, with the result that money simply disappears. It has to disappear for the logical reason that debt is money in our society. As I said earlier, the notes issued by the Federal Reserve Banks are our main currency supply. Pull in the notes (the credit) and you pull in the money, and you dry up checking account "money" as well. In our type of society we simply can't wait for the private bankers to recover their courage during a severe recession. We've got to keep money in circulation in one way or another, even if we have to borrow it or print it.

No, it isn't a communist plot. Deficit spending is an old idea expanded into a "system" by a very capitalistic Britisher, one who made a fortune buying and selling British pounds, American dollars, and other currencies in the open market. Once he became very rich he was able to devote more of his time to thinking up ways to keep the basic system operating. For all its value as an economic stimulant, the Keynes system does result in a more or less continuing inflationary spiral, barring the use of wage and price controls. And older people on pensions will continue to take a beating unless they organize into an effective political force. If the dollar is to continue to lose from 2 to 3 per cent of its value each year, you must see that your social security benefits are increased at the same pace. And from year to year, not five years after the inflation is officially recognized.

If this is the economic game we're going to play, older people should demand the same regular cost-of-living increases that labor unions, politicians, and executives demand—and get. Don't try to change the game unless you've got a better idea, just insist that you be dealt in. One vote means little or nothing, but 20 million votes can mean everything. Of course, we should insist on economy, in the sense of getting the most for our tax money, and there will be many times, when the economy is booming, in which taxes should be reduced. That would enable us to spend more money, rather than the government.

But at least let's try to make a little sense out of our pleas for economy. Let's not beat straw men to death. Take, if you will, a $100 billion national budget. If in a sudden fit of economy we were to dispense with all welfare programs and all Federal Government—in the civilian sense, we'd still have to spend about $80 billion a year. That is the built-in cost of war—past, present, and future. It includes interest on the war-incurred debt, payments to veterans, service to veterans, and the cost of maintaining a huge military establishment. And were you to deduct the cost of subsidies to farmers, the shipping industry, and other special interests from the remaining $20 billion, there would be very little left to run the government and provide for social welfare.

Keep this in mind when you write to your Congressman.

CONCLUSION

It's getting harder to be a loner

Our society was founded by rugged individualists who hated the very thought of group action, except in dire emergencies. Up until the early part of the twentieth century, the American hero was more or less a loner, even in his married life. While that image is still much revered in oratory, reality has begun to set in.

Pressure groups call the tune in our day. If you were to approach the typical lawmaker today, urging the passage of some bit of legislation, he would likely ask, "Who is behind you?" He would be counting heads and votes.

Each large American industry and each professional group has its own association today, working toward the economic betterment of its members. And because of lobbying pressures, a great deal of our legislative activity is devoted to keeping prices up, not down. But it was that way in ancient China, too, many hundreds of years ago. Maybe history just repeats itself as societies reach certain stages of development.

I mention this because it is almost impossible for individual consumers to make their voices heard today. I am all for self-reliance, or I wouldn't have written this book. But I also know how difficult it is for most persons to cope with the complex problems of today. If you would like to change certain things, give some thought to joining consumer groups. In case you have forgotten some of the problems I mentioned earlier, let me repeat a few, and add a few more.

1. Our weights and measures laws make price comparison very difficult. Simplicity and standardization has to come from Congress. Then there is the added problem of having to cope with odd sizes and weights. Consumers shouldn't be obliged to carry computers wherever they shop in order to buy intelligently.

2. Interest rates are difficult to compare because of the numerous methods used to express the rates. We might push for a uniform method of stating credit terms.

3. In some fields of commerce there seems to be no competition on price whatsoever. High-rate lenders make 99 per cent of their loans at the top rates allowed by law. Railroads aren't allowed to lower their rates without approval of a Federal agency. Steamship lines and airlines belong to "international rate conferences," which brook no price competition. Whenever farm prices slip, the Federal Government steps in to buy up the surpluses, sometimes at the expense of the consumer. In many of our professional associations, fee competition is frowned upon. To put it in another way, there is no really free play of the market working for the consumer.

Over the past few years, a number of our most respected industries and corporations have been indicted for price-fixing. If this sort of thing is considered respectable at the highest level of our business-oriented culture, the least we can do is admit that our values have changed and quit pretending.

4. Our tax laws are a disgrace. When some persons earning one million dollars a year pay less in income taxes than average wage earners, things are ripe for a change. At the very least, it seems to me we should take another look at our entire tax structure. It should be revised to achieve simplicity, justice, and economy of collection.

5. And finally, with eighteen million Americans buying shares in corporations, it is no longer practical to consider the stock exchanges as "rich men's clubs." Even if you never own a share of stock directly, there is a good chance that you are affected by what happens in the market. Some of your pension money may be in stocks; even some of your union money and life insurance cash value may be reflected in the Dow Jones averages. Wall Street should not be so dimly lighted.

If you would improve some of these things, give some thought to joining consumer groups in order to make your views effective.

And you can't be a "loner" in your marriage either. A husband and wife must cooperate in the economic area today in order to make a go of things. With most young wives working in the commercial arena, they are entitled to equal rights.

If nothing else, I hope I have impressed you with the importance of staying solvent even if you never get rich. Being rich is no sure path to happiness. Nor for that matter, will just staying solvent guarantee a long, serene life.

Insolvency is deadly. It dulls the spirit and saps one's energy. A little sacrifice, involving both partners to a marriage, will go a long way toward solvency and compatibility. Look at this another way. It is downright undignified to live behind the financial eight ball, always borrowing money, dodging bill collectors, and robbing Peter to pay Paul. When a married couple becomes financially insolvent, lack of mutual respect is inevitable. Then come fights and accusations.

To be sure, even a fool and a spendthrift can survive in our type of society. There are plenty of relief agencies willing to feed and clothe the profligates of our era. Even if a person retires heavily in debt, he won't go without shelter. Somehow or other we taxpayers and bleeding hearts will pick up the tab to keep him breathing. But what a way to end up after the hundreds of thousands of dollars he probably handled during his earning years. It's up to individuals to manage their finances with care.

Knowing you are getting ahead financially can be a genuine boost to your spirits. It can make you a *better* wage earner; it can improve your marriage; it can even improve your health. That is why I have provided a family bookkeeping system to help those who are determined to get ahead. It isn't a "simple" system—it is rather sophisticated. It assumes you have read this book with understanding. After all, money itself is a sophisticated subject.

There aren't many shortcuts to keeping on top of your finances. The only one I know of is making so much money you can't spend it fast enough.

The family bookkeeping system

a. What makes up a set of books

At this point you may want to go back to the section on Managing Your Income, which dealt with budgeting. Budgeting is not the same thing as bookkeeping, however. Let me use this example to clarify the difference. It is the duty of the top financial officer of each company to prepare a budget for the coming year. He must plan and project the spending of his firm for the year ahead. The President of the United States has to do that, too, although he receives a lot of help.

But in order to prepare an intelligent budget, a financial officer must look back at last year's spending. He has to know where the money has been going in the past in order to project for the future and revise percentages according to current conditions. Which means that someone in the firm—the bookkeeper—has to keep accurate records.

Of particular importance is the matter of deficits (overspending) or surpluses (savings). Furthermore, these must be proved. That is why a good set of books, family or business type, has two basic parts, which act as a check on each other.

One part is the income-expense comparison. The other is the asset-liability ratio. The first part shows how much money came in and where it went out. The second part shows what happened to the net worth of the family or firm. To put it in a simple way: if expenses were greater than income, the company lost ground. And that lost ground shows up in the asset-liability ratio, as a reduction in net worth. On the other hand, if expenses were less than income received, there was a profit, or savings. And that will show up in the asset-liability ratio in one of two ways: either the assets increased, or the liabilities (debts) decreased.

So I have prepared two sets of forms for those of you who wish to keep rather complete records and prove their accuracy. The first is the income-expense comparison, and the second is the asset-liability comparison or ratio. Those go to make up a set of family "books."

b. *How to use them*

(1) The Income Record

You will notice that the first sheet, the one on which to record your income for the year, deals with gross income. Forget about your take-home pay, record your total earnings. If you earn $200 a week, use that figure. For monthly purposes, use one-twelfth of your annual gross income, before anything is deducted. You can make pencil notations each month, for the previous month, perhaps at the time you pay all your bills. There are a number of columns to fill out, but remember this is for your own records, not for the income tax people. Some of your real income isn't taxable.

(2) The Expenses

I have broken down the expenses into Housing, Food, Basic Transportation, Medical, Clothing, Savings, Life Insurance, Cost of Owning Assets, Church, Entertainment, and Interest and Tax Cost. In other words, there are eleven major categories, with subdivisions under each. You can use the forms in the book or copy them onto sheets of paper.

Some of the expense sheets should be kept up monthly; others can be filled in only once a year. But read each sheet before using it, and make pencil notes, which can be erased.

You may want to do this just for fun, and only once in your lifetime. At the very least, you will have some eye-opening revelations about where your money is going. Each spending section has several columns. At the end of a year, total each column in each section. Then add the sums of all the columns to get your *total spending* under that particular section of the budget.

Under Housing or Rental you should quickly observe that there is no column for payments. Nor should there be, because as I explained before, the payments aren't a measurement of housing costs. Payments on debts of any kind show up in the Savings section, after allowing for the interest cost.

Under Food, watch that you don't include things you can't eat. The typical supermarket check-out slip is for 20 per cent nonedibles.

The other sections are quite self-explanatory. Read the instructions.

Whenever you decide to run a final total on your spending for a year, add each of the eleven sections in the places provided at the bottom of each sheet. Then carry all the totals over to their proper places under the *Accounting for Year*. There are spaces provided to show what percentage of your total income has been spent for each and every budget item. You may want to revise your spending, especially if you are spending over 100 per cent of your income.

(3) Trial Balance

Then go to the Trial Balance sheet. List the realistic value of all the things you own. Also itemize your debts or liabilities in the place provided. If your assets are larger than your debts, you have a "net worth," but if your debts are the greater, you are insolvent, "in the red." Keep your trial balance and compare it with next year's figures to see if you are progressing or falling behind. A surprisingly high number of families using consumer credit are "in the red." They may kid themselves by placing too high a value on their assets, and also by conveniently forgetting some of their debts. But it pays to face up to the true situation, unpleasant as it may be. Only by doing that can you hope to improve your own financial picture. And after all, this is your own record. You needn't show it to anyone.

It may surprise some persons that I set up a separate budgeting section for Interest and Taxes. Yet these two things together are the largest hidden drains on our incomes. Interest is rarely "frankly" stated, or itemized in advance. Some taxes are deducted from our checks; others are more or less incorporated in the prices we pay for things. I deliberately set up a section for Interest and Taxes to make people do some figuring—and some thinking.

But even in this section I did not include the hidden excise taxes, the kind placed on manufactured goods and passed on to the consumer. Those are too hard to uncover. Let's face the fact that part of what you are attributing to the various cost of living items is just taxes in disguise.

You may not want to use the bookkeeping forms at all. They may seem too complicated. They are, however, about as simple as I could make them without sacrificing honesty of accounting. I avoided using anything so complex as double entry books. The ones in this book are the most basic I could think up.

You may choose to get all your figures for the year together and take the forms to some bookkeeper, accountant, or financial counselor, to have him tie the whole thing together. At least use the forms in some manner.

Changes in our technology may make it much easier to transact financial dealings. In mid-1966, an "electronic money system" was introduced to the public. A firm by the name of Electronic Currency System offered a plan by which a person could run up bills at stores simply by inserting a specially designed credit card in a computer box. He would give the box his memorized identification number—to guard against some other person finding his card and using it—after which the box would "identify" him and then okay or reject his credit. The entire transaction would take place in under three seconds.

If the card user elected to, he could have the purchase added to his bank credit plan. Or he could simply charge at the store where he bought the merchandise or service. Theoretically, he could also use the card to ride subways, buses or taxis, if the firms involved subscribed to the electronic service. Furthermore, even if the card-carrying consumer ran up bills at a dozen different stores during any one month, he could pay all his bills by writing only one check to the electronic control center, which would then make the proper disbursements. There will be other systems of this kind, of course—some probably quite worthwhile.

But you must keep one thing in mind. These new services will never get commercial acceptance if they are designed to help you spend less. They will only be supported and encouraged by merchants, banks, and other credit firms if they are aimed at helping you spend more money, faster and with less red tape. So the need for discipline will remain on your shoulders. In other words, you'll be able to go broke faster and further tomorrow than you could today.

Many wealthy persons hire business managers. Almost all entertainers do. These business managers, in addition to helping with investments, pay bills and dole out allowances. A good business manager is a hardheaded fellow, able to say "no" to his client and get away with it. The typical charge for this service is 5 per cent of annual gross income.

And as I have indicated, millions of overindebted individuals already have been forced into having their entire financial affairs handled by debt counselors or court trustees. Between those persons with high incomes and those overburdened with debts is the vast middle area, made up of people struggling along on fair to excellent incomes. Neither rich nor poor, but finding it hard to get ahead, they usually are too embarrassed to ask for help, or too economy-minded to pay a manager.

Nevertheless, many solvent families earning from $10,000 to $25,000 per year have turned their affairs over to financial managers. In Los Angeles, a firm by the name of Financial Secretary, Inc. was serving some 500 or more middle-income families during 1966. Financial Secretary analyzes the financial situation of each client in a personal interview, sets up a budget, and then pays all the bills. Each month every client receives a complete accounting of not only where the money went, but also how the planned spending program is progressing. Each month the family also receives a form showing a "surplus" or a "deficit." Sometimes a client will need "special handling" for one reason or another.

Many of Financial Secretary's clients are engineers, professional men, junior executives, and entertainers. They have one thing in common; they dislike the details of money management. So they pay to have it done for them. The cost runs from 1½ per cent to 2 per cent of gross income, less than the highly paid business managers get, but enough to show a decent return to Financial Secretary. This firm relies heavily on automation, special checks, and electronically processed accounting forms. I have worked with Financial Secretary and know that most of its clients profit from such a system. I've performed this sort of work for many families over the years.

We have reached the stage in our society where almost any service is available if you desire it. It makes sense for a family with a decent income to hire a bookkeeper-secretary by sharing the otherwise high costs with numerous other families. There is no reason why you should struggle with your financial chores if you don't choose to, especially if you can earn additional money on your free time doing things you like better. With both adults in a family working, as is more and more the case, perhaps neither one has the time and energy to do a good job with the financial affairs.

This is somewhat the concept behind mutual funds, which enables a family with modest financial resources to share the costs of a professional investment team. The odds are, despite all the new ideas and technological innovations in the field of money and credit, each of us will find life a little more complex and a little more specialized. It may mean an increased reliance on the skills of others, including fund managers, debt managers, and income managers.

Nevertheless, the more you can do on your own, assuming you can do it reasonably well, the more money you can save. And without a decent understanding of money, you won't be able to comprehend what the specialists can do for you—or to you. Certainly it is up to you to decide on your own goals in life.

Money should be considered a means to an end, a means toward enjoying life. When you hoard money, or fritter it away, you are blocking off your dreams. If you will accept that thought alone, it will be reward enough for me for laboring over this book.

BOOKKEEPING FORMS

REAL INCOME FOR YEAR (GROSS)

Figure at end of year

This needn't agree with income tax filing

	Salary or wages (family unit)	Bonuses, tips, and odd jobs	Interest, dividends, etc.	Gifts of value rec'd.	Income from rental	Garden income, free rent, etc.
JANUARY						
FEBRUARY						
MARCH						
APRIL						
MAY						
JUNE						
JULY						
AUGUST						
SEPTEMBER						
OCTOBER						
NOVEMBER						
DECEMBER						

TOTAL $ ....

HOUSING OR RENTAL — Year____

Ignore house payment here—if you rent, use col. 5

Home value $____
Mortgage balance $____
Equity $____

	1. Utilities—gas, light, water, heat, phone—garbage	2. Repairs—upkeep roof, plumbing, yard, etc.	3. Insurance—fire, etc.	4. Taxes including assessments	5. Investment loss (figure once a year—at 3 to 4 per cent of your equity in the home)	6. Depreciation (figure once a year—at 2 to 3 % home value) Allow for neighborhood decay or improvement, age of home. Any long-term improvements can be added to home value, not shown as expenses. If value increased, subtract gain from other home expenses shown.
JANUARY						
FEBRUARY						
MARCH						
APRIL						
MAY						
JUNE						
JULY						
AUGUST						
SEPTEMBER						
OCTOBER						
NOVEMBER						
DECEMBER						
TOTAL						

TOTAL HOUSING COST FOR YEAR $ ....

373

FOOD

Only what you paid for

Eliminate nonfood items such as soap, beer, cigarettes, etc.

	Regular grocery bill	Milk and deliveries	Lunches—work and school	Cost of garden	Dinners out	Special costs
JANUARY						
FEBRUARY						
MARCH						
APRIL						
MAY						
JUNE						
JULY						
AUGUST						
SEPTEMBER						
OCTOBER						
NOVEMBER						
DECEMBER						

TOTAL $ ....

TRANSPORTATION
Only cash outgo

Do not include car purchase price,
payments, depreciation, or insurance

	Gasoline, oil, & tires	Parking fees and license	Bus, streetcar, or taxis	Minor car repairs & service	Car wash or polish	Special—such as car pool
JANUARY						
FEBRUARY						
MARCH						
APRIL						
MAY						
JUNE						
JULY						
AUGUST						
SEPTEMBER						
OCTOBER						
NOVEMBER						
DECEMBER						

TOTAL $ . . . .

MEDICAL
Only out-of-pocket costs, not debts

Do not list if paid by insurance
or if cost is paid by employer

	Medical insurance	Doctor and hospital	Dentist and cleaning	Private nurse	Medicine and drugs	Ambulance and misc.
JANUARY						
FEBRUARY						
MARCH						
APRIL						
MAY						
JUNE						
JULY						
AUGUST						
SEPTEMBER						
OCTOBER						
NOVEMBER						
DECEMBER						

TOTAL $ ....

375

CLOTHING

Only if actually paid for

	Regular clothing purchases	Dry cleaning	Laundry cost (soaps, etc.)	Shoeshines, pressing, etc.	Materials used in sewing	Special
JANUARY						
FEBRUARY						
MARCH						
APRIL						
MAY						
JUNE						
JULY						
AUGUST						
SEPTEMBER						
OCTOBER						
NOVEMBER						
DECEMBER						

TOTAL $ ....

SAVINGS

Figure at end of year compared to start of year
Ignore interest—show increase in equity or worth

	Increase in cash value of life ins.	Reduction in home mortgage	Reduction in other debts *(Subtract from other saving if your debts increased over the year)	PURCHASED DURING YEAR		
				Cash savings, trusts, etc.	Stocks, bonds, shares	Valuable jewelry, art, etc. (cost)
JANUARY						
FEBRUARY						
MARCH						
APRIL						
MAY						
JUNE						
JULY						
AUGUST						
SEPTEMBER						
OCTOBER						
NOVEMBER						
DECEMBER						

*Misc. debt start of year $ ____
Misc. debt now $ ____
Increase or decrease $ ____

NET SAVINGS (if any) $ ....

LIFE INSURANCE

Includes group insurance, G.I. insurance, term
insurance, and social security deductions

(Your insurance agent can help)
All you want to compute here is cost
of protection—the premium less the savings

	Premiums paid (total)	Less increase in cash value		Actual cost (net)
JANUARY				
FEBRUARY				
MARCH				
APRIL				
MAY				
JUNE				
JULY				
AUGUST				
SEPTEMBER				
OCTOBER				
NOVEMBER				
DECEMBER				

TOTAL $ ....

COST OF ASSETS

Figure only at end of year

You aren't to figure what you bought, but the cost of owning things and the amount they lost value during year

	Autos (depreciation) 25% a year of price—or use your own percentage	Furniture (depreciation) 5–10% a year of price	Appliances (depreciation) 10% a year of price	Cost of major service and repair	Profit or loss from sale	Auto ins., etc.
JANUARY						
FEBRUARY						
MARCH						
APRIL						
MAY						
JUNE						
JULY						
AUGUST						
SEPTEMBER						
OCTOBER						
NOVEMBER						
DECEMBER						

Price of auto $ _____
Price of appliances $ _____
Price of furniture $ _____

TOTAL $ ....

CHURCH, CHARITY, AND CONTRIBUTIONS

If actually paid

	Church pledge	Church plate	United campaign	Educational costs	Pots, kettles, and minor pledges	Gifts
JANUARY						
FEBRUARY						
MARCH						
APRIL						
MAY						
JUNE						
JULY						
AUGUST						
SEPTEMBER						
OCTOBER						
NOVEMBER						
DECEMBER						

TOTAL $ ....

FUN, ENTERTAINMENT, AND PERSONAL CARE

Do not list if you haven't paid the bill

	Vacations and travel	Parties	Shows, plays	Personal care	Liquor and smokes	Allowances not accounted for
JANUARY						
FEBRUARY						
MARCH						
APRIL						
MAY						
JUNE						
JULY						
AUGUST						
SEPTEMBER						
OCTOBER						
NOVEMBER						
DECEMBER						

TOTAL $ ....

INTEREST AND INCOME TAX COST*

* Other taxes shown in various items of budget

	Home mort-gage interest	Personal loan interest	Interest on time buying	Income taxes	Interest on insurance loan	Misc. union dues, etc.
JANUARY						
FEBRUARY						
MARCH						
APRIL						
MAY						
JUNE						
JULY						
AUGUST						
SEPTEMBER						
OCTOBER						
NOVEMBER						
DECEMBER						

TOTAL $ ....

ACCOUNTING FOR YEAR
(Use totals from each ledger sheet)

REAL INCOME FOR YEAR $_____

		% of income ?
SPENDING FOR YEAR		
HOUSING	$_____	_____
FOOD	_____	_____
TRANSPORTATION	_____	_____
MEDICAL	_____	_____
CLOTHING	_____	_____
SAVINGS (+ or −)	_____	_____
LIFE INS. COST	_____	_____
COST OF ASSETS	_____	_____
CHURCH, ETC.	_____	_____
FUN, ETC.	_____	_____
INTEREST, TAXES	_____	_____
TOTAL	$_____	_____
ERROR OR LEEWAY	$_____	_____

(Income and expenses should be about equal, since savings reflect difference between income and outgo)

Debts run up for other than long-lasting assets may give you a false picture of the way you are consuming your pay check. Payments made on such debts—as for food, clothing, medical, etc.— should be charged directly to such parts of your budget. Analyze your debts to see where you are overconsuming.

384

TRIAL BALANCE
(To see how you are doing each year)

Things of value	START OF BUDGET YEAR Dollar amount	ONE YEAR LATER Dollar amount
Cash on hand	$	$
Cash in bank	$	$
Value of house	$	$
Value of auto	$	$
Furniture and appliances	$	$
Stocks, shares, bonds	$	$
Cash value life ins.	$	$
Jewelry, antiques, or heirlooms	$	$
Amount other people owe me	$	$
Miscellaneous	$	$
Total assets	$	$

Debts or Liabilities

House mortgage	$	$
Balance due on car	$	$
Balance due on furniture or appliance	$	$
Other loans	$	$
Unpaid medical bills	$	$
Current bills unpaid	$	$
Total debts	$	$
Net worth (assets minus debts)	$	$
In the hole (if your debts are bigger than assets)	$	$

INDEX